GU00538454

SHIPS IN FOCUS 'RECORD 2017' is now available: an enlarged, 124-page, annual hardback with exactly the same mixture of accurate, well-researched features and photographs as our 64 four-monthly editions. It features owners old and not-so-old: British, Belgian and Anglo-Swedish; including Union-Castle, Cockerill and Burmah Oil. Coverage of shipbuilding runs from a small Welsh yard to the major figure of John Priestman. 'South West Scenes' rounds off our pictorial coverage of the diverse maritime activities at Falmouth, and there is the story of an epic Second World War convoy battle. It covers a range of vessels, from cargo liners, tramps, trawlers and tankers to coasters and other small vessels. More pages mean longer, complete articles. Hardback, 128 pages £17.50

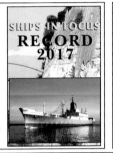

EVERARD OF GREENHITHE 2nd Edition K.S. Garrett this second edition takes the story through to its conclusion with the sale of the company in 2006. All ships bought since 1991 have been added to the fleet list, along with managed and time-chartered vessels. Many photographs from the 1st edition have been replaced h/b £36.00

THE ABERDEEN LINE George Thomson Jnr's Incomparable Shipping Enterprise Peter H King, lightly illustrated company history with brief fleet list h/b 256pp £25.00

SWANSEA DOCKS IN THE 1960s Mark Lee Inman s/b 128pp £12.99

SVITZER TUGS WORLDWIDE Bernard McCall full colour with captions 112pp s/b £10.95 also **SVITZER TUGS UK** Bernard McCall Photo album of Svitzer tugs working in the United Kingdom s/b A5 88pp £9.95

WARTIME STANDARD SHIPS Nick Robbins illustrated 160pp h/b £25.00

WARSHIP 2017 John Jordan 208pp h/b £40.00

THE HISTORY OF THE PORT OF LONDON A vast Emporium of All Nations Peter Stone, foundation, growth and evolution through to present day, its rise, fall and revival illustrated history from 18th century 248pp h/b £19.99

LIFE IN THE TONS Ton Class Association Stan Hudson illustrated s/b 156pp £13.99

DE SCHEPEN VAN DE VCK (Vereenigd Cargadoorskantoor, Amsterdam) 1915-1919 & 1952-1988 (Stegro No.23) Illustrated fleet list, Dutch language h/b 198pp £23.00

TO SAIL NO MORE IN COLOUR Part One Ian Buxton photos warships being scrapped 156pp h/b £25.00

HALF A CENTURY AND MORE OF SHIP PHOTOGRAPHY AT BARROW Ken Royall Warships and merchant ships seen at Barrow, photos with illustrative captions s/b £9.99

THE FOTOFLITE FILES Volume 1: RN Warships Steve Bush photos with descriptive captions 144pp s/b £17.99

THE UNSEEN OLYMPIC The Ship in Rare Illustrations now in soft back 112pp £19.99

ATLANTIC CONTAINER LINE 1967-2017 Philip Parker history with many illustration h/b 144pp £19.50

DANSKE REDERIER Volume 19 Bent Mikkelsen C.Clausen/Sonderborg Rederi A/S and Corral Line £29.50

SAILING PAST THE POINT Bernard McCall full colour with captions 80pp £16.00

THE FIRST ATLANTIC LINER Brunel's Great Western Steamship Helen Doe lightly illustrated h/b 292pp £20.00

CUNARD CRUISE SHIPS Ian Collard illustrated in black and white and colour s/b 96pp £14.99

THE SHIPS THAT CAME TO THE POOL OF LONDON From the Roman galley to HMS Belfast illustrated s/b 160pp £15.99

RMS QUEEN MARY – THE FINAL VOYAGE Michael Gallagher, Miles Cowsill and Richard Tennant, ship's final voyage out to Long Beach via Cape Horn in 1957 over 200 photos h/b 292pp £24.95

FERRIES 2018 features on Silja and Tallink and full listing of major UK and Northern European ferries h/b 224pp £18.75

QUEEN VICTORIA Miles Cowsill 2017 new edition includes her extensive refit in May 2017, h/b 96pp £16.00 (December)

THE BUILDING OF QUEEN ELIZABETH 2 –the world's most famous ship, not only the story of her building but also aborted Q3 project h/b 172pp £24.50

TOWNSEND THORESEN – THE FLEET covers Forde through to Pride of Dover, each ship detailed and with photo or illustration h/b 96pp £16.95 (December)

SHIPWRECKS OF THE P&O LINE Sam Warwick and Mike Roussel covers loss of Don Juan in 1837 through to Shillong in 1957. h/b 180pp £25.00

STRANDED IN THE SIX DAY WAR Cath Senker The story of the 14 ships trapped in the Suez Canal for eight years, illustrated s/b 192pp £13.50

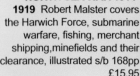

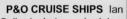

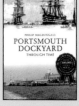

CLEARANCE SALE

The books listed on this and the following seven pages are offered for sale at 50% of their original retail price.

With many of the titles there is only one copy remaining so early ordering is recommended.

Post and packing will be charged at cost

TITLE	AUTHOR	NORMAL	REDUCED
…and Home There's No Returning	Renchington	£13.95	£6.98
100 Jahr Deutsche Fahrschifffahrt (100 Years of German Ferries (English, German and Danish language)	Kai Ortel	£48.00	£24.00
100 Jahr Neue Schleppdampfchiffgreederei Louis Meyer, Hamburg 1907-2007 (German Language)		£14.75	£7.38
100 Years of Shipping on the River Clyde	G C O'Hara	£9.99	£5.00
175 Years of Cunard with memories from Captains and Crew	Frame/Cross	£20.00	£10.00
200 Years of Clyde Paddle Steamers	Deayton/Quinn	£14.99	£7.50
21 Centuries of Marine Pilotage - The History of the United Kingdom Maritime Pilot's Association	Harry Hignett	£15.00	£7.50
750 Schiffe Aus Flesburg - Die Flensburger Schiffbau-Gesellschaft -yard list etc (German text)	Gert Uwe Detlefsen	£70.00	£35.00
7th U-Boat Flotilla, Donitz's Atlantic Wolves	Konstam and M Showell	£12.99	£6.50
A Bristol Channel Album	Chris Collard	£12.99	£6.50
A Century of Sand Dredging in the Bristol Channel Volume One: The English Coast	Peter Gosson	£16.99	£8.50
A Century of Sand Dredging in the Bristol Channel Volume Two: The Welsh Coast	Peter Gosson	£14.99	£7.50
A Century of Sea Travel - Personal Accounts from the Steamship Era	C Deakes and Tom Stanley	£30.00	£15.00
A Commodious Yard The Story of William Thomas & Sons Shipbuilders of Amlwch	Bryan D. Hope	£14.50	£7.25
A Floating Home and Born Afloat	Ionides, Atkins and Haig	£35.00	£17.50
A History of Shipbuilding at Lytham	Jack M.Dakres	£8.00	£4.00
A History of The Royal Navy - World War I	Farquharson Roberts	£25.00	£12.50
A MacBrayne Album	Deayton/Quinn	£14.99	£7.50
A Photographic History of P & O Cruises	Henderson/ Cremer/ Frame/Cross	£19.99	£10.00
A Sailors Life - The Life and Times of John Short of Watchet 1839-1933	Tom Brown	£12.00	£6.00
A Shipyard at War - Unseen Photographs from John Brown's, Clydebank, 1914-1918	Ian Johnston	£30.00	£15.00
A Thicket of Business	Peter Bowing	£19.95	£9.98
Admiralty Coastal Salvage Vessels	David Sowdon	£20.00	£10.00
Afridi to Nizam British Fleet Destroyers 1937-43	John English	£16.00	£8.00
Aground in the Rip - The wreck of the SS Time at Port Phillip Heads	Greg Wane	£11.00	£5.50
Aircraft-Carrying Ships of the Royal Navy	M Cocker	£16.99	£8.50
Alan Villiers, Voyager of the Winds	Kate Lance	£25.00	£12.50
Alte Hafen - Neue Aufgaben (German language)		£21.00	£10.50
Always Ready, West Coast Maritime Series No.2	S C Heal	£15.00	£7.50
Amphibious Assault - Manoeuvre from the sea- From Gallipoli to the Gulf - a definitive analysis	Tristan Lovering	£35.00	£17.50
An Eye on the Coast The Fishing Industry from Wick to Whitby	Gloria Wilson	£12.99	£6.50
An Illuminating Experience	G Medlicott	£14.99	£7.50
An Illustrated History of Cardiff Docks Vol 3 The Cardiff Railway Company and the docks at war	John Hutton	£19.99	£10.00
An Illustrated History of Thames Pleasure Steamers	Nick Robins	£19.99	£10.00
Arctic Adventure	Rob Ellis	£9.95	£4.98
Armed Merchant Cruisers 1878-1945	Osborne, Spong & Grover	£40.00	£20.00
Armorique	Bruce Peter	£16.00	£8.00
Artemis The Original Royal Princess	Sassoli-Walker & Poole	£19.99	£10.00
Astern Business 75 Years of U.K.Shipbuilding	George H.Parker	£5.00	£2.50
Aufbruch von der Weser Die Biographie des Segelschiffkapitans Johann Gerhard Lange (1810-1881)	Peter Ulrich	£25.00	£12.50
Australian Migrant Ships 1946-1977	P Plowman	£15.00	£7.50
B.E.F. Ships before, at and after Dunkirk	John de S.Winser	£16.00	£8.00
Baltic Ferries	Bruce Peter	£18.50	£9.25
Barrie Nairn The Den Line	D.C.E. Burrell	£6.00	£3.00
Battle Honours of the Royal Navy	B. Warlow RN	£19.95	£9.98
Bay Beacons - Lighthouses of the Chesapeake Bay	Linda Turbyville	£20.00	£10.00
Beardmore Built The Rise and Fall of a Clydeside Shipyard	Ian Johnston	£9.95	£4.98
Belfast Shipbuilders - A Titanic Tale	S Cameron	£16.00	£8.00
Bell's Comet How a Paddle Steamer Changed the Course of History	P.J.G. Ransom	£16.99	£8.50
Beneath the Surface - Submarines built in Seattle and Vancouver 1909 to 1918	Bill Lightfoot	£20.00	£10.00
Ben-My-Chree - Woman of my Heart, Isle of Man Steam Packet Steamer and Seaplane Carrier	Ian M Burns	£30.00	£15.00
Birds of the Sea - 150 Years of the General Steam Navigation Company	Nick Robins	£15.00	£7.50
Bishop Rock Lighthouse	E.Stanbrook	£16.00	£8.00
Blown to Eternity - The Princess Irene Story (1st edition)	John Hendy	£4.50	£2.25
Blue Star Line	Dovey & Bottoms	£28.50	£14.25
Blue Star Line Fleet List & History	Ian Collard	£19.99	£10.00
Boat Trips in Devon & Cornwall	Ian Boyle	£12.00	£6.00
Bombay to Elwick Bay	B & S Dennison	£7.95	£3.98
Boomsticks and Towlines, West Coast Maritime Series No 1	S C Heal	£15.00	£7.50
Boots - und Holzschiffbau an der Unterweser, small ships, lifeboats etc (German text)	Heinz D Janssen	£30.00	£15.00
Bore 100, 1897 - 1997, The Centenary Fleet List of the Ships Owned by Bore and Rettig Companies		£25.00	£12.50
Box Boats How Container Ships Changed the World	Brian J. Cudahy	£50.00	£25.00
Bremen and Europa - German Speed Queens of the Atlantic	J Russell Willoughby	£35.00	£17.50
Bremens letzte liner (German text - well illustrated)	Harald Focke	£30.00	£15.00
Breverton's Nautical Curiosities A Book of the Sea	Terry Breverton	£9.99	£5.00
Bristol Port and Channel Nostaslgia	M Cranfield	£16.00	£8.00
Britain's Lost Commercial Waterways	M. E. Ware	£14.99	£7.50
Britannia to Beira and Beyond One man's humorous experiences of Royal Navy life in the 1960's	Mike Critchley	£6.99	£3.50
British and Commonwealth Warship Camouflage of WW11 Volume 2 Battleships and Aircraft Carriers	Malcolm Wright	£30.00	£15.00
British Cruisers Two World Wars and After	N Friedman	£45.00	£22.50
British Invasion Fleets The Mediterranean and beyond 1942-1945	John de S.Winser	£20.00	£10.00
British Warships 1860 to 1906 - a photographic record	Nicholas Dingle	£35.00	£17.50
British Warships and Auxiliaries 2003/2004	Steve Bush	£6.95	£3.40
British Warships and Auxiliaries 2002/2003	Steve Bush	£6.95	£3.48
British Warships and Auxiliaries 2004/2005	Steve Bush	£6.95	£3.48
British Warships and Auxiliaries 2005/2006	Steve Bush	£6.95	£3.48
British Warships and Auxiliaries 2008/2009	Steve Bush	£8.99	£4.50
British Warships and Auxiliaries 2011/2012	Steve Bush	£8.99	£4.50
British Warships and Auxiliaries 2012/2013	Steve Bush	£8.99	£4.50
British Warships and Auxiliaries 2014/2015	Steve Bush	£8.99	£4.50
Brittany Ferries - 40 Memorable Years of Service, Hospitality and Holidays	Miles Cowsill	£17.50	£8.75
Buckie Lifeboats 150 Years of Gallantry	N. Leach	£5.99	£3.00
Building for Victory - The Warship Building Programmes of the Royal Navy 1939-1945	George Moore	£27.00	£13.50
Building the Biggest From Ironships to Cruise Liners	Geoff Lunn	£17.99	£9.00

Title	Author	Price	Price
Building the Steam Navy - Dockyard, Technology and the Creation of the Victorian Battle Fleet 1830 to 1906	David Evans	£30.00	£15.00
Bulk Carriers - The Ocean Cinderella	Nick Tolerton	£27.50	£13.75
Bulk Carriers Built for the Greeks 1956-1970	George M. Foustanos	£37.50	£18.75
But No Brass Funnel	J. Douglas Stewart	£17.95	£8.98
By Ro-Ro to the Baltic	Barry Mitchell	£10.95	£5.48
By Steamer to The Essex Coast	A Gladwell	£14.99	£7.50
By Steamer to the South Coast	A Gladwell	£14.99	£7.50
Caernarfonshire Sail	O F G Kilgour	£9.50	£4.75
CalMac An Illustrated History of Caledonian MacBrayne	Alistair Deayton	£19.99	£10.00
Camera on the Clyde	Glen & Peter	£18.00	£9.00
Captured at Sea - Merchant Ships captured in the South West Seas of Britain in the time of Napleon	Colin R Rees and Prof.Peter Clark	£16.00	£8.00
Carebeka 1939-1983	Anderiesse and others	£30.00	£15.00
Ceredigion Shipwrecks Tales of Great Courage and Shameful Behaviour	W. Troughton	£12.00	£6.00
Chapman of Newcastle	Lingwood & Appleyard	£6.00	£3.00
Charles Dixon And the Golden Age of Marine Painting	Stuart Boyd	£29.99	£15.00
Classic Dutch-Built Coasters	B McCall	£17.00	£8.50
Classic Liners - Ile de France and Liberte - France's Premier Post War Liners	William H Miller	£19.99	£10.00
Classic Liners - RMS Queen Mary	Andrew Briton	£19.99	£10.00
Classic Liners - SS Leviathan America's First Superliner	Brent I. Holt	£19.99	£10.00
Classic Liners - SS Pasteur / TS Bremen	Andrew Briton	£19.99	£10.00
Classic Narrow Boats	M. Ranieri	£19.99	£10.00
Closing Down Sail	W Martin Benn	£22.00	£11.00
Clyde River and Other Steamers Fourth Edition	Duckworth & Langmuir	£25.00	£12.50
Clydebank Battlecruisers - Forgotten Photographs from John Brown's Shipyard	Ian Johnston	£30.00	£15.00
Coast Lines Key Ancestors - M Langlands & Sons	N Robbins and C Tucker	£16.00	£8.00
Coast to Coast - The Great Australian Coastal Liners	Peter Plowman	£15.00	£7.50
Coasters 2007	B McCall	£13.00	£6.50
Coasters An Illustrated History	Roy Fenton	£20.00	£10.00
Coasters in 2009	B McCall	£13.00	£6.50
Coasters of South Devon	B McCall	£15.00	£7.50
Coasters of South Wales	B McCall	£17.50	£8.75
Coasters of the 1960s	B McCall	£16.00	£8.00
Coasters of the 1970s Volume 1,	B McCall	£17.00	£8.50
Coasters op Kaarten (Dutch language) interesting photos	Harry de groot	£26.00	£13.00
Coasting Bargemaster	Bob Roberts	£9.95	£4.98
Cochrane Shipbuilders Vol. 3 1940-1993	G Mayes and M Thompson	£19.50	£9.75
Cochranes of Selby - Yorkshire Shipbuilders	E Hammond & P D Coates	£20.95	£10.48
Comben Longstaff & Co Ltd	K.S.Garrett	£16.00	£8.00
Come Home Sailor	Eric Kemp	£16.95	£8.48
Conquest of the ATLANTIC Cunard Liners of the 1950s and 1960s	William H. Miller	£19.99	£10.00
Cory Towage Ltd. A Group History	W.J. Harvey	£20.00	£10.00
Cosens of Weymouth, 1848 to 1918. A History of the Bournemouth, Weymouth and Swanage Paddle Steamers	R. Clammer	£29.95	£14.98
Cosens of Weymouth, 1918-1996	R. Clammer	£29.00	£14.50
County Class Guided Missile Destroyers	Neil McCart	£25.00	£12.50
Cromer Lifeboats A pictorial history	N.Leach & P. Russell	£16.99	£8.50
Cross Channel and Short Sea Ferries - An Illustrated History	Ambrose Greenway	£30.00	£15.00
Crossed Flags The Histories of the New Zealand Shipping Co Federal Steam Navigation Co and their subsidiaries	Laxon/Farquhar/Kirby/ Perry	£27.50	£13.75
Cruise Ships The World's Most Luxurious Vessels	Peter C. Smith	£30.00	£15.00
Cruise Ships (3rd edition)	William Mayes	£22.00	£11.00
Cruise Ships (4th edition)	William Mayes	£22.00	£11.00
Cruisers and La Geurre de Course (Paintings)	Ian Marshall	£35.00	£17.50
Cruisers, Corsairs & Slavers An Account of the Suppression of the Picaroon, Pirate & Slaver by the Royal Navy during the 19th Century	Basil Lubbock	£35.00	£17.50
Cunard - A Photographic History	Janette Mc-Cutcheon	£19.99	£10.00
Cunard - A Photographic History (2008 edition)	Janette Mc-Cutcheon	£19.99	£10.00
Cunard - A Photographic History (2013 edition)	Janette Mc-Cutcheon	£19.99	£10.00
Cunard - The Golden Years in Colour	Miller and Logvinenko	£19.99	£10.00
Cunard Portraits	J H Isherwood	£4.00	£2.00
Cunard The Golden Years in Colour	W. H. Miller & Logvinenko	£19.99	£10.00
Cunarder - Maritime Paintings by Stephen J Card	Stephen J Card	£35.00	£17.50
Cunard's Modern Queens A Celebration	W. H. Miller	£19.99	£10.00
Cunard's Three Queens A Celebration	W. H. Miller	£25.00	£12.50
d/s Norden Rederikoncernens flade	O. S. Johannesen	£52.50	£26.25
Dampschifffahrts-Gesellschaft Neptun 1873-1998 Sloma Neptun Schiffahrts-Aftiendesellschaft (German text) Yard List	Reinhold Thiel	£30.00	£15.00
Danish Ship Design 1936 to 1991, the work of Kay Fisker and Kay Korbing	Bruce Peter	£16.00	£8.00
Dansk Illustreret Skibsliste 2008 Danish Illustrated List of Ships		£10.00	£5.00
Danske Rederier, Volume 01	B Mikkelsen	£29.50	£14.75
Danske Rederier, Volume 02	B Mikkelsen	£29.50	£14.75
Danske Rederier, Volume 03	B Mikkelsen	£29.50	£14.75
Danske Rederier, Volume 09	B Mikkelsen	£29.50	£14.75
Danske Rederier, Volume 10	B Mikkelsen	£34.50	£17.25
Danske Rederier, Volume 11	B Mikkelsen	£29.50	£14.75
Danske Rederier, Volume 13	B Mikkelsen	£29.50	£14.75
Das Schiffsportrait, Dekoration und Document Volume 1 (German text)	Boye Meyer-Friese	£30.00	£15.00
De Smit-Lloyd Story - Anywhere, Anytime, Anyway (Durch text)	Nico J Owehand	£34.00	£17.00
Den lige linie, Historien om Juelsminde-Kalundborg Overfarten (Danish)	Jan Vinther Christensen	£30.00	£15.00
Deutsche Reedereien Band 30	Uwe Detlefsen	£40.00	£20.00
Deutsche Reedereien Band 35 (Rickmers)	Uwe Detlefsen	£65.00	£32.50
Deutsche Reedereien Band 36	Uwe Detlefsen	£52.00	£26.00
Deutsche Reedereien Band 37	Uwe Detlefsen	£46.00	£23.00
Deutsche Reedereien Band 38 (Peter Dohle)	Uwe Detlefsen	£65.00	£32.50
Deutsche Reedereien Band 43	Uwe Detlefsen	£50.00	£25.00
Deutsche Reedereien Band 47 and 48 (cannot split) Hapag-Lloyd	Uwe Detlefsen	£95.00	£47.50
Deutsche Schoner Band IV (German text)	H. Kartind	£48.50	£24.25
Deutsche Schoner Band V (German text)	H. Kartind	£48.50	£24.25
Deutsche Schoner Band VII (German text)	H. Kartind	£48.50	£24.25
DFDS 1866-1991 Ship Development through 125 years		£30.00	£15.00
Die Deutsche Schiffsliste 2000 (List of German shipowners with ships) Illustrated with drawing and photos	Eckardt & Messtorff, Hamburg	£20.00	£10.00
Die Flub-und Hafenschiffahrt der Deutschen Dampfschifffahrts-Gesellschaft "Hansa"	Holger Patzer	£38.00	£19.00
Die Geschichte de Bremer Vulcan 1805-1997 Band II 1919-1945 German text	Reinhold Thiel	£25.00	£12.50
Die Geschichte der Hapag-Schiffe Band 1:1847-1900	Arnold Kludas	£25.00	£12.50
Die Geschichte und die Schicksale deutscher Serienfrachter, Volume 2	Uwe Detlefsen	£28.00	£14.00
Die Gesschichte der Hapag-Schiffe - Band 3, 1914 - 1932 (German text) Company history and fleet list	Arnold Kludas	£30.00	£15.00
Die Gesschichte der Hapag-Schiffe - Band 4, 1933 - 1970 (German text) Company history and fleet list	Arnold Kludas	£30.00	£15.00
Die Gesschichte der Hapag-Schiffe - Band 5, Seebaderschiffe, Seeschlepper, Hilfsschiffe German text.	Arnold Kludas	£30.00	£15.00
Die Neubauten der Hitzler-Werft, Lauenburg 1886 to 2011 (German language)	Hitzler and Detlefsen	£32.00	£16.00
Die Rettungsboote der DGzRS von 1865-2009	Wilhelm Esmann	£25.00	£12.50
Die Typeschiffe der Sietas-Werft, Register der Trockenfrachter (German text)	Uwe Detlefsen	£87.50	£43.75
Disasters in the Thames	Michael Foley	£14.99	£7.50
Dock Developments at Newport The Alexandra (Newport & South Wales) Docks and Railway Co.		£4.95	£2.48
Dockers The '95 to '98 Liverpool Lockout	Dave Sinclair	£17.99	£9.00

Title	Author	Price 1	Price 2
Dockland Apprentice	D Carpenter	£9.00	£4.50
Dockside Delights Dock, Harbour and Seaside Scenes by Lowestoft Photographer Ernest Graystone	Malcolm R. White	£9.75	£4.88
Douglas Head Ferry and Port Soderick Boats	Captain Stephen Carter	£8.50	£4.25
Dover Calais	John Hendy	£18.95	£9.48
DP&L A History of the Dundee, Perth & London Shipping Company Ltd and Associated Shipping Companies	Graeme Somner	£6.00	£3.00
DSB Ferries - Ships of the Danish State Railways	Bruce Peter	£22.00	£11.00
DSR-Lines, Die Deutsche Seereederei, Rostock with brief fleet list (German text)	Bonische, Wenzel and Stubner	£25.00	£12.50
Dun Laoghaire Holyhead 1826-2015, The Rise and Decline of ireland's Premier Route	Justin Merrigan	£19.50	£9.75
Dutch & Belgian Short Sea Shipping 1996-97	Fenton & McCall	£5.00	£2.50
Dutch Merchant Navy, 1930 - 1939 (1)	W. H. Moojen	£13.50	£6.75
E H Hain of St. Ives	O'Donoghue and Appleyard	£10.00	£5.00
Early 20th Century Ports and Ships	G. M. Foustanos	£20.00	£10.00
East a Half South	John Curry	£8.99	£4.50
East of Suez - Liners to Australia in the 1950s and 1960s	Miller and Noble	£19.99	£10.00
Ebb and Flow Evacuations and Landings by Merchant Ships in World War Two	Roy Martin	£18.99	£9.50
Elders & Fyffes A Photographic History	C. McCutcheon	£19.99	£10.00
Ellerman Lines Remembering a Great British Shipping Company	Ian Collard	£16.99	£8.50
Empress to the Orient - Canadian Pacific	W Kaye Lamb	£7.50	£3.75
Eventful Voyage HMS Arlanza 1915-16	Jerry Driscoll	£10.50	£5.25
Fastest to Canada - The Royal Edward from Govan to Gallipoli	Richard Oliff	£16.99	£8.50
Favourite British Liners	Anthony Cooke	£34.00	£17.00
Fearless and Intrepid, 1965 to 2002	Neil McCart	£24.00	£12.00
Ferger og passagerskibe I Denmark (published 2006)	Anders Riis	£29.50	£14.75
Ferries 2001 British Isles & N. Europe	Nick Widdows	£12.00	£6.00
Ferries 2004 - Southern Europe	May and Mayes	£15.00	£7.50
Ferries 2012 British Isles & N. Europe	Nick Widdows	£19.00	£9.50
Ferries 2014 British Isles & N. Europe	Nick Widdows	£18.50	£9.25
Ferries 2016 British Isles & N. Europe	Nick Widdows	£18.50	£9.25
Ferries 2017 British Isles & N. Europe	Nick Widdows	£18.50	£9.25
Ferries of Dover	John Hendy	£4.95	£2.48
Ferries of Dover through 5 decades 1960 - 2010	John Hendy	£16.00	£8.00
Ferries of Scotland, Volume 2,	John Hendy	£5.95	£2.98
Ferries of the English Channel - Past and Present Volume 2	Miles Cowsill	£4.75	£2.38
Ferries of the Lower Thames	Joan Tucker	£19.99	£10.00
Ferries of the Upper Thames	Joan Tucker	£19.99	£10.00
Ferry & Cruise Ship Annual 2009		£20.00	£10.00
Ferry and Cruise Ship Annual 2010		£18.95	£9.48
Ferry Malta Il-Vapuri Ta Ghawdex	Graeme Somner	£6.00	£3.00
Ferry Tales - Tyne-Norway Voyages 1864-2001	Dick Keys and Ken Smith	£5.99	£3.00
Fifty Ship Paintings by Francis Huswick	A.S.Davidson & A Tibbles	£25.00	£12.50
Figureheads and Ship Carvers	M. Stammers	£17.99	£9.00
Finnish Illustrated List of Ships 2003		£23.00	£11.50
Finnish Maritime Index 05-06		£10.00	£5.00
Finnish Maritime Index 08-09		£10.00	£5.00
Fire Skibe med navnet TJALDUR (Danish language)	Bjarni Akesson Filholm	£24.00	£12.00
Fishguard-Rosslare - The Album	Justin Merrigan	£15.00	£7.50
Fishing Boats of Campbeltown Shipyard	S Henderson & P Drummond	£14.99	£7.50
Fishing The European Coast	Mike Smylie	£14.99	£7.50
Floating Palaces The Great Atlantic Liners	William H. Miller	£19.99	£10.00
Flying The Red Duster A Merchant Seaman's First Voyage into The Battle of The Atlantic 1940	Morris Beckman	£12.99	£6.50
Folkestone for the Continent 1843 -2001	John Hendy	£21.50	£10.75
For The Kings Service - Railway Ships at War	A J Mullay	£12.50	£6.25
Forgotten Beacons - The Lost Lighthouses of the Chesapeake Bay	Hornburger and Turbyville	£20.00	£10.00
Forgotten Coast	Robert Simper	£12.50	£6.25
Forty Years on, Ships of the New Waterway in 1968	George Garwood	£15.00	£7.50
Frank C. Strick Co.	Belt & Appleyard	£12.00	£6.00
Freshening Breezes, Fishing Boats of Cleveland and North Yotkshire	Gloria Wilson	£14.99	£7.50
From Comet to CalMac - Two Centuries of Hebridean and Clyde Shipping	Meek and Peter	£21.00	£10.50
From High Arctic to Antarctica Ships of Thom Companies on the Seven Seas	Matti Pietikainen	£52.00	£26.00
From Plymouth to Pieta HMS Hibernia, L-Arbanja at the Grand Harbour Malta	Michael Cassar	£10.50	£5.25
From The Revolution to The Cold War a History of the Soviet Merchant Fleet from 1917-1950	Martin J. Bollinger	£39.00	£19.50
From the Wheelhouse, Tugboaters tell their own stories (from Canada)	Doreen Armitage	£25.00	£12.50
Gale Warning - aerial photographs of ships in rough seas	Flying Focus	£16.75	£8.38
Gammle Saltens Bater (Norwegian ferries)	Johan Arnt Strom	£15.00	£7.50
Genesis of a Queen: Cunard Lines Queen Mary 2	The Naval Architect	£20.00	£10.00
George Gibson & Company	G. Somner	£6.00	£3.00
Giants of the Seas The Ships that Transformed Modern Cruising	Aaaron Saunders	£30.00	£15.00
Glasgow & South Western and other Steamers	Alistair Deayton	£12.99	£6.50
Glory Days - British Ferries	D L Williams	£16.99	£8.50
Glory Days - Clyde Steamers	Brian Patton	£16.99	£8.50
Goliath i Aalborg - En Lille Bi Kan Osse Stikke	Ole Mehder	£29.50	£14.75
Gone....	Bill' Cumming	£55.00	£27.50
Great American Passenger Ships	W H Miller	£19.99	£10.00
Great Classic Sailing Ships	K. Giggal with paintings by Cornelis de Vries	£25.00	£12.50
Great French Passenger Ships	W. H. Miller	£19.99	£10.00
Great Liners at War	S. Harding	£17.99	£9.00
Great Passenger Ships 1910-1920	W. H. Miller	£19.99	£10.00
Great Passenger Ships 1920-1930	W. H. Miller	£19.99	£10.00
Great White Fleet Celebrating Canada Steamship Lines Passenger Ships	John Henry	£20.00	£10.00
Greek Coastal Service 1945 to 1995	G M Foustanos	£37.50	£18.75
Greek Passenger Liners	W H Miller	£19.99	£10.00
H.Hogarth & Sons Limited Baron Line A short history and fleet list	A.A.McAlister & Leonard Gray	£8.00	£4.00
Hadley	W.J.Harvey	£10.00	£5.00
Hafn Hamburg (German text - well illustrated)	Kurt Groecker	£30.00	£15.00
Hamburg Tugs	Dollenbacher Schnake	£8.00	£4.00
Hearts of Steel - The Warship Paintings of Paul Wright		£19.99	£10.00
Henry Trengrouse - The Cornish Inventor of the Rocket Life-saving Apparatus	R & B Larn	£3.99	£2.00
Heroic, Forceful and Fearless - Australia's Tugboat Heritage	Randi Svensen	£70.00	£35.00
Herring A History of the Silver Darlings	Mike Smylie	£12.99	£6.50
High Seas High Risk The Story of the Sudburys	Pat Wastell Norris	£16.00	£8.00
Hine Brothers of Maryport - The Sailing Fleet based in Liverpool then Maryport, Volume 1	Robert Peel	£25.00	£12.50
Historic Sail Britain's Surviving Working Craft	Paul Brown	£16.99	£8.50
History and Fleet List 1948-1992 London & Overseas Freighters PLC	K J O'Donoghue	£8.00	£4.00
Hitler's Armada The Royal Navy & The Defence of Great Britain April-October 1940	Geoff Hewitt	£19.99	£10.00
HMS Ark Royal - Zeal does not rest 1981 - 2011	A Graham and E Grove	£29.99	£15.00
HMS Glory, 1945 to 1961	Neil McCart	£19.95	£9.98
HMS HQS Wellington	A D Munro	£10.00	£5.00
Hollandsche Stoomboot Maatschappij, De vaart op het Verenigd Koninkrijk en West Afrika, Volume 1, Rederijgeschiedenis. (Holland Steamship Company)	William H Moojen	£29.50	£14.75
HollandscheStoomboot Maatschappij, De vaart op het Verenigd Koninkrijk en West-Afrika, Volume 1 - Rederijgeschiedenis (Dutch language)	Willem H Moojen	£29.50	£14.75
HollandscheStoomboot Maatschappij, De vaart op het Verenigd Koninkrijk en West-Afrika, Volume 2 - De Vloot (Dutch language)	Willem H Moojen	£29.50	£14.75

Title	Author	Price	Price
Holyhead to Ireland Stena and its Welsh Heritage	J. P. Merrigan & I. H. Collard	£17.99	£9.00
Holyhead's Royal Visit - Queen Victoria's Return from Her Last Journey to Ireland	Jones/Robinson/Carr	£5.95	£2.98
Hovercraft - The Story of a Very British Invention	Arthur W J G Ord-Hulme	£16.00	£8.00
How to Pilot a Submarine A Fascinating Insight into The Life of a Submariner		£8.99	£4.50
Howard Smith Shipping - Enterprise and Diversity	Ian J Farquhar	£17.50	£8.75
Huddart Parker - A Famous Australasian Shipping Company 1876 to 1961	WA Laxon	£23.50	£11.75
Huddart Parker - A Famous Australian Shipping Company, 1876 to 1961	W A Laxon and others	£23.50	£11.75
Hunstanton Lifeboats	N.Leach	£12.99	£6.50
Hurricane Hutch's Top 10 Ships of the Clyde	R L Hutchison	£20.00	£10.00
Ile de France and Liberte France's Premier Post-War Liners	William H. Miller	£19.99	£10.00
Illustrert norsk skipliste Del 1-2006	Krohn Johansen	£10.00	£5.00
Illustrert norsk skipliste Del 2-2004	Krohn Johansen	£10.00	£5.00
Illustrert norsk skipliste Del 2-2008	Krohn Johansen	£10.00	£5.00
Illustrert norsk skipsliste Del 1-2004	Krohn Johansen	£10.00	£5.00
Illustrert norsk skipsliste Del 2-2004	Krohn Johansen	£10.00	£5.00
Illustrert norsk skipsliste Del 3-2004	Krohn Johansen	£10.00	£5.00
Illustrert norsk skipsliste Del 3-2006	Krohn Johansen	£10.00	£5.00
Illustrert norsk skipsliste Del 3-2007	Krohn Johansen	£10.00	£5.00
Images of England Weymouth and Portland	G Pritchard & A Hutchings	£12.99	£6.50
Images of Wales Butetown and Cardiff Docks	Brian Lee	£12.99	£6.50
Imperial Japanese Navy WWII	John Atkinson	£10.00	£5.00
In Fair Weather and Foul - 30 Years of Scottish Passenger Ships and Ferries	Colin J Smith	£12.95	£6.48
Irish Ferries - An ambitious voyage	Cowsill and Merrigan	£19.75	£9.88
Irish Sea Schooner Twilight The Last Years of the Western Seas Traders	Richard J. Scott	£24.99	£12.50
Isle of Man Shipping The Twilight Years	Ian Collard	£12.99	£6.50
Islenska Sjomanna Almanakid	F. A. Jonsson	£10.00	£5.00
J Fredrichs & Co, Fredrichswerft. , brief yar list (German text)	Diercks & Thiel	£25.00	£12.50
J Samuel White & Co. Shipbuilders	Williams and De Kerbrecht	£12.99	£6.50
J.Lauritzen, Skibene i arene Volume 1, 1888-1952	Ole Stig Johannesen	£44.00	£22.00
J.Lauritzen, Skibene i arene Volume 2, 1952 - 2013	Ole Stig Johannesen	£55.00	£27.50
Jaarboek Binnenvaart 2014	de Alk	£15.00	£7.50
Jaarboek Binnenvaart 2015	de Alk	£15.00	£7.50
Jackspeak A Guide to British Naval Slang & Usage	Rick Jolly & Tuss	£11.95	£5.98
Japanese Ferries	Peter & Ishiyama	£19.75	£9.88
Jebsens - A Group History	W J Harvey	£27.00	£13.50
John Kelly Ltd - a history (reprint from Sea Breezes)	Ian Wilson	£7.50	£3.75
Kelly's Navy John Kelly Ltd., Belfast A Group History	W.J. Harvey	£19.00	£9.50
Kent Seaways, Hoys to Hovercraft	M Langley	£16.95	£8.48
Kings of the Oceans 1948-1956	G. M. Foustanos	£30.00	£15.00
Kings of the Oceans 1967-1970	G. M. Foustanos	£30.00	£15.00
Kings of the Oceans 1975-1980	G. M. Foustanos	£30.00	£15.00
Kings of the Oceans 1991-2000	G. M. Foustanos	£30.00	£15.00
Kings of the Oceans 2001-2003	G. M. Foustanos	£30.00	£15.00
Kompagniets Skibe - Motorskibene fro OK under Dansk Flag East Asiatic motorships (Danish with English translation of introduction)	Ole Stig Johannesen	£45.00	£22.50
Kurs England, Mit der Hamburg Nach Harwich	Gert Uwe Detlefsen	£15.00	£7.50
La Marine Marchande Francaise 1939-1945	J I Brouard G Mercier M Saibenre	£42.00	£21.00
La Societe Generale Des Transports Maritimes a Vapeur	Alain Croce	£42.50	£21.25
Lakeland Steamers	A. Gladwell	£14.99	£7.50
Lancashire Coast Pleasure Steamers	A. Gladwell	£12.99	£6.50
Landing Craft from 1926	John Atkinson	£8.00	£4.00
Larrinaga Line 1863-1974	David Eccles	£19.00	£9.50
Last of the Line (lighthouses)	P Gumbrell	£14.95	£7.48
Launching History - The Saga of Burrard Dry Dock (includes yard list)	Francis Mansbridge	£30.00	£15.00
Leander Class Frigates	Osbourne and Sowden	£20.00	£10.00

Title	Author	Price	Price
Les Navires Hopitaux Francais Au XX Siecle, French Hospital Ships during the XX Century	Alain Croce	£15.00	£7.50
Liberty en Guerre	J-I Brouard	£35.00	£17.50
Lifeboat Stations of North East England From Sunderland to the Humber Through Time	Paul Chrystal	£14.99	£7.50
Light Vessels of the United Kingdon and Ireland 1820-2006, Illustrated Fleet List	Philip Simons	£15.00	£7.50
Linjer Rundt Jorden - Historien om Norsk Linjefart Cargo Liners (Norwegian)	Dag Bakka Jr	£25.00	£12.50
Lisbon of the World's Route - Lisbon Cruise Ships (English and Portuguese)	Luis Miguel Correia	£15.00	£7.50
Lisbon on the World's Routes - Cruise ships	Luis Miguel Correia	£15.00	£7.50
Lobo Marinho 2003 (Navios Portugueses)	Luis Miguel Correia	£13.00	£6.50
London and North Western Railway - Garston Docks (Reprint)	Mike G Fell	£15.00	£7.50
London's Docklands A History of the Lost Quarter	Fiona Rule	£19.99	£10.00
Looking Back at Bristol Channel Shipping	A. Wiltshire	£16.00	£8.00
Looking Back at Refrigerated Ships	A. Wiltshire	£16.00	£8.00
Looking Back at Traditional Cargo Ships	Andrew Wiltshire	£17.00	£8.50
Lowestoft Fishing Vessel Remembered. Wrecked Sunk and Missing Vessels of the Lowestoft Fleet 1939-1991	Malcolm White	£12.95	£6.48
Lundy Packets	Mike Tedstone	£24.00	£12.00
Lusitania - an illustrated Biography of the Ship of Splendour	J Kent Layton	£20.00	£10.00
Lusitania, An Illustrated Biography	J.Kent Layton	£40.00	£20.00
Lymington - Yarmouth, The New Generation	John Hendy	£6.00	£3.00
MacBrayne Ships	A Deayton	£19.99	£10.00
Maerskfladen - Skibene I arene 1976 to 1990 Text in Danish/English, Fleet list Danish but easy to follw	Ole Stig Johannesen	£46.00	£23.00
Marco Polo, Celebrating Fifty Golden Years of Ocean Travel	Richard Clammer	£15.99	£8.00
Marine Art and Ulster - a chronicle of sail, steam and flag codes	A S Davidson	£39.95	£19.98
Marine Pilot	John Foot	£12.95	£6.48
Mariner's Book of Days 2007	P H Spectre	£9.95	£4.98
Mariner's Launch	Ray Solly	£16.95	£8.48
Mariner's Voyage	Ray Solly	£16.99	£8.50
Maritiem Verleden in Beeld - Nostalgie (1)	W H Moojen	£13.50	£6.75
Maritime Greenwich	David Ramzan	£12.99	£6.50
Maritime Hartlepool - Two Thousand Years of History and Enterprise	Bert Spaldin	£12.95	£6.48
Maritime History, (Ship Models) Volume 6, (The Zomp, Dammes Eve, Zwarte Zee III)	Lanasta	£10.00	£5.00
Maritime History,(Ship models) Volume 5, (Batavier II, Witsen's yacht, Prins Willem Frederik Hendrik)	Lanasta	£10.00	£5.00
Maritime Royalty The Queen Mary and the Cunard Queens	William H. Miller	£19.99	£10.00
Maritime Wales	John Richards	£18.99	£9.50
Masting & Rigging The Clipper Ship & Ocean Carrier	Harold A. Underhill	£22.00	£11.00
Med Faergen fra Grenaa til Hundested	Jan Vinther Christensen	£60.00	£30.00
Mediterranean Ferries	Richard Seville	£16.00	£8.00
Medway & Swale Shipping Through Time	Geoff Lunn	£14.99	£7.50
Memories of the Clyde - Duchess of Fife 1903-1953 plans and photographs		£4.95	£2.48
Merchant Fleets 28 - Holland America Line	Duncan Haws	£11.00	£5.50
Merchantmen in Action, Evacuations and Landings by Merchant Ships in the Second World War	Roy V Martin	£20.00	£10.00
Merseyside - The Indian Summer, Volume 2 - Return to Pier Head Wallasey, Liverpool and the Hinterland	Cedric Greenwood	£19.99	£10.00
Minenschiffe 1939-1945 German language)	Kutleben and others	£20.00	£10.00
Mit Weselmann ging es Voran (german)	Uwe Detlefsen	£37.50	£18.75
Modern Mersey Shipping	Ian Collard	£16.00	£8.00
MS Corvo of 2007 (in Portuguese and English)	Luis Miguel Correia	£15.00	£7.50
MS Europa	A Dolling	£15.00	£7.50
MV Balmoral The First 60 Years	A Deayton & I Quinn	£14.99	£7.50

N.P.1840 The Loss of the Atlantic Conveyor	Chalres Drought	£9.99	£5.00
Nautical Training Ships An Illustrated History	Phil Carradice	£17.99	£9.00
Naval Accidents since 1945	M Maclean	£30.00	£15.00
Nederlandse Koopvaardij in Beeld - 1920 - 1929 (1)	William H Moojen	£13.50	£6.75
Nederlandse Koopvaardij in Beeld - 1950 - 1959 (1)	William H Moojen	£13.50	£6.75
Nederlandse Koopvaardijschepen in beeld, No.03, Passagiersvaart	Dick Gorter	£14.00	£7.00
Nederlandse Koopvaardijschepen in beeld, No.05, Kleine I landelsvaart (1)	Dick Gorter	£14.00	£7.00
Nederlandse Koopvaardijschepen in beeld, No.06, Lijnvaart (2)	Dick Gorter	£14.00	£7.00
Nederlandse Koopvaardijschepen in beeld, No.07, Koelvaart	Dick Gorter	£16.50	£8.25
Nederlandse Koopvaardijschepen in beeld, No.08, Kleine Handelsvaart (2)	Dick Gorter	£16.50	£8.25
Nederlandse Koopvaardijschepen in beeld, No.09, Lijnvaart (3)	Dick Gorter	£16.50	£8.25
Nederlandse Koopvaardijschepen in beeld, No.10, Wilde vaart (2)	Dick Gorter	£16.50	£8.25
Nederlandse Koopvaardijschepen in beeld, No.11, Kleine Handelsvaart (3)	Dick Gorter	£16.50	£8.25
Nederlandse Koopvaardijschepen in beeld, No.12, V.M.S.	Dick Gorter	£16.50	£8.25
Nederlandse Koopvaardijschepen in beeld, No.14, Tankvaart - Buiten- landse eigenaren Nederlandse vlag	Dick Gorter	£21.50	£10.75
Nederlandse koopvaardijschepen in beelt No.16 Nedlloyd	Dick Gorter	£22.50	£11.25
Nederlandse Kottervisserij in Beeld - 1960 - 1969	Jurie van den Burgh	£13.50	£6.75
Neutral Shores, Ireland and the Battle of the Atlantic	Mark McShane	£17.50	£8.75
New Zealand Maritime Images - The Golden Years	Emmanuel Makarios	£15.00	£7.50
No Higher Purpose - The Official Operational History of the Royal Ca- nadian Navy in the Second World War 1939 to 1943, Volume 2, Part 1	Douglas, Sarty and Whitby	£40.00	£20.00
No More Paraffin-Oilers	Ian Cassells	£20.00	£10.00
No Port in a Storm (working on Light Ships)	B MacAlindin	£13.95	£6.98
No Tides to Stem Volume 2 A History of the Manchester Pilot Service	Derek A. Clulow	£9.75	£4.88
Norddeutscher Lloyd Hamburg- Bremer Africa-Linie (German)	Reinhold Thiel	£30.00	£15.00
Norddeutscher Lloyd Roland Linie 1905-1992 (German)	Reinhold Thiel	£30.00	£15.00
Nordsoens Hurtiglobere - Historien om Englandsbadene Kronprins Frederik og Kronprinsesse Ingrid (in Danish and well illustrated)	BjarniAkesson Filholm	£26.50	£13.25
Nordsovaerftet	B Mikkelsen	£29.50	£14.75
North Sea Ferries - Across Three Decades	Barry Mitchell	£6.95	£3.48
North Wales Pleasure Steamers	A Gladwell	£14.99	£7.50
Norwegian America Line 1910-1995	B Pedersen & F.W. Hawks	£12.00	£6.00
Nothing Over the Side Examining Safe Crude Oil Tankers	Ray Solly	£19.99	£10.00
Nourse Line	F.W.Perry & W.A.Laxon	£6.00	£3.00
Obdurate to Daring, British Fleet Destroyers 1941 - 1945	John English	£33.00	£16.50
Ocean Freighter Finale	Nigel Jones	£16.00	£8.00
Ocean Liner Chronicles	William H. Miller	£16.95	£8.48
Ocean Liner Odyssey 1958-1969	T. W. Scull	£10.95	£5.48
Ocean Liner Posters	G. Cadringher	£25.00	£12.50
Oinoussian Steamships 1905-1940	G.M. Foustanos	£40.00	£20.00
On a Broad Reach - The History of the St Anne's on the Sea Lifeboat Station, 1881 to 1925	G I and J E Mayes	£12.50	£6.25
Oriana & Aurora Taking UK Cruising into a New Millenium	S Polle & A. Sassoli-Walker	£19.99	£10.00
Out of Harms Way - Moving Ameri- ca's Lighthouse,	Mike Booher and Lin Ezell	£20.00	£10.00
Owen & Watkin Williams of Cardiff 'The Golden Cross Line'	David Jenkins	£6.00	£3.00
P & O at 175 - A World of Ships and Shipping since 1837	Peter & Daw- son	£24.50	£12.25
P & O Princess The Cruise Ships	Roger Cart- wright	£19.99	£10.00
P & O, The Fleet, (about 2010)	Hendy/Cowsill	£6.00	£3.00

Paddle Steamer Kingswaer Castle and Steamers of the River Dart	Clammer and Kittridge	£14.00	£7.00
Paddle Steamers of the Thames	Peter Box	£12.99	£6.50
Palm Oil & Small Chop	John Goble	£16.99	£8.50
Paquebots autor du monde	Jean-Francois Durannd	£23.00	£11.50
Passage to the Northern Isles - Ferry services to Orkney and Shetland 1790-2010	Cowsill and Smith	£17.50	£8.75
Passagiersschepem Uit Nederland - De Oceaanlijners van CA 1880 Tot I leden (Dutch text)	Arne Zuidhoek	£30.00	£15.00
Passenger Liners Scandinavian Style	Bruce Peter	£27.00	£13.50
Passenger Steamers of the River Conwy Serving the Famous Trefriw Spa	Richard Clam- mer	£14.99	£7.50
Passenger Tugs and Tenders	Nick Robins	£15.00	£7.50
Passing Ships	Gordon Gray	£17.99	£9.00
Piers of the Hebrides & Western Isles	A. Deayton	£14.99	£7.50
Pilots, The World of Pilotage under Sail and Oar, Volume 1 - Pilot Schooners of North America and Great Britain	Tom Cunliffe	£50.00	£25.00
Pilots, The World of Pilotage under Sail and Oar, Volume 2, Schooners and Open Boats of the European Pilots and Watermen	Tom Cunliffe	£50.00	£25.00
Porthmadog Ships	E.Hughes and A.Eames	£8.00	£4.00
Ports of Scotland 2007		£12.50	£6.25
Ports of Scotland 2010		£12.50	£6.25
Ports of Scotland 2012		£12.50	£6.25
Ports of Scotland 2014		£15.00	£7.50
Ports of Scotland 2015		£15.00	£7.50
Ports of Scotland 2015		£15.00	£7.50
Post War Canadian Pacific Liners - Empresses of the Atlantic	William H Miller	£19.99	£10.00
QE2 Forty Years Famous	Carol Thatcher	£25.00	£12.50
QM2 - a photographic journey	Frame & Cross	£25.00	£12.50
Queen Elizabeth - a photographic journey	Frame & Cross	£25.00	£12.50
Queen Mary 2 - A Book of Compari- sons		£12.50	£6.25
Queen Victoria - A photographic jour- ney (hard back)	Frame & Cross	£25.00	£12.50
Queen Victoria - A Celebration of Tra- dition for 21st century Ocean Travel	Philip Dawson	£16.00	£8.00
Queen Victoria - a photographic jour- ney (soft back)	Frame and Cross	£18.99	£9.50
Queens of the Tyne	Ken Smith	£6.99	£3.50
Railways to New Holland and The Humber Ferries	A J Ludlam	£8.95	£4.48
Rats, Rust & Two Old Ladies	David Creamer	£18.99	£9.50
Red Sky in the Morning The Battle of the Barents Sea 1942	Michael Pear- son	£16.99	£8.50
Reederei Karl Schluter Rendsburg (German and English)		£30.00	£15.00
Reefer Ships - The Ocean Princesses	Nick Tolerton	£27.50	£13.75
Register der Deutschen Kumos sowie anderer Fracht - und Containerschiffe von 500 bis 1600BRT und bis BRZ 5000 (1945 to 1999) In two volumes	Detlefsen and Abert	£137.50	£68.75
Remembering the Chunnel Beaters - The Pride of Dover and the Pride of Calais	John Hendy	£9.95	£4.98
Remembering the Free Enterprise - Townsend's trend setting ferry	R P Blowers	£7.95	£3.98
Remembcring thc Lord Wardcn	John Hondy	£12.00	£6.00
Remembering the Thoresen Vikings - Townsend Thoresen trendsetters	Cowsill and John Hendy	£15.00	£7.50
Reminiscences of John Jones Griffith	J. Maxwell	£5.95	£2.98
Rendel's Floating Bridges	Alan Kittridge	£12.50	£6.25
Rendsburger Schiffsregister - Schrift- en des Rendsburger Schiffahrtsar- chives No.1.	Dr Jens-Peter Schluter	£38.50	£19.25
Rendsburger Schiffsregister No. 1	Schluter and Detlefsen	£38.00	£19.00
Rendsburger Schiffsregister -Schriften des Rendsburger Shiffahrtsarchives No.1. (German language)	Uwe Detlefsen	£38.50	£19.25
Report into the Loss of the SS Titanic	S Halpern	£20.00	£10.00
Rescue at Sea - An International History of Lifesaving, Coastal Rescue Craft and Organisations	Clayton Evans	£35.00	£17.50
Reuben Chappell - Pierhead Painter	Robert Jones	£29.99	£15.00
Ritsons' Branch Line	M Cooper	£16.00	£8.00
River Clyde from Source to Sea	R Harper & Mark Steward	£16.99	£8.50

Title	Author	Price	Price
RMS Lusitania The Ship & Her Record	Eric Sauder	£14.99	£7.50
RMS Majestic The 'Magic-Stick'	Mark Chirnside	£19.99	£10.00
RMS Queen Elizabeth 2 The Last Great Liner	Janette Mc-Cutcheon	£19.99	£10.00
RMS Queen Elizabeth The Beautiful Lady	Janette Mc-Cutcheon	£19.99	£10.00
RMS Queen Mary	Andrew Britton	£19.99	£10.00
RMS Queen Mary 2 - Owners's Workshop Manual	Stephen Payne	£21.99	£11.00
RN Battleships and Battlecruisers in Focus	David Hobbs	£14.99	£7.50
RN Cruisers in Focus	Ben Warlow	£14.99	£7.50
RN Frigates in Focus	Ben Warlow	£14.95	£7.48
RN Submarines in Focus	David Hobbs	£14.99	£7.50
Robert Schmidt - Hamburg, von Seemann zum marinemaler (German)	Hormann/ Muller	£25.00	£12.50
Rock Lighthouses of Britain	C Nicholson	£25.00	£12.50
Round The Horn Before The Mast	Basil Lubbock	£16.00	£8.00
Royal Navy Handbook, 1914 -1918	David Wragg	£25.00	£12.50
Royal Navy Submarine Service Losses in WWII	John Atkinson	£9.95	£4.98
Royal Navy Trawlers Part 2, Requisitioned Trawlers	Gerald Toghill	£24.95	£12.48
Royal Yachts	Alan Major	£20.00	£10.00
Russian Sea/River Ships	Bernard Mc-Call	£17.50	£8.75
S.S.United States - Fastest Ship in the World, 50th Anniversary Maiden Voyage Edition	Frank Braynard and R H Westover	£24.95	£12.48
Safmarine - The South African Marine Corporation Ltd - A Group History	Harvey/Mackenzie	£24.00	£12.00
Sailing Barge Master - The Story of a Victorian Bargemen	Captain George Winn	£12.95	£6.48
Sailing Seven Seas A History of the Canadian Pacific Line	Peter Pigott	£23.00	£11.50
Sailing to Success - The Union Company Cadet Scheme	Ra McGregor	£28.00	£14.00
Sally Line, The Complete Story	Breeze/Cowsill/Hendy	£4.50	£2.25
Saltens Bater II, Gammel og ny tid moites, (Norwegian ferries)	J.A. Strom and B I Strom	£15.00	£7.50
Scheepvaart 2003	G.J.de Boer	£10.00	£5.00
Scheepvaart 2011	G.J.de Boer	£10.00	£5.00
Schiffahrt im Bild - Behordenschiffe (Harbour craft)	Uwe Detlefsen	£14.50	£7.25
Schiffahrt im Bild - Containerschiffe (II)	Uwe Detlefsen	£14.50	£7.25
Schiffahrt im Bild - Containerschiffe (III)	Uwe Detlefsen	£14.50	£7.25
Schiffahrt im Bild - Norddeutsche Fahren	Uwe Detlefsen	£14.50	£7.25
Schiffahrt im Bild - Passagierschiffe	Uwe Detlefsen	£14.50	£7.25
Schiffahrt im Bild - Schiffe des Norddeutschen Lloyd	Uwe Detlefsen	£14.50	£7.25
Schiffahrt im Bild - Spezialfrachter	Uwe Detlefsen	£14.50	£7.25
Schiffahrt im Bild - Tanker (I)	Uwe Detlefsen	£14.50	£7.25
Schiffahrt im Bild - Tanker (II)	Uwe Detlefsen	£14.50	£7.25
Schiffahrt im Bild - Tanker (III)	Uwe Detlefsen	£14.50	£7.25
Schiffahrt im Bild - Trampschiffe (I)	Uwe Detlefsen	£14.50	£7.25
Schweizer Reeder in aller Welt Schweizer Schiffahrtsgeschichte des 19 Jahrhumderls (German)	Walter Zurcher	£40.00	£20.00
Scotland's East Coast Fishing Industry	Mark I'Anson	£7.99	£4.00
Scotlands Turntable Ferries	Beale & Hendy	£16.00	£8.00
Scrap & Build	D.C.E.Burrell	£8.00	£4.00
Sea Like a Mirror	Alan Jones	£16.99	£8.50
Sealink and beyond	M Murtland and R Seville	£24.50	£12.25
Sealink Memories	Hendy & Merrigan	£18.00	£9.00
Seaspray and Whisky Tale of a Turbulent voyage	Norman Freeman	£9.99	£5.00
Secret Victory Ireland and the War at Sea 1914-1918	Laim Nolan & John E. Nolan	£19.50	£9.75
Selandia The World's First Oceangoing Diesel Vessel	Anders Riis	£36.00	£18.00
Severn & Wye & Severn Bridge Joint Railway Lydney Harbour, Docks, & Canal Dues, Bye-laws, & C November 1902		£3.95	£1.98
Severn Bridge Disaster 25th October 1960	Chris Witts	£4.95	£2.48
Shakespeare's Avon - The History of a Navigation	Jamie Davies	£8.95	£4.48
Shaw Savill and Albion - A Fleet History	Spong/Osborne	£45.00	£22.50
Shield of Empire - The Royal Navy and Scotland	Brian Lavery	£30.00	£15.00
Shipcraft 7 -British Battle Cruisers or the Second World War	Steve Backer	£15.00	£7.50
Ship-Pax - Designs 07 Ferry, Cruise and Ro-Ro Newbuilding Yearbook		£12.00	£6.00
Ship-Pax - Designs 08 Ferry, Cruise and Ro-Ro Newbuilding Yearbook		£12.00	£6.00
Ship-Pax - Guide 06 Ferry, Cruise and Ro-Ro Register Yearbook		£12.00	£6.00
Ship-Pax - Market 07 - report and analysis of passenger and ro-ro shipping		£12.00	£6.00
ShipPax Designs 06 - Ferry, Cruise and RoRo Newbuilding Yearbook		£45.50	£22.75
ShipPax Guide 07, Ferry, Cruuise and RoRo Register		£12.00	£6.00
ShipPax Guide 09, register of ferries, cruise liners and Ro-Ro vessels		£12.00	£6.00
ShipPax Market 07 - reports and analysis of passenger and ro-ro shipping		£57.50	£28.75
ShipPax Market 08		£12.50	£6.25
Shipping of the Bosphorus	C Brooks and S Smith	£16.00	£8.00
Shipping of the River Forth	W F. Hendrie	£12.99	£6.50
Ships & Shipbuilders Pioneers of Design and Construction	Fred M. Walker	£25.00	£12.50
Ships for a Nation, John Brown and Company, Clydebank 1847-1971	Ian Johnston	£25.00	£12.50
Ships for All Nations John Brown & Co. Clydebank 1847-1971	Ian Johnston	£40.00	£20.00
Ships of North Cornwall	John Bartlett	£35.00	£17.50
Ships of the Solent	Colin Hall	£12.95	£6.48
Ships of the White Star Line	R de Kerbrecht	£19.99	£10.00
Shipwrecks of Sussex	W Hughes	£12.99	£6.50
Shipwrecks of the Forth and Tay	Bob Baird	£18.99	£9.50
Shipwrecks of the Irish Coast Volume 1, 1105-1993	Edward J Bourke	£11.99	£6.00
Shipwrecks of the Irish Coast Volume 3 1582 to 2000	Edward J Bourne	£11.99	£6.00
Shipyards of the Upper Mersey	Robert Ratcliffe	£16.99	£8.50
Short Sea Shipping 1999/2000	Mayes/McCall	£6.00	£3.00
Short Sea Shipping 2001/2002	Gilbert Mayes	£3.50	£1.75
Short Sea: Long War Cross-Channel Ships Naval & Military Service in World War 11	John de S.Winser	£21.00	£10.50
Showing the Flag, West Coast Maritime Series No.4	S C Heal	£15.00	£7.50
Significant Ships of 1996		£35.00	£17.50
Significant Ships of 1997		£35.00	£17.50
Significant Ships of 1998		£35.00	£17.50
Significant Ships of 1999		£35.00	£17.50
Significant Ships of 2002		£33.00	£16.50
Significant Ships of 2003		£41.00	£20.50
Significant Ships of 2007		£45.00	£22.50
Significant Ships of 2009		£47.00	£23.50
Significant Small Ships of 2004		£27.50	£13.75
Significant Small Ships of 2006		£29.00	£14.50
Significant Small Ships of 2009		£30.00	£15.00
Significant Small Ships of 2010		£27.00	£13.50
Silent Warriors Submarine Wrecks of the United Kingdom Volume Three	P Armstrong & R Young	£19.99	£10.00
Silja Line from Samseglande to Tallink	Kalle Id	£22.00	£11.00
Sink the French At War With Our Ally-1940	David Wragg	£19.99	£10.00
Six Stars of the Ocean -Seven Seas Navigator - A dream cruise ship for the 21st Century	Maurizeo Eliseo	£32.50	£16.25
Six Wonderful Days - Italian Liners		£29.00	£14.50
Skegness Lifeboats An Illustrated History	N. Leach	£9.99	£5.00
Skoubadene - skibene fra rederiet Ove Skou	Ole Stig Johannesen	£31.00	£15.50
Sleep & Duwboten 2001		£10.00	£5.00
Sleep & Duwboten 2007		£10.00	£5.00
Sleep & Duwboten 2010		£23.00	£11.50
Sleep & Duwboten 2016		£10.00	£5.00
Sloops 1926-1946 (marked cover)	Arnold Hague	£14.00	£7.00
Smoke, Ash and Steam, West Coast Steam Engines, 1st edition (from Canada)	R Sheret	£14.00	£7.00
Smoke, Ash and Steam, West Coast Steam Engines, 2nd edition (from Canada)	R Sheret	£14.00	£7.00
Solent Seaways, Wight Link Isle of Wight Ferries	John Hendy	£16.00	£8.00
South West Harbours, Ships and Trades	M Langley	£16.95	£8.48
Spanish Civil War Blockade Runners	Paul heaton	£20.00	£10.00
SS Rotterdam of 1959	Miller/Correia	£9.00	£4.50
SS United States Speed Queens of the Seas	William H. Miller	£19.99	£10.00

Title	Author	Price	Price
Standaard Schepen 1939-1945 in de Nederlandse en Belgische koopvaardij, Volume 1 History (Dutch language)	Drs D Gorter and G J de Boer	£32.50	£16.25
Standaard Schepen 1939-1945 in de Nederlandse en Belgische koopvaardij, Volume 2 Fleet List (Dutch language)	G J de Boer and Drs D Gorter	£32.50	£16.25
Steadfast Boats and Fisher-People	Gloria Wilson	£12.99	£6.50
Steamers of the Clyde (paintings with description)		£6.95	£3.48
Steamers of the Clyde and Western Isles (paintings with description)		£6.95	£3.48
Steamers of the Clyde The White Funnel Fleet	Alistair Deayton	£12.99	£6.50
Steamers of the Forth, Volume 2, Firth Services and Excursions	Ian Brodie	£7.50	£3.75
Steamers of the Tay	Ian Brodie	£7.50	£3.75
Steamers to Arran	Andrew Clark	£10.00	£5.00
Steamers to Rothesay and the Isle of Bute	Andrew Clark	£10.00	£5.00
Steamship Travel in the Interwar Years Tourist Third Cabin	Coon & Varias	£9.99	£5.00
Stena	W.J. Harvey	£31.00	£15.50
Stena Line - celebrating 50 years of service	Bruce Peter	£18.95	£9.48
Stena Line - The Fleet (1997)	W J Harvey	£4.75	£2.38
Still Passing the Point	B McCall	£16.00	£8.00
Sunrise Coast	Robert Simper	£12.50	£6.25
Sussex Beach Trades, Sea Coal to Trippers	M Langley	£16.95	£8.48
Swan Hunter Built Warships	Ian Buxton	£17.99	£9.00
Tall Ships on the Tyne	Dick Keys and Ken Smith	£3.99	£2.00
Thames & Medway Pleasure Steamer from 1935	Andrew Gladwell	£14.99	£7.50
Thames-side Kent Through Time	Anthony Lane	£14.99	£7.50
The "Type 35" Torpedoboats of the Kriegsmarine	M.J.Whitley	£6.00	£3.00
The Aberdeen Steam Navigation Company Ltd	Graeme Somner	£6.00	£3.00
The Anatomy of a Ship -The *Fairmile D* Motor Torpedo Boat	John Lambert	£15.00	£7.50
The Anatomy of Canals The Early Years	A Burton & D Pratt	£15.99	£8.00
The Australian National Line History and Fleet List	Clark, Rex and Robertson	£8.00	£4.00
The Battle of Jutland	G Bennett	£20.00	£10.00
The Battleship Builders Constructing and Arming British Capital Ships	Ian Johnston and Ian Buxton	£30.00	£15.00
The Bell Rock Light -Robert Stevenson's account of its building	Robert Louis Stevenson	£20.00	£10.00
The Blockade Busters Cheating Hitler's Reich of Vital War Supplies	Ralph Barker	£19.99	£10.00
The British Cruise Ship - An Illustrated History 1945-2014	Ian Collard	£19.99	£10.00
The British Cruise Ship An Illustrated History 1844-1939	Ian Collard	£19.99	£10.00
The British Excursion Ship	Nick Robbins	£28.00	£14.00
The Caledonian Canal, Lochs, Locks and Pleasure Steamers	Guthrie Hutton	£7.99	£4.00
The Caledonian Steam Packet Company An Illustrated History	A Deayton	£19.99	£10.00
The Canal Builders	A Burton	£16.99	£8.50
The Canals of Harley Crossley An Artist's View of Boats and Waterways	Barbara Crosssley	£19.99	£10.00
The Clyde Shipping Company, Glasgow, 1815 - 2000	W J Harvey, P J Telford	£20.00	£10.00
The Cockleshell Canoes British Military Canoes of World War Two	Quentin Rees	£19.99	£10.00
The Comet and her creators - The men who built the PS Comet, and her career	J Craig Osborne	£6.00	£3.00
The Conway History of Seafaring in the 20th Century	Various	£20.00	£10.00
The Cornish Fishing Industry - an illustrated history	John McWilliams	£16.99	£8.50
The Cornish Fishing Industry - an illustrated history	J McWilliams	£16.99	£8.50
The Crew A Portrait of Merchant Seamen at the End of the Tramp Steamer Era	Tom Peppitt	£17.00	£8.50
The Currie Line of Melbourne	W A Laxon	£7.50	£3.75
The Currie Line of Melbourne (Company History and Fleet List)	W A Laxon	£7.50	£3.75
The Daily Telegraph Guide to Britain's Maritime Past	Anthony Burton	£14.99	£7.50
The Daniel Adamson - A Unique Survivor		£8.00	£4.00
The Down Easters The Story of the Cape Horners	Basil Lubbock	£22.00	£11.00
The Edwardian Superliners - A Trio of Trios	J.Kent Layton	£40.00	£20.00

Title	Author	Price	Price
The Enigmatic sailor	Alan Peacock	£14.95	£7.48
The Evolution of the British Ferry	Nick Robins	£7.95	£3.98
The Fatal Flaw Collision at Sea & The Failure of the Rules	David Thomas	£12.00	£6.00
The Ferry - a drive through history (hard back - abridged version)	Peter and Dawson	£21.50	£10.75
The Ferry - a drive through history (soft back - original version)	Peter and Dawson	£32.50	£16.25
The Fighting Civilians	Charles Daly	£8.99	£4.50
The First Atlantic Liners - Seamanship in the age of Paddle Wheel, Sail and Screw	P Allington and B Greenhill	£35.00	£17.50
The Fishbourne Car Ferry - Portsmouth to the Isle of Wight	John C H Failkner	£15.99	£8.00
The Fourth Force, The Untold Story of the Royal Fleet Auxiliary since 1945	Geoff Puddlefoot	£25.00	£12.50
The Fred Olsen Line and its Passenger Ships	Anthony Cooke	£21.00	£10.50
The Glamorganshire and Aberdare Canals	S Rowson and Ian L Wright	£30.00	£15.00
The Gloucester & Sharpness Canal An Illustrated History	Hugh Conway-Jones	£16.99	£8.50
The Gorthon Shipping Companies 1915-1985	Kjell A. Axelson & Tomas Johannsson	£6.00	£3.00
The Gozo - Malta Connection	M Cassar	£33.00	£16.50
The History of World War One - Naval Warfare 1914-1918 - From Coronel to the Atlantic and Zeebrugge	Tim Benbow	£25.00	£12.50
The House that Percy Built Growing up on Merseyside	Syd Heal	£10.00	£5.00
The Illustrated History of Canal and River Navigations	Edward Paget Tomlinson	£24.99	£12.50
The Irish Boats Volume 1 Liverpool to Dublin	Malcolm McRonald	£19.99	£10.00
The Isle of Man Steam Packet Through Time	Ian Collard	£14.99	£7.50
The Kent Coast, Gravesend to Margate through time	Anthony Lane	£14.99	£7.50
The Last Atlantic Liners 'Getting there is Half the Fun'	William H. Miller	£19.99	£10.00
The Last of the Windjammers Volume 1	Basil Lubbock	£30.00	£15.00
The Last of the Windammers Volume 11	Basil Lubbock	£30.00	£15.00
The Last White Empresses	Clive Harvey	£17.95	£8.98
The LD Lines Story	G Holland	£9.95	£4.98
The Life and Adventures of a Trinity Boy	Roy Jones	£4.99	£2.50
The Life and Times of the Steam Packet	J Shepherd	£11.95	£5.98
The Lifeboats of Rosslare Harbour and Wexford	Nicholas Leach	£19.99	£10.00
The Lifeboats Story	E Wake-Walker	£8.99	£4.50
The Liner - Retrospective and Renaissance	Philip Dawson	£30.00	£15.00
The Log of the "Cutty Sark"	Basil Lubbock	£24.00	£12.00
The Log Ships	S.C.Heal	£12.00	£6.00
The Lugger Coast	Robert Simper	£12.50	£6.25
The Marine Art of Harley Crossley	Harley Crossley	£19.99	£10.00
The Mariner's Book of Days 2009	P H. Spectre	£9.95	£4.98
The Mariner's Book of Days 2010	P H. Spectre	£9.95	£4.98
The Martingale Chronicles Part One (1933-41)	John L. Winstone	£10.50	£5.25
The Martingale Chronicles Part Two (1942-53)	John L. Winstone	£10.50	£5.25
The Naval Service of Canada 1910-2010, The Centennial Story	Richard H Gimblett	£24.00	£12.00
The Nitrate Boats	David Burrell	£6.00	£3.00
The North Atlantic Front The Northern Isles at War	James Miller	£20.00	£10.00
The North Boats, The Story of the North of Sctoland, Orkney & Shetland Shipping Company	Alastair W McRobb	£6.95	£3.48
The North Herring Fishing Ring Net Fisherman in the Minches	Angus Martin	£13.99	£7.00
The Old Forth and Clyde Canal	Guthrie Hutton	£10.00	£5.00
The Once-Ubiquitous Paddle Steamer	John Hannavy	£9.99	£5.00
The Opium Clippers	Basil Lubbock	£24.00	£12.00
The Ostend Ferry from Start to Finish	S Pattheeuws	£19.75	£9.88
The Port Talbot Railway and Docks Co., Handbook of Rates etc. (fascimile)		£7.50	£3.75
The Prowess of Charlie Fielder	Wood/Walsh	£13.50	£6.75
The Pyman Story - Fleet and Family History	Hogg and Appleyard	£10.00	£5.00
The QE2 Story	Frame/Cross	£8.99	£4.50
The Real Price of Fish - the story of Scotland's Fishing Industry and Communities	Linda Fitzpatrick	£6.95	£3.48
The Royal Navy 1914-1918 - A Photographic Record	Adrian Vicary	£25.00	£12.50

Title	Author	Price	Price
The Royal Navy at Devonport since 1900	Ben Warlow	£14.95	£7.48
The Royal Navy Day by Day	Sainsbury & Phillips	£35.00	£17.50
The Royal Navy Handbook - The Definitive MOD Guide		£14.99	£7.50
The Royal Navy in Focus 1980-1989	Steve Bush	£14.99	£7.50
The Sail and Steam Navy List - All the Ships of the Royal Navy 1815 to 1889	D Lyon & Rif Winfield	£60.00	£30.00
The Sail of Cardiff Bay Volume Two	Alan Roy Thorne	£13.99	£7.00
The Saint George Steam Packet Company	Greenwood & Hawks	£6.00	£3.00
The Salty Shore	John Leather	£10.95	£5.48
The Schooner - Its design and Development from 1600 to the present	David R Mac-Gregor	£14.95	£7.48
The Sealink Legacy - 30 Years since Privatisation	Iain McCall	£9.95	£4.98
The Secrets of HMS Dasher	John Steele & Noreen Steele	£9.99	£5.00
The Shamrock Shipping Company	W.J. Harvey	£20.00	£10.00
The Ships of Ellis Island	W H, Miller	£19.99	£10.00
The Short-Sea Route Dover Calais 1st Edition 2009	John Hendy	£18.50	£9.25
The Thames - a photographic journey from source to sea	Derek Pratt	£19.99	£10.00
The Thames Sailing Barge Compendium - A Schedule of Sailing Barge Data arranged alphabetically and by last known location	John White	£20.00	£10.00
The Torm Ships - The Torm Fleet Through 120 Years	Ole Stig Johannesen	£56.00	£28.00
The Towns	Arnold Hague`	£20.00	£10.00
The Townsend Eight	Cowsill/Hendy	£8.00	£4.00
The Trades Increase A Centenary History of Norex plc	J Lingwood & K O'Donoghue	£10.00	£5.00
The Ultimate Shipwreck Guide Whitby to Berwick	Ron Young	£19.99	£10.00
The Unseen Lusitania, The Ship in Rare Illustrations	Eric Sauder	£25.00	£12.50
The Voyage is Done & The Winds Don't Blow	Robert A. Wilson	£10.00	£5.00
The War in the Mediterranean	B Ireland	£19.95	£9.98
The Western Ocean Packets	Basil Lubbock	£22.00	£11.00
Thomas Watson	K.S.Garrett	£16.00	£8.00
Those Beautiful Coastal Liners	R D Turner	£19.00	£9.50
Three Greenwich built ships	D C Ramzan	£17.99	£9.00
Three Greenwich Built Ships (Princess Louisa, clipper Hallowe'en and RN Dolphin	David C Razman	£17.99	£9.00
Titanic - A fresh look at the evidence by a former Chief Inspector of Marine Accidents	John Lang	£20.00	£10.00
Titanic & Her Sisters A Postcard History	Janette & Campbell McCutcheon	£19.99	£10.00
Titanic in Picture Postcards	R McDougall & R Gardiner	£19.99	£10.00
Titanic's Predecessor - The SS Norge Disaster of 1904	Per Kristian Sebak	£25.00	£12.50
To Western Scottish Waters by Rail and Steamer to the Isles	Robert N. Forsythe	£16.99	£8.50
Town Class Cruisers	Neil McCart	£29.00	£14.50
Traditional Fishing Boats of Britain & Ireland	Mike Smylie	£19.99	£10.00
Traditional Fishing Boats of Europe	Mike Smylie	£19.99	£10.00
Tramp - Norwegian Tramp Shipping 1945-1985 (In Norwegian and English)	Dag Bakka Jr	£22.50	£11.25
Trampskibe Myren og Progress Orient og Motortramp	Ole Stig Johannesen	£45.00	£22.50
Trawlerman Life at the Helm of the Toughest Job in Britain	Jimmy Buchan	£7.99	£4.00
Tug World Review 1997-1998		£30.00	£15.00
Tug World Review 1999-2000		£30.00	£15.00
Tug World Review 2005-2006		£30.00	£15.00
Tug World Review 2006-2007		£30.00	£15.00
Tugs and Offshore Supply Vessels 2009/10 (U.K. and Ireland)	J Dodds and B McCall	£12.50	£6.25
Tugs in Camera	D & B McCall	£19.50	£9.75
Tugs in Colour - British Built	B McCall	£17.00	£8.50
Tugs in Colour - UK	B McCall	£14.00	£7.00
Tugs in Colour - Worldwide	B McCall	£16.50	£8.25
Tugs, Booms and Barges	R Sheret	£15.00	£7.50
Two Ships - One New Era P & O Ferries Spirit of Britain and Spirit of France	John Hendy	£18.50	£9.25
Tying the Knot	S C Heal	£15.00	£7.50
U-Boat Operations of the Second World War, Volume 2 - Career Histories, U511 to UIT25	Kenneth Wynn	£30.00	£15.00
U-Boat War Patrol - The hidden photographic diary of U564	Lawrence Paterson	£25.00	£12.50
U-Boat Warfare - The Evolution of the Wolf Pack	Jak P Mallmann Showell	£24.99	£12.50
U-Boats under the Swastika	Jak P Mallmann Showell	£16.99	£8.50
Under Tow - A History of Tugs and Towing (Canada)	Donal M Baird	£30.00	£15.00
Union-Castle Liners - From Great Britain to Africa 1946-1977	William H. Miller	£19.99	£10.00
United States Lighthouse Service Tenders 1840 to 1939 (includes fleet list)	Douglas Peterson	£25.00	£12.50
Unter Fremder Flagge - Schicksale deutscher Frachter	Uwe Detlefsen	£25.00	£12.50
Vickers Barrow Built Warships	Jon Wise	£17.99	£9.00
Vickers' Master Shipbuilder - Sir Leonard Redshaw	Leslie M Shore	£24.99	£12.50
Visserij in Vogelvlucht - A Bird's Eye View of the Dutch Fishery (captions in Dutch and English)	Flying Focus	£16.75	£8.38
Vliedende stor - het vervolg - aerial photos merchant ships in bad weather - Dutch text	Flying Focus	£16.75	£8.38
Vliegen Boven Vissers - aerial photos of fishing vessels - Dutch text	Flying Focus	£16.75	£8.38
Vliegende storm - aerial photos merchant ships in bad weather - Dutch text	Flying Focus	£16.75	£8.38
Vognmandsruten (Danish ferries/Danish language) (Superflex ferries)	Frederik Naumann	£38.00	£19.00
Vom Dampfboot zum Katamaran, Die Gesschichte der Flensburger Fordeschiffahrt und aller Tochterfirmen	Detlefsen, Moltsen and Schneider	£35.00	£17.50
Vom Ewer zum Containerschiff, die Geschichte der deutschen Kustenschiffahrt	Uwe Detlefsen	£31.50	£15.75
Von Der Hanse Kooge zum Containerschiff. 500 Jahre Schiffbau in Deutschland (in 2 volumes) (listing of ships built in German yards)	Cai Boie	£167.50	£83.75
Von Der Weser in Die Welt Band III, Bremen, Bremeerhave, Geestemunde (German text)	Peter-Michael Pawlik	£50.00	£25.00
von Stapel gelaufraf - Eine schiffahrtshistorische Ruckschau (German text)	Karl-Hartman Necker	£30.00	£15.00
Warship 2008	Conway	£30.00	£15.00
Warships for Export, Armstrong Warships 1867 - 1926	Peter Brock	£28.50	£14.25
Warships in Focus - The Naval Photography of Michael Lennon, Volume 1	Michael Lennon	£19.99	£10.00
Waverley, last of the Clyde Steamers	Andrer Clark	£10.00	£5.00
Wells-next-the-Sea Lifeboats	N Leach and P Russell	£12.99	£6.50
West Highland Steamers	Duckworth and Langmuir	£25.00	£12.50
Weston Shipping	K.S.Garrett	£8.00	£4.00
Weymouth to the Channel Islands - A Great Western Railway Shipping History	L Jackson	£13.95	£6.98
White Star Line A Photographic History	J McCutcheon	£19.99	£10.00
Whitehaven Harbour Through Time	A Routledge	£14.99	£7.50
William Sloan & Co Ltd, Glasgow 1825-1968	G E. Langmuir & G H. Somner	£6.00	£3.00
Wilson Line	John Harrower	£16.00	£8.00
With a Flower upon the Ocean	E T Wilkins	£7.50	£3.75
With a Pinch of Salt A collection of nauticl expressions and other stories	Captain Nick Bates	£7.95	£3.98
World Cruise Ships - The History and Development of Cruising	Norman L Middlemiss	£20.00	£10.00
World War 1 Verschollen U Boat Losses	D R Messimer	£22.00	£11.00
Wreck, Rescue & Salvage	Dick Jolly	£16.99	£8.50
Yacht-und Bootswerft Burmester, Bremen 1920-1979 (German text)	Klaus Auf dem Garten	£30.00	£15.00
You and Your Ships	Jim Davis	£14.95	£7.48

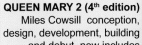

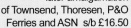

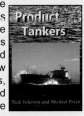

CONTENTS

Ships in Focus Publications

Correspondence and editorial:
Roy Fenton
18 Durrington Avenue
London SW20 8NT
020 8879 3527
roy@rfenton.co.uk

Orders and photographic:
John & Marion Clarkson
18 Franklands, Longton
Preston PR4 5PD
01772 612855
shipsinfocus@btinternet.com

Printed by Amadeus Press Ltd.,
Cleckheaton, Yorkshire.
Designed by Hugh Smallwood, John
Clarkson and Roy Fenton.

SHIPS IN FOCUS RECORD
ISBN 978-0-9928264-0-6

SHIPS IN FOCUS RECORD 2017

Welcome back to 'Record', now appearing as an enlarged, yearly edition. We intend to include in these annuals exactly the same mixture of accurate, well-researched features and photographs as in our 64 four-monthly editions of 'Record'. Thus we have features on owners old and not-so-old: British, Belgian and Anglo-Swedish. Coverage of shipbuilding runs from a small Welsh yard to the major figure of John Priestman. 'South West Scenes' rounds off our pictorial coverage of Falmouth, and there is the story of a major Second World War convoy battle. Readers' letters and follow-ups of recent articles complete the mix. We have also covered a fair range of vessels, from cargo liners, tramps, trawlers, tankers, coasters and some small fry: only passenger ships are neglected, but there are more than enough of those in other journals. More pages mean we can encompass longer, complete articles which, in the 64-page format, we would have split over two or three editions to ensure each issue had a spread of topics.

The feature on Sir John Priestman in this issue began simply as an attempt to chronicle his Tower ship design, an apparent attempt to get round the patents on Doxford's Turrets and Ropner's Trunks. Material on these ships proved sparse, but it soon became apparent that Priestman himself was an interesting character. Hence the original article morphed into coverage not only of his Towers, but of his history as a shipbuilder, typical vessels built and Priestman's role as a ship owner which became necessary when he could not sell the ships he built in the 1920s. A lesson learned before in such investigations is how often facts in books and on the 'web have been parroted without being checked. As always it is essential to refer to reliable sources, like the well-researched fleet lists held by the World Ship Society, and the official ships' registration papers. We hope we have our facts correct, but if not the ever vigilant readers will no doubt tell us.

We have accumulated much material for this edition but, despite extending it to 128 pages, some has had to be left out. Nevertheless, we would encourage existing and potential authors to submit material for publishing in 2018. And please keep the feedback coming!

John Clarkson   Roy Fenton

November 2017

John Priestman's Sunderland yard built almost exclusively dry cargo ships, but occasionally ventured into slightly more exotic vessels, like the two-funnelled Greek passenger ship *Moraitis* of 1907, later *Themistocles*. See page 7. *[George Foustanos collection]*

Front cover: *Southampton Castle [Ian Shiffman]*. See page 51.
Back cover upper: *Snow Hill [Dave Salisbury]*. See page 61.
Back cover lower: *Solent Star [Nigel Kirby]*. See page 66

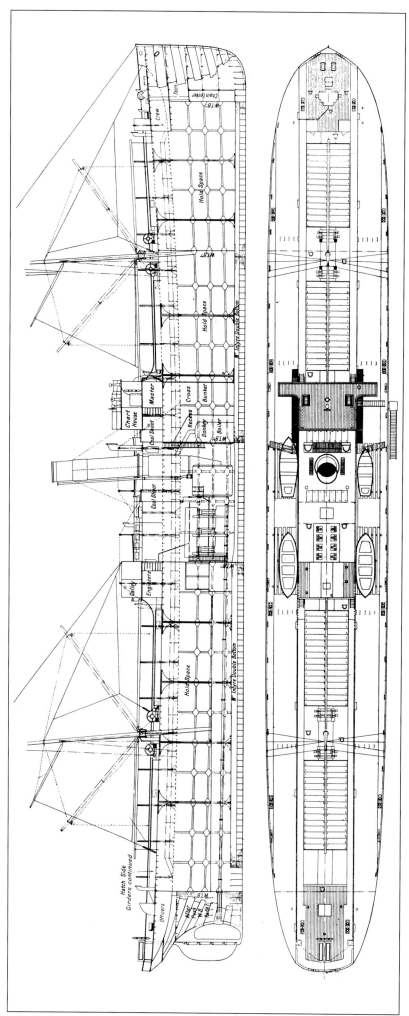

Top: General arrangement drawings of a Tower Deck ship. Note the narrowness of the hatches.

Bottom left: A further view of *Enfield* in the Avon, probably on the same occasion as the one on the opposite page judging by the stains on the Tower Deck, which show up particularly well in these photographs.
[J. and M. Clarkson]

Bottom right: A sad looking *Enfield* towards the end of her career, probably when she was laid up in the River Torridge off Bideford. Just how little she was now worth is demonstrated by her 1932 sale for just £750 to a British owner, who put her under the Panama flag. *[Roy Fenton collection]*

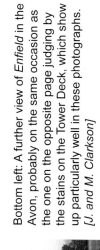

PRIESTMAN AND THE TOWER DECK SHIPS

Roy Fenton

By the 1890s, the ocean-going iron or steel cargo ship with a triple-expansion engine was so well proven and established that building of large sailing ships had all but ceased, at least for British owners. A number of yards were competing strongly for orders for steamers, especially those on the Wear, Tees, Tyne and Clyde. With the marine steam engine now regarded as reaching almost its maximum potential, the search for innovation turned to hull forms. Doxfords were pioneers in patenting a novel design, the Turret Deck. After a slow start, this enjoyed a period of considerable success amongst both tramp and liner operators. This was not because of its enhanced strength or seaworthiness, which were claimed (and disputed), but largely because its narrow main deck reduced certain harbour and canal dues.

Doxford's success inevitably spawned competing designs, several of which appear to be simply attempts to achieve the same narrow main deck whilst circumventing Doxford's patent. The most numerous of these were Ropner's Trunk Deck ships which were detailed in 'Record' 2 and 3. Amongst several others were the Tower Deck design, built between 1896 and 1898. The design was patented by John Priestman and Co. who completed all the examples. The ships had a narrow main deck, as in Turrets and Trunks, but below this the plating sloped down at an angle of 45 degrees to narrow walkways which ran the length of the ship. Besides reducing dues thanks to a low net tonnages for the ship's size, a further advantage claimed was that the funnel-shape produced by the Tower made the ships self-trimming. As with the Turrets, it was claimed that the high main deck

would remain dry in all weather conditions.

There is some controversy over which ships were built to Priestman's design, most authors claiming there were three, but disagreeing about which ships they were. Frank Bowen, in one of his excellent portraits of shipbuilders published in 'Shipbuilding and Shipping Record', names three, *Unique*, *Enfield* and *Universe*. Other authors ignore the *Unique*, asserting that *Enfield* was the first, but include the *Kilmaho* (yard number 74; 2,155/1898). Although her dimensions were similar as was her ratio of net to gross tonnage, the *Kilmaho* is the only one not described in 'Lloyd's Register' as having a 'trunk deck', and she is almost certainly an imposter.

Little has been found of owners' or crews' experience with Tower Deck ships, although Bowen claimed the stability of *Unique* to have been excellent, and that her success led to the ordering of *Universe* by the same owner. However, it is notable that Priestman provided a mortgage of £8,000 to help encourage Charles Ormston to order the *Enfield* and no other British owner took delivery of a Tower Deck ship. Both *Enfield* and *Universe* survived serious strandings, the former managing almost 38 years of service, suggesting that Priestman built them well, as he did with his other ships.

Priestman's Tower Deck ships

These are listed in chronological order with yard numbers preceding the name, but note that – as with many of the Southwick yard's ships – these do not reflect the order in which ships were launched or completed.

Enfield in the Avon. [World Ship Photo Library]

63. UNIQUE/HAUGASTØL

2,036g 1,298n.
280.0 x 40.1 x 17.0 feet.
T. 3-cyl. by North Eastern Marine Engineering Co. Ltd., Wallsend-on-Tyne; 210 NHP, 12½ knots.
9.1896: Launched by John Priestman and Co., Southwick, Sunderland (Yard No. 63).
11.1896: Completed for Hjalmar Røed, Tønsberg, Norway as UNIQUE.
1900: Transferred to A/S Unique (Hjalmar Røed, manager), Tønsberg.
1905: Manager became Sigurd Røed, Tønsberg.
1906: Transferred to A/S United (Sigurd Røed, manager), Tønsberg.
1908: Manager became O.M. Milberg.
1909: Sold to Dampsk. A/S Glittre (Fearnley& Eger, managers), Christiania, Norway and renamed HAUGASTØL.
29.11.1917: Torpedoed and sunk by the German submarine UB 35 ten miles south by west half west of Start Point whilst on a voyage from Glasgow to Rouen with a cargo of coal.

70. ENFIELD 1897-1932

O.N. 106626 2,124g 1,364n.
288.0 x 40.0 x 19.4 feet.
T. 3-cyl. by William Allan and Co. Ltd., Sunderland; 210 NHP, 1,050 IHP, 9 knots.
27.10.1897: Launched by John Priestman and Co., Southwick, Sunderland (Yard No. 70).
24.11.1897: Registered in the ownership of Charles W. Ormston, Newcastle-upon-Tyne as ENFIELD.
31.8.1898: Transferred to the Enfield Steam Ship Co. Ltd. (Charles W. Ormston and Co., managers), Newcastle-upon-Tyne
27.1.1905: Manager became Thomas Speeding of Speeding, Marshall and Co., Sunderland.
4.10.1915: Damaged by a mine two and a half miles west by south of Folkestone whilst on a voyage from Newcastle-on-Tyne to St. Nazaire with a cargo of coal. The mine had been laid by the German submarine UC 5.
6.1.1916: Manager became Septimus Marshall, Sunderland.
4.12.1918: Stranded in fog on the east side of Lundy, about half a mile north of the South Lundy Light, whilst outward bound from a South Wales port with 3,000 tons of coal. Although later salvaged, extensive bottom damage meant she was declared a constructive total loss. Later repaired.
13.1.1920: Register closed.
7.5.1920: Re-registered in the ownership of Claude Langdon Ltd., London.
21.5.1920: Sold to Jeffree Line Ltd. (John C. Jeffree, manager), Cardiff.
23.6.1924: Taken over by mortgagees and transferred to the James Tucker Steamship Co. Ltd. (John Cory and Sons Ltd., managers), Cardiff.
7.71924: Transferred by mortgagees to Orders and Handford Steam Ship Co. Ltd. (John Cory and Sons Ltd., managers), Cardiff.
8.11.1932: Register closed on sale for £750 to Trading and Shipping Co. Ltd., London and renamed SANCTA RITA under the Panama flag.

1935: Broken up in Italy during the second quarter.

71. UNIVERSE/SAMBRO/ HEATHCOTE 1898-1917

O.N. 129040 2,535g 1,634n.
300.0 x 42.5 x 20.2 feet.
T. 3-cyl. by North Eastern Marine Engineering Co. Ltd., Wallsend-on-Tyne; 210 NHP, 10½ knots.
28.9.1898: Launched by John Priestman and Co., Sunderland (Yard No. 71).
11.1898: Completed for A/S Universe (Hjalmar Røed), Tønsberg, Norway as UNIVERSE.
1906: Transferred to A/S United (Sigurd Røed), Tønsberg.
25.4.1907: Wrecked at Seal Cove, White Haven, Nova Scotia whilst on a voyage from New York to Pictou.
13.6.1907: Refloated.
22.9.1909: Registered at London in the ownership of the Halifax Graving Dock Co. Ltd., Halifax, Canada as SAMBRO.
6.10.1910: Sold to Hector McInnes, Halifax, Nova Scotia.
6.11.1909: Renamed HEATHCOTE.
27.12.1915: Transferred to Dominion Shipping Co. Ltd. (Hector McInnes, manager), Halifax, Nova Scotia.
25.7.1917: Sunk in collision with the Dutch steamer KELBERGEN (4,751/1914) in the Cabot Strait whilst on a voyage from Port au Port, Newfoundland to Sydney, Cape Breton with a cargo of limestone.
18.9.1917: Register closed.

PRIESTMAN'S SHIPBUILDING

Although almost single-handedly founding a highly successful shipyard, John Priestman (1854-1941) did not have a shipbuilding background, but was the son of baker from Bishop Auckland. He began work as a 14-year-old apprentice in the drawing office of John Blumer's yard at Sunderland. Having displayed his ability as a ship designer, he eventually became Chief Draughtsman, moving on to the same appointment for William Pickersgill's yard. He is credited with producing the plans for Pickersgill's first iron ship, *Camargo* completed in 1880, somewhat belatedly perhaps, as Pickersgill was the last major yard on the Wear to move from wood to iron.

William Pickersgill was killed in an accident in his yard in 1880, and at this time Priestman decided to start on his own, taking over from a John Gulston the Castletown Yard at Southwick, to the west of Pickersgill's establishment. It was a propitious time, with the change from sail to steam and wooden to iron hulls gaining momentum, both transitions in which British yards were in the lead. Priestman had backers at this time, but kept management firmly in his own hands, and gradually bought out his backers until he was sole proprietor. Throughout his career his aim was to provide well-built hulls at the lowest reasonable price. He made no effort to add engine or boiler shops to his yard, relying on the well-established marine engineering companies with which the north east was well provided.

The Castleton Yard's first ship launched was the iron-hulled *Troutbeck* (yard number 3; 817/1882) for Fisher, Renwick on 1st August 1882. However, presumably because it had been laid down first, yard number 1 was the 1,149 gross ton *Isle of Cyprus* launched in February 1883. A seemingly haphazard approach to yard numbering was apparent at various periods of the yard's life, the system breaking down completely during Priestman's final years.

Sir John Priestman (1854-1941)

4

Although the yard launched 7,500 tons of shipping in its first full year of operation, after its promising start it closed between 1885 and 1888. When work resumed the first steel hull was completed, the *Gemini* (yard number 16; 996/1888) for Cardiff owners. Thereafter the yard prospered and during its first quarter century was numbered amongst the top five on the River Wear for output. In 1900 a total of 20,302 tons was launched, all for overseas owners. The yard eventually had four berths up to 600-feet long, and its typical output was four ships each year. Although unable to expand the yard further, Priestman maximised its output by carefully organised building work.

Although fairly basic tramps and large coasters were the mainstay of Priestman's work, notable ships included two large cattle carriers built for de Freitas and Co. of Hamburg, but quickly making their way to the fleet of Hamburg Amerika Line, *Granada* (yard number 80; 5,140/1899) and *Sevilla* (yard number 81; 5,156/1900), the biggest ships yet built at the yard. An emigrant ship completed for Greek owners, the twin-screw *Moraitis* (yard number 120; 6,045/1907), was 400-feet long and the largest hull the yard produced, and probably the only one with two funnels. Cargo liners were built for, amongst others, Furness, Wilson and Prince Lines.

During the First World War the yard kept up their annual output. The shipping controller ordered a number although, again, sources differ as to quantity and types. Mitchell and Sawyer list one B-type standard and four C-types, of which only the B and one C type were completed before the Armistice. The last C-type emerged in January 1920 in modified form as Strick's *Muristan* (yard number 284; 3,062/1920). During the war a number of cargo ships were also built for private owners including two for Priestman himself or for a company in which he had an interest. Thereafter, times became much harder, and once wartime orders were completed a significant number of the ships laid down were for Priestman's own account or for companies in which he had a large shareholding. As some ships

were built to definite orders, but not delivered, the situation becomes complex. Ships launched from the beginning of 1920 are listed below, again in order of yard number (but not launch or completion date). Yard numbers 272, 273 and 297 were not used; 281 to 284 were allocated to ships ordered by the Shipping Controller and launched in 1919. The yard was virtually closed for long periods in 1921 and 1922, and there were no launches in 1926.

The list below suggests that 11 of the 26 ships were laid down and launched for either Priestman's own account or for a company in which he had a significant shareholding, with a further two hulls taken over before delivery. Thus fully half of the yard's post-1920 output was more-or-less self-financed.

Work in the yard ceased after the Danish *Finland* was delivered in October 1930. Yard number 299 was then left on the stocks after the Norwegian who had ordered her defaulted on payment. An attempt was made to auction her, but the best bid, of just £20,000, received the derisory answer from the auctioneer as to which part of the ship the bidder wanted. Work eventually recommenced and the ship was launched in May 1933 but she could not be sold until 1937, becoming *Rio Novo*. She became an early conversion to a liquefied petroleum gas carrier. During the Second World War the West Yard of William Pickersgill and Sons Ltd. was built on the Priestman site, although only two berths were operated.

Despite his yard's closure, Priestman died a rich man, leaving over £1.5 million including very substantial donations to charity. His philanthropy extended to Sunderland Technical College where his money enabled a full-sized mould loft to be installed and also benefited the college's library. He was a shrewd investor, making money especially from South African goldfields, but also from collieries and from the tramp ship companies for whom he built ships. He was knighted in 1923 and made a baronet in 1934 in recognition of his work on local public bodies and massive donations to charity.

No.	Launch name	Launch	GT	Owner	Notes
267	LANDAAS	24.2.1920	4,248	J. Erland, Bergen	
268	UNDEN	1.6.1920	4,252	G. Carlsson, Gothenburg	
269	STORNES	15.9.1920	4,252	H.J. Hansen, Oslo	Became STORNEST (below)
270	LIFJELD	25.1.1921	4,274	H.G. Martens, Bergen	Completed NESTLEA (below)
271	BARBARA MARIE (1)	15.2.1923	4,266	Cliffside Sg. Co. Ltd.	See below
274	EASTLEA	20.2.1924	4,267	Cliffside Sg. Co. Ltd.	See below
275	WESTLEA	16.10.1924	4,218	Cliffside Sg. Co. Ltd.	See below
276	FERNLEA	2.11.1925	4,212	Cliffside Sg. Co. Ltd.	See below
277	FRANCES MASSEY	28.7.1927	4,212	W.A. Massey, Hull	
278	BARBARA MARIE (2)	6.3.1928	4,223	Cliffside Sg. Co. Ltd.	See below
279	HOLMELEA	18.6.1928	4,223	Cliffside Sg. Co. Ltd.	See below
280	FARNDALE	3.10.1928	4,235	Morrison Steamship Co. Ltd.	See below
285	COQUETDALE	14.6.1923	1,597	S. Marshall, Sunderland	See below
286	PENHALE	23.11.1923	4,071	Chellew S.N. Co. Ltd.	
287	BRINKBURN	3.6.1924	1,598	S. Marshall, Sunderland	
288	CHELDALE	11.2.1925	4,218	Morrison Steamship Co. Ltd.	See below
289	BOREAS	2.9.1925	1,376	Torp & Wiese, Bergen	See GAUNLESS below
290	FRANK SEAMANS	8.12.1927	4,271	I.A. Christensen, Oslo	
291	ASHLEA	12.12.1928	4,222	Cliffside Sg. Co. Ltd.	See below
292	KNIGHT OF THE CROSS	10.4.1929	3,857	Pardoe-Thomas, Newport	
293	KNIGHT OF THE ROSE	21.6.1929	3,856	Pardoe-Thomas, Newport	
294	KNIGHT OF THE REALM	18.12.1929	3,856	Pardoe-Thomas, Newport	
295	THORNLEA	21.10.1929	4,261	J. Priestman	See below
296	GLENLEA	9.7.1930	4,252	J. Priestman	See below
298	FINLAND	10.9.1930	2,302	O.H. Christensen, Copenhagen	
299	---	10.5.1933	2,490	Øivind Lorentzen, Oslo	Completed as RIO NOVO

Although given Priestman's first yard number, *Isle of Cyprus* (1,021/1883) was actually the fourth ship to be launched, on 22nd February 1883. She was for Dixon, Robson and Co. of Newcastle-upon-Tyne, who went on to have the slightly smaller *Isle of Dursey* completed later that year as yard number 5. *Isle of Cyprus* was sold to Swedish owners in 1897 as *Britannia*, becoming *Bjornvik* in 1916. The Estonians who bought her in 1934 did not change this name, which she was still carrying when broken up at Copenhagen by Petersen & Albeck late in 1936. *[Roy Fenton collection]*

Reindeer (yard number 60; 2,424/1896) was built for the Reindeer Steamship Co. Ltd., managed by Jackson Brothers and Cory of London. Her career was singularly uncomplicated, but had a tragic and mysterious conclusion. She passed through the Downs on 15th November 1916 whilst bound from Dieppe to Middlesbrough in ballast, and was not seen again, possibly a victim of a mine. *[E.N. Taylor/J. and M. Clarkson]*

Priestman built a series of three ships for A.C. de Freitas of Hamburg around the beginning of the twentieth century. Of these, *Sevilla* (yard number 81, 5,156/1900) was claimed as a war reparation in 1919, was sold to Christian Salvesen in 1922 and converted to a whale factory ship, as seen here. Under British and subsequently Norwegian ownership, she had a long and at times controversial career, as detailed in our recent book 'Whale Factory Ships and Modern Whaling' by Ian Hart. Decommissioned as a factory ship about 1938, she served as a depot ship in the Clyde during the Second World War, being deemed too slow and unreliable for Atlantic convoys. She was broken up at Ghent in 1946. *[B. and A. Feilden/J. and M. Clarkson]*

Moraitis (yard number 120; 6,045/1907) was the largest and probably the most sophisticated ship built by Priestman, hence her being made the subject of an advertisement for the yard. She was completed for D.G. Moraitis of Piraeus but within a year had moved on to the Hellenic Transatlantic Steam Navigation Co. Ltd. who renamed her *Themistocles*. Then, in 1915, owners became the National Steam Navigation Co. Ltd., of Greece, for whom she was managed by Embiricos Brothers. She went to breakers at Savona in 1933, having spent some time laid up in Piraeus. *[George Foustanos collection]*

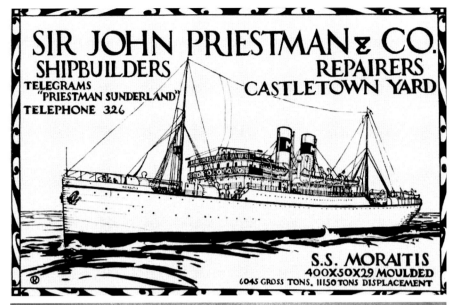

Bottom: *Portuguese Prince* (yard number 236; 4,981/1912) was built for a cargo liner company, Prince Line Ltd., by a yard whose major customers were operators of tramp ships. Ending her career with Prince, she was broken up by the West of Scotland Shipbreaking Co. Ltd. at Troon during 1934. *[Ships in Focus]*

One of several ships completed during the First World War for private ship owners was *Maindy Court* (yard number 260, 3,792/1917) for Maindy Shipping Co. Ltd., managed by Jenkins, Richards and Evans Ltd. This was one of a number of Cardiff companies formed during the First World War whose ambition seemed to know no bounds. Initial excellent profits encouraged reckless expansion, with the consequence that Maindy folded ignominiously in the lean years between the wars. *Maindy Court* became *White Fan* in 1932, finding her way on to the Greek register as *Aegeus* in 1933. On 9th May 1937 she was sunk in collision with the United States steamer *Nashaba* (6,062/1921) 32 miles south east of Bornholm whilst on a voyage from Gdynia to Rosario with coal. *[York collection]*

Sunland (yard number 263; 4,879/1918) in the original colour scheme of the Sun Shipping Co. Ltd., her funnel bearing the 'CM' monogram of her managers, Mitchell, Cotts and Co. of London, who later adopted plain white funnels with black tops. *Sunland* was sold to Lykiardopulo in 1934 as the Greek-flagged *Daphne*. Her final name, still in Greek ownership, was *Embiricos Nicolaos*, as which she was bombed and sunk whilst escaping from Piraeus to Port Said on 23rd March 1941. *[Ships in Focus]*

Of the three ships launched for management by Pardoe-Thomas and Co. Ltd. of Newport in 1929, the first was *Knight of the Cross* (yard number 292; 3,857/1929), owned by the Newport – Africa Line Ltd. and seen here at Waterford. She was sold to the Scindia Steam Navigation Co. Ltd. of Bombay in 1935 and renamed *Jalapadma*, and was so badly damaged by the explosion of the *Fort Stikine* (7,142/1942) in her home port on 14th April 1944 that she was sold for scrapping. *[Roy Fenton collection]*

Coquetdale (yard number 285; 1,597/1923) (top) and her sister *Brinkburn* (middle) (yard number 287; 1,598/1924) were built for companies managed by Sunderland's Septimus Marshall and Co., who would have known Priestman (who later provided a mortgage for *Coquetdale*). *Coquetdale* is seen at Preston in 1929 with a cargo of esparto grass. Neither survived the war, *Coquetdale* being sunk by German aircraft on 8th August 1940 west of the Isle of Wight whilst returning from Portsmouth to the Clyde in ballast. *Brinkburn* lasted slightly longer, torpedoed by *U 73* on 21st June 1943 whilst on a voyage from Swansea to Gibraltar. *[Both: J. and M. Clarkson]*

Frances Massey (yard number 277; 4,212/1927) is lying at buoys in the Thames off Charlton on 21st September 1932 (bottom). Built for W.A. Massey and Sons Ltd. of Hull, she was one of only a handful of post-First World War completions not funded by Priestman or one of his companies. Nevertheless, she was identical in size to the yard's other ships of the period. She also shared the fate of most of her sisters during the Second World War. On 6th June 1940 she was torpedoed and sunk by the German submarine *U 48* in position 53.33 north, 08.26 west whilst on a voyage from Wabana, Newfoundland to Glasgow with a cargo of iron ore. *[R.A. Snook/F.W. Hawks]*

Priestman built no tankers, indeed apart from the occasional passenger ship his yard's entire output consisted of dry cargo ships, mainly ocean-going with a few large coasters or medium-sized hulls. But the very last ship, although conventional enough when she was finally delivered, became a pioneer of what is, today, a signicant and growing segment of the tanker market, the liquid petroleum gas carrier. Yard no. 299 was acquired in February 1937 by Øivind Lorentzen of Oslo and named *Rio Novo*. She tramped conventionally until 1949 when she was taken in hand and converted to a gas carrier, remaining with Lorentzen but now named *Ultragaz*. Her name was changed several times, to *Gasbras Sul* in 1954 (top) and to *Mundogas Sul* in 1961, but Lorentzen remained her beneficial owner, although she was transferred in 1963 to a company he controlled in Panama, and reflagged to that country. After what must be judged a successful career, she was broken up at Rio de Janeiro in 1967. Her hull had then been in service for 30 years, but taking into account that it had lain in the shipyard for some years, it was somewhat older. *[Fotoflite incorporating Skyfotos]*

Penhale (yard number 286; 4,071/1924) was completed in January 1924 for R.B. Chellew Steam Navigation Co. Ltd., a company founded in Truro but by now operating out of Cardiff (above). She was almost unique as a Priestman-built ship in surviving the Second World War, and served Chellew until 1954 when, more or less on her thirtieth birthday, she was sold to

Turkish owners as *Preveze*. The Turks were then renowned for squeezing a few extra years out of superannuated steam tramps, but with *Preveze* they obtained a relatively modest seven years before she was broken up at Beograd in Yugoslavia in 1961. She was photographed in London on 3rd October 1953, shortly before her sale to Turkey. *[Ships in Focus]*

PRIESTMAN'S SHIP OWNING

Alongside his other investments, Priestman put his money into shipping companies. In the 1920s, when orders were short, he laid down a number of steamers either as a speculation or on behalf of two shipping companies in which he invested and which were managed by John Morrison and Son. The managers were an old-established Newcastle family company, ship owners since before 1876 and also ships stores merchants, but by 1920 they had no

ships. Indeed, in post-war years, Morrisons entire efforts as managers were devoted to ships owned or partly financed by Priestman.

The fleets owned in Priestman's own name and by the two companies in which he invested, Cliffside Shipping Co. Ltd. and the Morrison Steamship Co. Ltd., are described and listed separately below, but they were managed and operated as one unit. Besides tramping, the ships' main employment was in the West Africa to Europe trade, probably on charter to United Africa Company or others. The ship's relatively modest size, just 365 feet in length, suited them for this trade where ports were small or simply non-existent with cargo loaded from surf boats. Outward loading was often in the Baltic, with sawn softwood for South Africa.

The photograph of Priestman's *Westcliff* shows a black funnel with a broad white band, with a letter P for Priestman. Later ships under all three ownerships wore the managers' funnel colours, black with a white band carrying a red Maltese Cross, the houseflag echoing the band. In several cases, the Maltese Cross appears to have been white on a wholly-black funnel. However, in a number of photographs the ships have a plain funnel with a black top, almost certainly representing a charterer's marking, and possibly those of the United Africa Company.

Priestman and the Cliffside company did not hesitate to sell a ship when the opportunity arose, as in 1924 with the first *Barbara Marie*, which was named after Priestman's only daughter. The only second-hand ship acquired was the Priestman-built *Gaunless*, most likely taken over when the Norwegian owners defaulted on mortgage payments. Considerably smaller than the rest of the combined fleet, which consisted of more-or-less standard shelter-deck steamers, *Gaunless* was sold after just four years, but became one of if not the last Priestman-built ship afloat.

Transfers between Priestman and Cliffside complicate the picture, but the number laid down appears to total eleven: two for Priestman (with two others taken over after completion), six for Cliffside (with one acquired) and three for Morrison.

Owned by John Priestman

The first of six ships owned in Priestman's own name was the *Cliffside*, delivered in April 1917. As at that stage in the war he would have had no problem in selling the ship at a considerable profit, his holding on to it is a measure of his business acumen, as its value would have risen enormously by 1919 when he sold her to Norwegian owners. *Westcliff* of 1919 was sold to Norway even more quickly and presumably at least as profitably.

The next acquisition came in much less prosperous times, as *Stornes* was left on the builder's hands in March 1921 when a Norwegian who had ordered it defaulted on payment. A modest renaming to *Stornest* gave it a less Scandinavian feel. Two months later a similar default saw the *Lifjeld* registered in Priestman's name as the *Nestlea*. The two further ships owned in the builder's name, *Thornlea* of 1929 and *Glenlea* of 1930, were almost certainly laid down on speculation to keep the yard occupied. The –Lea prefix to the names which were also applied to the ships of the Cliffside Steamship Co. Ltd. was probably Priestman's own idea, as during their ship owning days the managers John Morrison and Son had used Scottish names, mainly of mountains.

Despite being named after his only daughter, *Barbara Marie* was sold to a Hull owner in 1924. The four remaining ships were transferred to Cliffside Shipping in 1936.

1. CLIFFSIDE/EASTCLIFFE 1917-1919

O.N. 133599 4,969g 3,737n.
350.0 x 50.9 x 31.5 feet.
T. 3-cyl. (25, 41, 67 x 45 inches) by North Eastern Marine Engineering Co. Ltd., Sunderland; 325 NHP, 1,750 IHP, $9^7/_8$ knots.
24.1.1917: Launched by John Priestman and Co., Sunderland (Yard No. 259).
4.1917: Completed.
19.4.1917: Registered in the ownership of John Priestman, Sunderland (Wilfrid Reay-Smith and John W. Morrison, Newcastle-upon-Tyne, managers) as CLIFFSIDE.
17.6.1918: Renamed EASTCLIFFE.
24.12.1919: Register closed on sale to Ivar An. Christensens Rederi A/S (I.A. Christensen, manager), Christiania, Norway as MODIG.
1923: Owners became A/S Ivarans Rederi (I.A. Christensen, manager), Christiania.
3.8.1934: Registered in the ownership of Clare Shipping Co. Ltd. (Arthur H. Lilley, manager), London as CLARE LILLEY.
17.3.1942: Wrecked near Portuguese Cove, in the entrance to Halifax, Nova Scotia whilst on a voyage from New York to Halifax and Liverpool with general cargo.
28.5.1942: Register closed.

Cliffside as *Clare Lilley*, locking out into the Thames.

2. WESTCLIFF 1919-1920

O.N. 142826 4,747g 2,963n.
350.0 x 50.8 x 31.5 feet.
T. 3-cyl. (25, 41, 67 x 45 inches) by George Clark Ltd., Sunderland; 384 NHP, 1,900 IHP, 10¼ knots.
19.12.1918: Launched by John Priestman and Co., Sunderland (Yard No. 264).
3.1919: Completed.
4.3.1919: Registered in the ownership of John Priestman and Co. (W. Reay-Smith and John W. Morrison, managers), Newcastle-upon-Tyne as WESTCLIFF.
18.3.1920: Register closed on sale to Grefstad Rederi A/S (B.J. Grefstad), Arendal, Norway and renamed ULLSTAD.
1922: Manager became P. Dedekam.
1931: Managers became Prebensen & Blakstad, Risør, Norway.

1936: Sold to L.A. Embiricos, Andros, Greece and renamed RINOS.
2.11.1942: Torpedoed and sunk by the German submarine U 402 in position 52.30 north, 45.30 west whilst on a voyage from Halifax to Hull with general cargo and vehicles.

3. STORNEST 1921-1936
O.N. 145454 4,265g 2,543n.
365.0 x 51.5 x 25.2 feet.
T. 3-cyl. (25, 41, 69 x 48 inches) by George Clark Ltd., Sunderland; 375 NHP, 1,775 IHP, $9^7/_8$ knots.
25.9.1920: Launched by John Priestman and Co., Sunderland (Yard No. 269).
3.1921: Completed for H.J. Hansen, Christiania, Norway as STORNES but immediately laid up.
15.8.1921: Registered in the ownership of John Priestman and Co., Sunderland (John Morrison and Co., Newcastle-upon-Tyne, managers) as STORNEST.
21.2.1936: Transferred to the Cliffside Shipping Co. Ltd. (John Morrison and Co., managers), Newcastle-upon-Tyne.
24.11.1941: Sold to Charles Strubin and Co. Ltd. (William C. Green, manager), London.
12.10.1942: Torpedoed by the German submarine U 706 in position 54.25 north, 27.42 west whilst on a voyage from Swansea and Belfast Lough to Boston with a cargo of 6,000 tons of coal.
14.10.1942: Foundered during heavy weather with the loss of all 39 crew and ten gunners.
30.1.1943: Register closed.

4. NESTLEA 1921-1936
O.N. 145450 4,274g 2,473n.
365.0 x 51.5 x 25.2 feet.
T. 3-cyl. (25, 41, 69 x 48 inches) by George Clark Ltd., Sunderland; 375 NHP, 1,775 IHP, $9^7/_8$ knots.
25.1.1921: Launched by John Priestman and Co., Sunderland (Yard No. 270) for H.G. Martens, Bergen, Norway as LIFJELD.
5.1921: Completed.
22.7.1921: Registered in the ownership of John Priestman and Co., Sunderland (John Morrison and Co., Newcastle-upon-Tyne, managers) as NESTLEA.
21.2.1936: Transferred to the Cliffside Shipping Co. Ltd. (John Morrison and Co., managers), Newcastle-upon-Tyne.
18.11.1940: Bombed, straffed and sunk in position 100 miles west south west of the Old Head of Kinsale in position 50.38 north, 10.00 west whilst on a voyage from Takoradi to Workington with a cargo of 7,150 tons of manganese

Westcliff. Note the lattice derricks and the letter P for Priestman on her funnel. *[Bristol Series/J. and M. Clarkson]*

Stornest in the Mersey, wearing what is probably the buff funnel of the United Africa Company. *[B. and A. Feilden/J. and M. Clarkson]*

Nestlea, again with a buff funnel. *[Roy Fenton collection]*

ore. The crew of 38 and one gunner were saved.
16.12.1940: Register closed.

5. BARBARA MARIE (1) 1923-1924
O.N. 145520 4,266g 2,587n.
365.0 x 51.6 x 25.2 feet.
T. 3-cyl. (25, 41, 69 x 48 inches) by George Clark Ltd., Sunderland; 374 NHP, 1,775 IHP, $9^7/_8$ knots.
15.2.1923: Launched by John Priestman and Co., Sunderland (Yard No. 271).
5.1923: Completed.
1.5.1923: Registered in the ownership

of John Priestman and Co. (John Morrison and Son, managers), Newcastle-upon-Tyne as BARBARA MARIE.

21.5.1924: Sold to the Sea Steamship Co. Ltd. (William Brown, Atkinson and Co. Ltd., managers), Hull.

15.12.1924: Renamed PORTSEA.

6.11.1933: Register closed on sale to 'Nivose' Societa di Navigazione (A. Scinicariello, manager), Naples, Italy and renamed CIPRO.

1937: Sold to Biagio Borriello (Lauro & Montella, managers), Torre del Greco, Italy and renamed STELLA.

14.8.1941: Captured by the armed merchant cruiser HMS CIRCASSIA in approximate position 25 north, 40 west while trying to reach Bordeaux from Recife.

30.9.1941: Registered in the ownership of the Ministry of War Transport, London (Golden Cross Line (Bristol Channel) Ltd., Cardiff, managers), as EMPIRE PLANET.

20.7.1943: Re-registered in the ownership of the Ministry of War Transport, London (Montague C. Thomas, Cardiff, manager).

20.3.1946: Owners become the Ministry of Transport, London.

15.7.1946: Sold to Stuart T. Williamson, Hong Kong.

24.3.1947: Renamed INCHKEITH.

3.4.1947: Transferred to the Inchkeith Steamship Co. Ltd. (Williamson and Co., managers), Hong Kong.

2.3.1955: Aground on a reef outside Port Meadows, Andaman Islands in approximate position 12.01 north, 92.47.30 east whilst on a voyage from Calcutta to Cochin and Bombay with a cargo of coal and timber. Abandoned the same day.

Later declared a constructive total loss.

4.7.1955: Register closed.

6. THORNLEA 1929-1936

O.N. 161544 4,261g 2,548n.
367.5 x 51.5 x 25.1 feet
T.3-cyl. (25, 41, 69 x 48 inches) by North Eastern Marine Engineering Co. Ltd., Sunderland; 380 NHP, 2,158 IHP, $10^3/_8$ knots.

21.10.1929: Launched by Sir John Priestman and Co., Sunderland (Yard No.295).

11.1929: Completed.

14.11.1929: Registered in the ownership of Sir John Priestman and Co. (John Morrison and Co., managers), Newcastle-upon-Tyne as THORNLEA.

21.2.1936: Transferred to the Cliffside

The first *Barbara Marie* in later life as *Inchkeith*. [V.H. Young]

Thornlea at Avonmouth with her funnel colours painted out, probably because of a charter: note the houseflag, which is not that of Morrison. *[Bristol Series/Roy Fenton collection]*

Glenlea in Morrison's colours at Mombasa in 1934. Note the awning over her forecastle. *[R. Moffat-Scott/Roy Fenton collection]*

Shipping Co. Ltd. (John Morrison and Co., managers), Newcastle-upon-Tyne.

2.9.1940: Torpedoed and sunk by the German submarine U 46 in position 55.14 north, 16.40 west whilst on a voyage in convoy OB 206 from Swansea to Montreal with a cargo of 6,400 tons of coal. Three of the crew of 37 were lost.

21.1.1941: Register closed.

7. GLENLEA 1930-1936

O.N. 161557 4,252g 2,541n.
367.5 x 51.5 x 25.1 feet.
T. 3-cyl. (25, 41, 69 x 48 inches) by George Clark Ltd., Sunderland; 375 NHP, 1,775 IHP, $9^7/_8$ knots.

9.7.1930: Launched by Sir John Priestman and Co., Sunderland (Yard No. 296).

8.1930: Completed.

5.8.1930: Registered in the ownership of Sir John Priestman (John Morrison and Son, managers), Newcastle-upon-Tyne as GLENLEA.

21.2.1936: Transferred to Cliffside Shipping Co. Ltd. (John Morrison and Son, managers), Newcastle-upon-Tyne.

30.4.1942: Transferred to the Morrison Steamship Co. Ltd. (John Morrison and Son, manager), Newcastle-upon-Tyne.

7.11.1942: Torpedoed and sunk by the German submarine U 566 in position 50 north, 30 west whilst on a voyage from Cardiff and Belfast Lough to Durban and Suez with 5,000 tons of coal, trucks and 1,000 tons of general cargo. Of the crew of 42, 39 were lost plus five of the six gunners. The master was taken prisoner.

31.5.1943: Register closed.

Glenlea is seen again in charterer's colours (United Africa?). [World Ship Society Ltd.]

Cliffside Shipping Co. Ltd., Newcastle-upon-Tyne

The larger of the two owning companies in which Priestman invested was the Cliffside Shipping Co. Ltd., formed in 1917. Although its founding documents have not survived in the National Archives, it is almost certain that Priestman was both a subscriber and a major investor: even the company's name echoed that of his home, 'Cliffside' in Roker. It was also the name chosen for the first ship owned in Priestman's name in 1917. Further evidence of Priestman's intimate involvement with the company comes from the 1936 transfers between ownership in his own name and that of the company: presumably the transfers had tax advantages in a period when earnings and profits from shipping were at last improving.

Cliffside appears to have been dormant until 1924 when the first of what might be regarded as Priestman's speculative completions, *Eastlea*, arrived after which the fleet grew steadily, punctuated by sale of *Westlea* and *Fernlea* to a

company managed by Ridley, Son and Tully. As mentioned, enhancement came in 1936 through transfer of four ships from Priestman's personal ownership.

The fleet's Second World War experience was unusually brutal. On the outbreak of war, the company had eight ships of which *Stornest* was sold in November 1941 (only to be lost within a year). Losses began quickly with *Ashlea* captured and sunk by *Admiral Graf Spee* in the South Atlantic in October. 1940 saw the second *Barbara Marie* and *Thornlea* torpedoed by U-boats in June and September, respectively and *Nestlea* bombed and sunk off Ireland in November. February and March of 1941 saw *Holmlea* sunk by gunfire from a U-boat, and *Eastlea* disappear, presumed also sunk by a submarine. The last of the pre-war ships, *Glenlea*, was transferred to the Morrison company in April 1942, only to be lost in November, again to a submarine torpedo.

1. EASTLEA 1924-1941

O.N. 148057 4,267g 2,582n.
365.0 x 51.6 x25.2 feet.
T. 3-cyl. (25, 41, 69 x 48 inches) by Richardson, Westgarth and Co. Ltd., Sunderland; 378 NHP, 1,900 IHP, 10 knots.

20.2.1924: Launched by John Priestman and Co., Sunderland (Yard No. 274)

3.1924: Completed.

28.3.1924: Registered in the ownership of the Cliffside Shipping Co. Ltd. (John Morrison and Son, managers), Newcastle-upon-Tyne as EASTLEA.

23.3.1941: Missing since sailing from St. Vincent, Cape Verde whilst on a voyage from Famagusta to Newport News with a cargo of cotton seed and general cargo. She is presumed to have been sunk by submarine about 30.3.1941.

17.3.1942: Register closed.

2. WESTLEA 1924-1927

O.N. 148107 4,218g 2,554n.
365.0 x 51.5 x 25.1 feet.

T. 3-cyl. (25, 41, 69 x 48 inches) by George Clark Ltd., Sunderland; 375 NHP, 1,775 IHP, 9⁷/₈knots.

10.10.1924: Launched by Sir John Priestman and Co., Sunderland (Yard No. 275).

11.1924: Completed.

26.11.1924: Registered in the ownership

of the Cliffside Shipping Co. Ltd. (John Morrison and Son, managers), Newcastle-upon-Tyne as WESTLEA.

7.5.1927: Sold to Tyneside Line Ltd. (Jno. Ridley, Son and Tully, managers), Newcastle-upon-Tyne.

29.6.1927: Renamed NEWTON ELM.

22.10.1937: Sold to the Arlon Steam Ship

Eastlea. [World Ship Society Ltd.]

Co. Ltd., London (Sir James German and Co. Ltd., Cardiff, managers).
16.11.1938: Renamed BECHEVILLE.
11.2.1944: Register closed on sale to the Ministry of War Transport, London.
4.5.1944: Re-registered in the ownership of the Ministry of War Transport, London (Christian Salvesen and Co., Leith, managers).
9.6.1944: Sunk to form part of Gooseberry No. 5, Normandy Beachhead.
5.7.1944: Register closed.

3. FERNLEA 1925-1927
O.N. 149403 4,212g 2,548n.
365.0 x 51.5 x 25.1 feet.
T. 3-cyl. (25, 41, 69 x 48 inches) by Richardson, Westgarth and Co. Ltd., Sunderland; 380 NHP, 1,900 IHP, 10 knots.
2.11.1925: Launched by Sir John Priestman and Co., Sunderland (Yard No. 276).
12.1925: Completed.
16.12.1925: Registered in the ownership of the Cliffside Shipping Co. Ltd. (John Morrison and Son, manager), Newcastle-upon-Tyne as FERNLEA.
23.5.1927: Sold to Tyneside Line Ltd. (Jno. Ridley, Son and Tully, managers), Newcastle-upon-Tyne.
26.5.1927: Renamed NEWTON PINE.
28.1.1941: Sold to Graig Shipping Co. Ltd. (Idwal Williams and Co. Ltd.), Cardiff.
16.10.1942: Torpedoed and sunk by the German submarine U 704 in approximate position 55 north, 30 west on a voyage from Hull and Loch Ewe to Halifax in ballast. The entire crew was lost.
19.1.1943: Register closed.

4. BARBARA MARIE (2) 1928-1940
O.N. 149464 4,223g 2,535n.
365.0 x 51.5 x 25.1 feet.
T. 3-cyl. (25, 41, 69 x 48 inches) by George Clark Ltd., Sunderland; 375 NHP, 1,775 IHP, 9⁷/₈ knots.
6.3.1928: Launched by Sir John Priestman and Co., Sunderland (Yard No. 278).
4.1928: Completed.
16.4.1928: Registered in the ownership of the Cliffside Shipping Co. Ltd. (John Morrison and Son, managers), Newcastle-upon-Tyne as BARBARA MARIE.
12.6.1940: Torpedoed and sunk by the German submarine U 46 in position 44.16 north to 13.54 west whilst on a voyage from Pepel to Workington with a cargo of ore.
12.9.1940: Register closed.

Westlea as *Newton Elm*, photographed on the River Scheldt. *[World Ship Society Ltd]*

Fernlea as *Newton Pine* unloading coal at Mombasa. Note the chutes over the side. *[R. Moffat-Scott/Roy Fenton collection]*

The second *Barbara Marie*. *[Bristol Series/J. and M. Clarkson]*

5. HOLMELEA 1928-1941
O.N. 149476 4,223g 2,535n.
365.0 x 51.5 x 25.1 feet.
T. 3-cyl. (25, 41, 69 x 48 inches) by George Clark Ltd., Sunderland; 375 NHP, 1,775 IHP, 9⁷/₈ knots.

18.6.1928: Launched by Sir John Priestman and Co., Sunderland (Yard No. 279).
30.7.1928: Registered in the ownership of the Cliffside Shipping Co. Ltd. (John Morrison and Son, manager),

Newcastle-upon-Tyne as HOLMELEA.
8.1928: Completed.
28.2.1941: Shelled and sunk by the
German submarine U 47 in position
54.24 north, 17.25 west whilst on a
voyage from Rosario to Hull with a
cargo of grain, linseed and maize.
11.9.1941: Register closed.

6. ASHLEA 1928-1939
O.N. 149491 4,222g 2,532n.
367.4 x 51.5 x 25.1 feet.
T. 3-cyl. (25, 41, 69 x 48 inches) by
George Clark Ltd., Sunderland; 375
NHP, 1,775 IHP, $9^7/_8$ knots.
12.12.1928: Launched by Sir John
Priestman and Co., Sunderland (Yard
No. 291).
2.1929: Completed
1.2.1929: Registered in the ownership
of the Cliffside Shipping Co. Ltd.
(John Morrison and Son, manager),
Newcastle-upon-Tyne as ASHLEA.
7.10.1939: Captured and sunk by
German heavy cruiser ADMIRAL
GRAF SPEE in approximate position
09 south, 03 west whilst on a voyage
from Durban to Falmouth with a cargo
of sugar.
20.1.1940: Register closed.

7. GAUNLESS 1933-1937
O.N. 161570 1,381g 772n.
245.7 x 37.0 x 16.2 feet.
T.3-cyl. (17½, 29, 48 x 33 inches) by
North Eastern Marine Engineering Co.
Ltd., Sunderland; 163 NHP, 9¾ knots.
2.9.1925: Launched by Sir John
Priestman and Co., Sunderland (Yard
No. 289).
9.1925: Completed by A/S D/S Boreas
(Torp & Wiese), Bergen, Norway as
BOREAS.
1927: Sold to Skibs A/S D/S Boreas
(Johan C. Wiese, manager), Bergen.
10.1.1933: Registered in the ownership
of the Cliffside Shipping Co. Ltd.
(John Morrison and Son, manager),
Newcastle-upon-Tyne as GAUNLESS.
15.1.1937: Register closed on sale to
O/Y FinskaInsjö A/B (Fred. Nichols and
Son), Helsingfors, Finland as ULEÅ.
1946: Managers became A/B Edv.
Bjorklund O/Y.
1947: Sold to Rederi A/B Inter (A.H.
Vang), Helsingfors and renamed INGER.
1949: Transferred to Rederi A/B Ergo,
Helsingfors.
1955: Sold to the U.S.S.R. and renamed
KHARLOV.
1970: Deleted from 'Lloyd's Register'
for lack of up-to-date information. She
was reported trading in 1957.

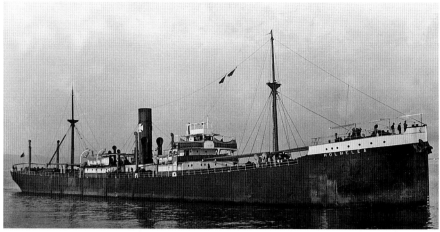
Holmelea. [World Ship Society Ltd.]

Ashlea. [World Ship Society Ltd.]

Above*: Gaunless post-war as Inger. [World Ship Society Ltd.]*
Below*: Gaunless in her final incarnation as Kharlov. [World Ship Society Ltd.]*

8. STORNEST 1936-1941
See Priestman no. 3.

9. THORNLEA 1936-1940
See Priestman no. 6.

10. GLENLEA 1936-1942
See Priestman no. 7.

Stornest fitted out for war, photographed on 7th August 1942 - two months before being lost. *[J. and M. Clarkson collection]*

Morrison Steamship Co. Ltd., Newcastle

This owning company was incorporated in March 1920 with a nominal capital of £100,000, although it had no ships until *Cheldale* was delivered in 1924. John Priestman was a subscriber to the Morrison Steamship Co. Ltd., one of those who put his name and his money to the company's articles, but the two directors were John and Samuel Morrison who were initially the largest investors. However, after the issue of 50,000 preference and 50,000 ordinary shares in 1925, Priestman gradually increased his holding until he had some 25% of the issued capital. He was also to provide a total of £58,500 in mortgages on *Farndale* and *Cheldale*. The company's name and the difference in naming scheme, with the Morrison ships not sharing the –*Lea* prefix of Priestman's other operations, is indicative of control by the Morrison family rather than Priestman, despite the latter's significant investment.

Figures for the Morrison company's profits are available only for certain years. In March 1927 a total profit for the previous two years of £5,881 was reported on an investment of £96,395 in ships. Figures improved during the 1930s: almost £8,000 was reported in 1932, £13,500 in 1936, peaking at over £23,000 in 1939. The war years were less remunerative, with for instance just over £14,000 earned in 1944, but even so an extraordinary amount considering that by then no ships were owned.

Both *Farndale* and *Cheldale* were lost within weeks of each other in 1940, but the company was encouraged to order a new ship with the offer of a mortgage of £95,000 from the Ministry of Shipping. This resulted in the *Elmdale* being completed as Burntisland yard number 241 in February 1941. Unfortunately she too became a loss, torpedoed in November 1942. The recently transferred *Glenlea* also became a U-boat victim just seven days later. With no ships left, early in 1947 it was resolved to voluntarily wind up the Morrison Steamship Co. Ltd., and eventually almost £233,000 was distributed to its shareholders. As the paid-up capital was around £75,000, this represented almost £3 for each holder of a £1 share. It is not surprising that Priestman's estate was so valuable.

1. CHELDALE 1925-1940
O.N. 148121 4,218g 2,536n.
365.0 x 51.5 x 25.1 feet.
T. 3-cyl. (25, 41, 69 x 48 inches) by Richardsons, Westgarth and Co. Ltd., Sunderland; 380 NHP, 1,900 IHP, 10 knots.
11.2.1925: Launched by Sir John Priestman and Co., Sunderland (Yard No. 288).
27.3.1925: Registered in the ownership of the Morrison Steamship Co. Ltd. (John Morrison and Son, managers), Newcastle-upon-Tyne as CHELDALE.
17.2.1940: Sunk in collision with the motor ship GREYSTOKE CASTLE (5,853/1928) 24 miles off Durban in position 29.49 south, 31.30 east whilst on a voyage from Rangoon to Durban and the west coast of Africa with a cargo of gunnies and rice.
19.6.1940: Register closed.

Cheldale. [Bristol Series/J. and M. Clarkson]

2. FARNDALE 1928-1940
O.N. 149482 4,222g 2,533n.
T. 3-cyl. (25, 41, 69 x 48 inches) by North Eastern Marine Engineering Co. Ltd., Sunderland; 380 NHP, 2,150 IHP, $10\frac{3}{8}$ knots.
365.0 x 51.5 x 25.1 feet.

3.10.1928: Launched by Sir John Priestman and Co., Sunderland (Yard No. 280).
25.10.1928: Registered in the ownership of the Morrison Steamship Co. Ltd. (John Morrison and Son, manager), Newcastle-upon-Tyne as FARNDALE.
11.1928: Completed.

30.3.1940: Caught fire while loading at Takoradi during a voyage from Port Harcourt to the United Kingdom with a cargo incuding palm kernels, ground nuts and cocoa.
1.4.1940: Beached but later declared a constructive total loss and abandoned.
20.6.1940: Register closed.

3. GLENLEA 1942
See Priestman no. 7.

4. ELMDALE 1941-1942
O.N. 165808 4,872g 2,810n. 441.0 (424.2) x 57.0 x 25.8 feet.
T.3-cyl. by Rankin and Blackmore Ltd., Greenock; 451 NHP, 1,900 IHP, 10½ knots.
14.12.1940: Launched by the Burntisland Shipbuilding Co. Ltd., Burntisland (Yard No. 241).
15.3.1941: Acquired by Morrison Steamship Co. Ltd. (John Morrison and Son, manager), Newcastle-upon-Tyne.
21.3.1941: Registered in the ownership of the Ministry of Shipping, London (John Morrison and Son, Newcastle-upon-Tyne, manager) as ELMDALE
4.1941: Completed.
6.4.1942: Damaged by gunfire from a Japanese submarine in position 6.52 south, 78.50 east whilst on a voyage from Karachi to Durban.
1.11.1942: Torpedoed and sunk by the German submarine U 174 in position 00.17 north, 34.55 west whilst on a voyage from Baltimore via Trinidad to Alexandria with a cargo of coal, military stores and general cargo. Five of the 36 crew and one of the six DEMS gunners were lost.
10.6.1943: Register closed.

Note that ELMDALE was registered *after* her sale by Ministry of Shipping to Morrison.

Farndale in the Mersey, in charterer's colours (upper middle) and again with Morrison's funnel colours (lower middle) . *[B. and A. Feilden/J. and M. Clarkson; F.W. Hawks]*

The short-lived tea-pot bowed *Elmdale* on trials in February 1941. *[Roy Fenton collection]*.

ABERDEEN MOTOR TRAWLERS LTD.
Peter Myers

Aberdeen's ageing post-1945 steam trawler fleet caused serious anxiety to some of the city's fish merchants, who became alarmed at the prospect of declining fish supplies. They resolved to set up a company which would later be in the vanguard of introducing new diesel-engined trawlers to the port's fleet in the 1950s. Aberdeen Motor Trawlers Ltd. (A.M.T.) had eight vessels built for it between 1957 and 1965, some of which were among the port's most profitable trawlers and helped vindicate the merchants' faith in their venture.

The elderly profile of Aberdeen's fleet of steam trawlers in the late-1940s and early 1950s was a source of concern to local fish merchants. The old-timers included, from left, *Strathglass* (A.62), *Pointer* (A.943) and *Strathalva* (A.757) seen here in the port's Albert Basin. *[Aberdeen Art Gallery and Museums]*

It had been hoped that Aberdeen's first new motor trawler, *Star of Scotland* (285 gt), completed by local yard Hall, Russell and Co. Ltd. in September 1947 for the Walker Steam Trawl Fishing Co. Ltd., would mark the start of a modernisation programme but this proved to be a false dawn. No further new motor trawlers followed until 1953 despite the favourable impression the *Star of Scotland* had made during her trials when she exceeded all expectations in terms of speed, manoeuvrability and dragging the trawl, while her 700 BHP British Polar oil engine meant she could call on extra power when needed.

Star of Scotland was Aberdeen's first new motor trawler and was completed in September 1947 by the local yard of Hall, Russell for the Walker Steam Trawl Fishing Co. Ltd. *[World Ship Society Ltd.]*

The moving spirit behind A.M.T. was fish merchant Byron S. Bellamy, who had moved from Grimsby to Aberdeen. He approached leading trawler owner Basil Parkes in 1949 about joining a group of merchants with the purpose of building a fleet of motor trawlers. Parkes took a financial stake in Aberdeen Motor Trawlers Ltd., which was incorporated on 26th November 1955 with Bellamy as chairman. In the previous month, Aberdeen shipbuilder John Lewis and Sons Ltd. had completed the 120-foot motor trawler *Mount Everest* (303 gt) for the Seafield Fishing Co. Ltd. of Aberdeen and in size and performance she pointed the way to the future for the Aberdeen fleet, giving an extra incentive to A.M.T.'s backers. She also had the distinction of being the first trawler to be built for the local fleet under the White Fish Authority's grant-and-loan scheme, which provided a 25% grant and loaned 80% of the building costs.

Mount Everest (A42) arriving Aberdeen 29th June 1977 when she was a part of the British United Trawlers (Aberdeen) Ltd. fleet. *[J. and M. Clarkson]*

Parkes's Boston Deep Sea Fishing and Ice Co. Ltd., which then owned and managed 28 motor trawlers, recommended that, from experience, boats of just under 115 feet in length were the most suitable for fishing the near and middle waters successfully. The Boston company's boss, who later became Sir Basil Parkes, agreed to find a third of the capital required for each trawler built and there was also the added bonus of the White Fish Authority's grant-and-loan scheme. Parkes was also ready to provide skilled staff to operate and manage the fleet, to train engineers and to have a resident superintendent engineer at Aberdeen. In practice, though, it was the 1902-established Don Fishing Co. Ltd. of Aberdeen who managed A.M.T.'s trawlers.

Initial orders from Aberdeen

A.M.T. placed an initial order for three trawlers, and soon afterwards the firm was converted into a public company at the end of January 1956, a move which coincided with a donation of £1,100 from a firm, which although it had no direct links to the fishing industry, appreciated the efforts being made by Aberdeen's fleet replacement scheme. A.M.T. expanded in September 1956 when it took over Distributors' Fishing Co. (Aberdeen) Ltd., which operated three motor seine-net fishing vessels.

The first of A.M.T.'s trawlers to take to the water was the 113-foot *Aberdeen City* (A.113) from the old-established Aberdeen yard of Alexander Hall and Co. Ltd. on 14th January 1957. She was launched on the same day as another motor trawler, the 118 ft 6 in *David Wood*, which came from John Lewis's Torry yard at the port. The *Aberdeen City* (263 gt) was fitted with a Mirrlees four-stroke oil engine and had a bunker capacity of 58 tons. The accommodation for the 16 crew was nothing short of revolutionary compared with the old steam trawlers. The skipper's cabin was abaft the wheelhouse while the chief engineer and the mate had single cabins. The remaining crew members were accommodated in two and four-berth cabins and two mess rooms were provided. The accommodation was heated throughout by hot water radiators supplied by an automatic oil-fired heating boiler in the engine room. She sailed from Aberdeen on her maiden trip on 1st May 1957 and during her first year she made 24 trips over 330 days and her catches grossed a total of £62,500. At the end of July 1957, there was a race home from the fishing grounds between the *Aberdeen City* and the coal-fired steam trawler *Star of Orkney*. The latter was given an hour's start and was narrowly pipped by the newer vessel which was tying up at Aberdeen fish market when the veteran arrived at the port. It was an impressive performance by the *Star of Orkney*, built by Hall, Russell in 1936 and whose design was the basis for the eight 'Round Table' class of naval trawlers launched in 1941-42 at Aberdeen yards.

Aberdeen Merchant of 1957 was lengthened by 10 feet in 1965, which helped improve her performance. *[Aberdeen City Libraries]*

Aberdeen Distributor of 1958 was owned originally by Distributors' Fishing Co. (Aberdeen) Ltd., a subsidiary of A.M.T, and is shown passing Hall, Russell's shipyard, circa 1959. *[World Ship Society]*

Aberdeen City was the first trawler built for Aberdeen Motor Trawlers Ltd. and served the company from June 1957 until wrecked on Sanday, Orkney in September 1963. She is shown passing George Gibson's short-sea trader *Ettrick* at Atlantic Wharf while outbound from Aberdeen. *[World Ship Society Ltd.]*

The *Aberdeen City* was followed from Alexander Hall by the similar 115 ft 6 in *Aberdeen Merchant* (A.134) which was completed in June 1957 and landed her maiden catch that month after a round 140-hour trip to Faroe. She was off again within 24 hours, which was something difficult to achieve with a coal-burning steam trawler. Both vessels were painted in the A.M.T. livery of black hull, red boot-topping and brown upper works. The black-topped red funnel bore the company's white house flag with the blue letters A M T within a blue circle. The *Aberdeen City* added to her appearance in March 1960 when she flew the Blue Ensign at her stern because her skipper, William Henderson, and four of his crew were active members of the Royal Naval Reserve.

The company's third vessel also came from Alexander Hall and was named *Aberdeen Distributor* (A.211) in deference to her registered owners, Distributors' Fishing

Co. (Aberdeen) Ltd., which was a subsidiary of A.M.T., although her ownership was later transferred to A.M.T. in May 1970. She was launched on 1st May 1958, ran her sea trials in Aberdeen Bay on 7th July 1958 and later in the month made her maiden trip to Faroe from which she returned with a catch of 850 hundredweight, which sold for £2,200 at the market. The new boats had been commanded on their maiden trips by Alex Elder, A.M.T.'s commodore skipper, who had first gone to sea as a deckie apprentice in 1937.

In his autobiography, 'Trawlings of a Lifetime' (1991), Sir Basil Parkes said the capital of A.M.T. was increased several times and, whenever any of the shareholders did not wish to take up their allocation, his company took up the shares, with the result that eventually the Boston company owned more than 50% of A.M.T. Boston also had a stake in Aberdeen Near Water Trawlers Ltd. which was incorporated on 11th August 1958 and was a sister company of A.M.T. with Byron Bellamy as its chairman. Its four new trawlers were designed to fish the near waters and are described in my article 'Aberdeen's Scratcher Trawlers' in 'Record' 59, page 178.

Trawlers from the Tyne
Down on the River Tyne, Thomas Mitchison of Gateshead built the *Aberdeen Enterprise*, which was launched on 31st January 1957 and ran her trials off the Tyne in June. She was

said to have been the first trawler to be built on the river in 30 years and for older Tynesiders revived memories of the erstwhile yards of J.T. Eltringham, of Willington Quay, and Charles Rennoldson of South Shields, who had specialised in building trawlers and tugs. Mitchison had been founded as ship-repairers in 1919 and did not start shipbuilding at its Friar's Goose yard until 1955, concentrating on coasters, tugs, barges and trawlers.

The *Aberdeen Enterprise*'s all-welded hull was of the hydroconic design, a feature she shared with her sister-ships *Aberdeen Progress* and *Aberdeen Fisher* which followed from the Tyne yard. The hydroconic principle was basically a hull with a series of hard chines rather than a smooth curve and had been patented by consultant naval architects Burness Corlett, and a number of builders were licensed to construct vessels to this design.

The Tyne-built *Aberdeen Progress* served A.M.T. from 1957 until sold to Argentine owners in 1974. *[Aberdeen City Libraries]*

Aberdeen Enterprise was the first of three trawlers built for A.M.T. by T. Mitchison, Gateshead in 1957-58. *[Aberdeen City Libraries]*

Bellamy said the hydroconic hull with stabilising fins made 'an extraordinarily good fishing platform' and it allowed 'progress to be maintained much above average in all weathers'. In fact, the *Aberdeen Enterprise* (A.114) had her stabilising fins fitted on the pontoon dock at Aberdeen harbour only after her third fishing trip which was to Faroe. Alex Elder had assessed her on that trip and rated her as powerful and a good sea boat. Her fishing performance was considered 'very satisfactory' after she caught 900 boxes of fish which sold for £3,300. The *Aberdeen Progress* (A.157) was officially named on 24th July 1957 although her launch was delayed for some weeks. The two Gateshead-built trawlers performed well enough for A.M.T. to order a third vessel from the Tyneside yard in March 1958. The new boat was named *Aberdeen Fisher* (A.218) and arrived at Aberdeen from Gateshead in December that year. She was commanded by Alex Elder for her initial fishing trips and by the beginning of May 1959 she had included two trips to Icelandic waters which yielded 2,700 boxes of fish and fetched £8,100 at the market. The 113-foot *Aberdeen Fisher* was reported at the time to be the smallest British trawler operating off Iceland.

A.M.T. returned to Aberdeen builders for its seventh new vessel and placed an order with Hall, Russell and Co. Ltd. for one of its Hall 'Economy' series of trawlers. The 115 feet 10 inches *Aberdeen Venturer* (A.488) was duly named on 6th June 1960 but her launch was postponed until four days later because of a strike by 70 carpenters at the yard. The new ship, which had a gross tonnage of 298 tons, was characterised by a lantern-style wheelhouse. Two other Hall 'Economy' trawlers built that year were the *Boston Wasp*

Boston Wasp (LT238) sailing from Lowestoft in August 1977. She had been transferred from Grimsby to Lowestoft in September 1968. *[J. and M. Clarkson]*

and *Princess Royal*. The design featured a transom stern and some boats had a quadpost mast which allowed improved forward visibility for the helmsman and also a much larger working space on deck.

The waters around Orkney and Shetland had taken their toll of trawlers in the inter-war period and this continued after 1945 with 19 being lost around Orkney. Among them was A.M.T.'s first vessel, *Aberdeen City*, which went aground at Start Point, Sanday, early on 16th September 1963 while outbound for Faroese waters. All 12 crew members were taken off by the Sanday lifeboat. During refloating operations the trawler turned on her side and was later declared a constructive total loss.

The Ministry of Transport's subsequent inquiry blamed the *Aberdeen City*'s loss on the failure of her skipper, William Henderson, to keep a lookout while being in the wheelhouse alone. It was found that as she drifted towards rocks at Start Point he had been preoccupied with investigating the breakdown and repair of the ship's radar instead of attending to her safety. The findings stated: 'There should have been a hand at the wheel, leaving the skipper in control of the vessel to keep a lookout and navigate her without any distraction.' It added that the skipper was not entitled to assume she would clear Start Point and drift north-north-east with the tide as she had done before. It was found that Skipper Henderson, who had first gone to sea at the age of 18, was guilty of an error of judgment rather than negligence and his certificate was suspended for six months.

Mannofield take control

An emerging force in the Aberdeen trawling industry was the Mannofield Fishing Co. Ltd. which had been incorporated on

25th June 1962 and soon moved to take control of A.M.T.'s trawlers. Skipper Alex Elder came ashore in 1963 to become the Mannofield group's Trawler Manager and then its Assistant Managing Director in 1965. In that year the *Aberdeen Merchant* was lengthened 10 feet forward of her wheelhouse at a Humber shipyard with the aim of improving her fishing performance and extending the length of her trips. She made two disappointing trips after the work had been completed, prompting Alex Elder to take temporary command for a five-day return trip to Faroe from which her 230 hunderweight catch fetched £1,200 at market. He reported enthusiastically after the trip: 'She's a better sea boat, faster by half-a-knot and she has proved she can make a paying trip.'

A more momentous occasion for A.M.T. in 1965 was the completion of the company's largest trawler, the 139-foot *Aberdeen Explorer* (425 gt), by Hall, Russell. She had been ordered in August 1964 as a replacement for the ill-fated *Aberdeen City* and her size meant she could prosecute the more distant grounds if required. She was launched on 17th May 1965 and sailed to Faroe on her maiden trip three months later under the command of Skipper William Walker. The new ship had the same hull design as the yard's *Prince Philip*, but was equipped for fishing from both sides. Her 1,100 BHP Mirrlees seven-cylinder, four-stroke, turbo-charged, direct-reversing diesel engine enabled her to make swift passages to and from the fishing grounds. The trawler's insulated fish room had a capacity of about 11,500 cubic feet and the trawl winch was electrically operated. Her fishing performance was impressive and despite her late start was Aberdeen's fifth top-grossing trawler in 1965, totalling £30,381 over 124 days with a daily average of £245. The *Aberdeen Venturer* was the eighth top trawler that year, grossing £62,299 over 279 days with a daily average of £225.

Aberdeen Venturer is launched from Hall, Russell's yard in June 1960. In the background at Matthews Quay is the 1955-built *St Rognvald* of the North of Scotland, Orkney and Shetland Shipping Co. Ltd. *[Aberdeen Journals Ltd.]*

Mutiny and poaching allegations
Two other A.M.T. trawlers were also in the news in 1965 but for less positive reasons. The *Aberdeen Enterprise* put into the Faroese port of Thorshavn for repairs in June after a collision with another trawler, believed to be British. No-one was injured in the incident and damage to the boat was only slight. Later in the year, five of the *Aberdeen Distributor*'s crew burst into her wheelhouse and tried to take control of her as she sailed from her home port. The incident was described as 'a minor mutiny' in court and the two worst offenders were each jailed for 60 days while the other three were fined £20 each.

The inbound *Aberdeen Distributor* reaches the safety of the Navigation Channel at Aberdeen harbour as a huge sea crashes against the South Breakwater. *[Aberdeen Art Gallery and Museums]*

The *Aberdeen Explorer* (A.765) did not stay long at Aberdeen because in March 1966 she moved to Fleetwood where she was operated by the Boston group, with which A.M.T. had close ties, and was subsequently renamed *Boston Explorer* (FD.15) in 1968.

Aberdeen trawlers had the occasional encounter with Royal Danish Navy warships which were engaged in fishery-protection duties off Faroe. In January 1961 the *Aberdeen Merchant* was boarded after she was ordered to stop by H.D.M.S. *Niels Ebbesen* when she was suspected of fishing inside the limit for British trawlers in Faroese waters. The Royal Navy frigate H.M.S. *Malcolm* arrived on the scene and after a discussion between the frigates' captains, in which they agreed there was no clear proof of illegal fishing, the *Aberdeen Merchant* was allowed to continue on her way.

A more serious incident occurred on 3rd January 1967 when the *Aberdeen Venturer* was shelled by H.D.M.S. *Vaedderen* off Faroe after being suspected of fishing within the 12-mile limit. The crew of the Danish frigate's Sud-Aviation Alouette III helicopter said they found the trawler four miles inside the limits and that her crew appeared to be getting rid of their fishing gear. A.M.T. denied their boat had been poaching and said she had lost her gear while making the final haul of the trip, adding that attempts to recover the gear had been hampered by the inclement weather. The *Vaedderen* fired a warning shot and then came alongside the *Aberdeen Venturer*, ordering her to stop, which Skipper Joe Glass, senior, did. When he noticed a boarding party being assembled on the frigate's deck he was not prepared to have his ship seized and got under way at full speed. The frigate opened fire and brought down part of the trawler's radio antenna, but there was no other damage. The pursuit continued until it was broken off when the *Aberdeen Venturer* was 26 miles off the coast of Faroe. By coincidence the *Vaedderen* had made a courtesy call at Aberdeen the previous October.

The Danish frigate H.D.M.S. *Hvidbjornen* made a similar visit to Aberdeen in late-November 1974 when her captain was amused to learn that his ship was nicknamed the 'Polar Bear' by Scottish fishermen but said that, on the whole, Aberdeen trawlers did not give him much trouble. However, less than a month later, on 26th December, the *Hvidbjornen* was involved in an incident with the *Aberdeen Fisher*, commanded by Skipper John Ogston. She was one of six trawlers alleged to be fishing within Faroese fishing limits and was singled out by the *Hvidbjornen* which fired at her in an attempt to halt the fleeing trawler. A year earlier Britain had signed an agreement with Denmark, acting on behalf of the Faroe Islands, which allowed British vessels to catch up to 18,000 tonnes of cod and haddock during 1974, plus unlimited quantities of other demersal species. The deal also specified certain areas outside the Faroese 12-mile limit that would be closed during certain periods.

Aberdeen Fisher was involved in an incident with a Danish fishery-protection frigate while fishing off the Faroe Islands in December 1974. *[Press Association]*

Change of control

The trawling company of John Wood and Son (Aberdeen) Ltd. made an important move when it was announced on 5th January 1967 that the management of A.M.T.'s trawlers was being transferred to the company, who would take a large financial interest in A.M.T. The nine A.M.T. trawlers involved in the new arrangement were the *Aberdeen Distributor, Aberdeen Enterprise, Aberdeen Fisher, Aberdeen Merchant, Aberdeen Progress, Aberdeen Venturer, Admiral Hawke, Admiral Nelson* and *Admiral Vian.* The three 'Admiral' trawlers had previously been acquired by Mannofield in September 1962 before being transferred to the ownership of A.M.T. in April 1964 (*Admiral Nelson*) and February 1966 (*Admiral Hawke* and *Admiral Vian*). The *Admiral Hawke* (225/1961), *Admiral Nelson*, ex-*Princess Royal*-63 (300/1960) and *Admiral Vian*, ex-*Mannofield*-62 (226/1961) were all products of Hall, Russell's yard. John Wood took full control of the Mannofield company in November 1967. The acquisitions had been masterminded by John Wood's son, Ian, who in later years described Aberdeen's fishing industry of the late-1960s as being 'static and parochial, a situation compounded by a languishing local economy'. Ian Wood, who was knighted in 1994, was the architect of the Wood Group's huge expansion after it diversified into the offshore energy industry.

It was traditional practice for most of Aberdeen's trawling fleet to be tied up over the Hogmanay and New Year holiday, but some skippers were keen to take advantage of the high market prices which prevailed at this time when fish supplies were scarce. On 3rd January 1967, four A.M.T. trawlers – *Aberdeen Distributor, Aberdeen Enterprise, Aberdeen Fisher* and *Admiral Nelson* – grossed almost £19,000 at their home port when they landed their catches from the Faroe and North Sea grounds. A few months earlier the *Admiral Vian* had been in the headlines after she netted a mine off Shetland in October 1966. Her crew had to live with the lethal wartime relic for five days until it was made safe and later dumped at sea.

Admiral Nelson (A469) docking at Aberdeen in July 1979 was converted to an offshore standby vessel in 1980. *[J. and M. Clarkson]*

The *Aberdeen Merchant* was sold for demolition and left her home port on 26th March 1971 for the breaker's yard at Bo'ness on the Firth of Forth under the tow of the John Wood trawler *Burwood* (249/1961). A few years earlier the *Aberdeen Progress* had also put her towing capabilities to good use when she towed the Grimsby distant-water trawler *Ross Resolution* (564/1948) 60 miles to Aberdeen in August 1968 after the latter had developed engine trouble while outbound for the fishing grounds.

In 1974 there were further disposals of the original A.M.T. fleet when the *Aberdeen Distributor, Aberdeen Enterprise* and *Aberdeen Progress* were sold to Ribazon S.A., Mar del Plata, Argentina to make way for new 86-foot pocket trawlers built by John Lewis's yard. The trio were renamed respectively *Ribazon Mar Platense, Ribazon Dorine* and *Ribazon Ines.* They were repainted at Aberdeen for their new owners and the author discovered them at Albert Quay on 15th April 1974 as they were being prepared for the long voyage to South America with a call at the Canary Islands for bunkers. The vessels all bore Mar del Plata as their new port of registration and they looked quite spruce in their new livery of red hull, white upper works and maroon over blue bands on a black funnel. The *Aberdeen Progress* had continued to perform well in her last months of fishing from Aberdeen and was one of the top boats in her class during December 1973 when she grossed £21,000 from two trips to Faroe under the command of John Smith.

The drink problem on some trawlers and its effect on shipboard discipline always gave cause for serious concern particularly during the mid-1970s when several high-profile incidents attracted unwelcome publicity for the industry. The worst occurred when the *Aberdeen Venturer* collided with another Aberdeen trawler, the *Ben Tarbert* (280/1960), off Peterhead's Bay of Refuge on 28th November 1975. The *Ben Tarbert* was stopped when she was struck amidships by the *Aberdeen Venturer* and sank within three minutes. Two crew members of the *Ben Tarbert* drowned in the collision. Both vessels had developed faults with their radar sets and intended lying off Peterhead to await radar technicians. The *Aberdeen Venturer* was manoeuvring to lie alongside the *Ben Tarbert* when the collision occurred. At the subsequent trial at Banff Sheriff Court, the *Aberdeen Venturer*'s skipper and second engineer were both fined after being found guilty of culpable homicide. The court had heard that the second engineer had failed to respond to telegraphed orders because he was drunk while on duty.

Decline

The sharp decline of Britain's trawling industry from the mid-1970s affected Aberdeen and among the older motor trawlers which ceased fishing from the port was the *Aberdeen Fisher*, whose withdrawal from service, for economic reasons, was announced in October 1976. She was sold for demolition soon after and was among a number of the port's redundant motor trawlers dating from the 1950s which were towed away to the breakers' yards in 1976-77.

The slump had a severe impact on Fleetwood and the port's *Boston Explorer*, which had briefly set up a port record for a 140-foot vessel in 1973 when she grossed £25,000 for a 19-day Iceland trip, was laid up at the end of October 1978 because of recurring losses and the fact that there were fewer grounds where she could fish. The former *Aberdeen Explorer* was soon snapped up by the North Star Fishing Co. Ltd., a subsidiary of prominent Aberdeen fishing company George Craig and Sons Ltd., and converted into an offshore standby vessel to lie off oil rigs and platforms in the United Kingdom Continental Shelf. Her features included accommodation for 250 evacuated personnel and a clear deck space aft to allow a helicopter to winch up personnel and equipment. She was renamed *Grampian Explorer* and went on show in her new role at Aberdeen for the first time on 19th December 1978.

Just a few days later it was announced that the *Aberdeen Venturer*, the sole remaining trawler in A.M.T. livery at Aberdeen, would be returning to sea after repairs and an overhaul following a period of idleness. A.M.T.

had transferred ownership of her to associated company Aberdeen Near Water Trawlers Ltd. in June 1972. The *Aberdeen Venturer* had traditionally fished off Faroe, but now there were severe restrictions at those grounds and there was little surprise when she was decommissioned in 1979. She arrived at Bo'ness on 2nd November 1979 after being sold to Bo'ness Shipbreakers and Scrap Merchants (S.G. Dalton) for demolition. Her departure was symbolic of the Aberdeen trawling industry's dramatic decline during that year. At the start of 1979 there were 80 trawlers fishing out of the port but that had slumped to just 53 vessels in December. In 1975 there had been 120 trawlers employing 1,200 fishermen but that had fallen to just 520 men at the end of the decade. In March 1979, an official of the Aberdeen Trawl Officers' Guild lamented the parlous state of the port's trawling industry and called for government intervention to help revive the sector. He added: 'It is heartbreaking for those of us who have spent all our lives in the industry to remember the days when trawlers were treble-berthed all the way along the market from the cross-berth in Market Street to the bottom of Commercial Quay waiting their turn to be discharged. Now a day's landings could be accommodated in the small section of Palmerston Quay at the top of the market.'

Grampian Explorer at Scrabster, Caithness on 13th May 1979 (above right) while employed in laying buoys for an underwater survey. *[Author]*

Aberdeen Explorer was the last and largest trawler built for A.M.T., but fished from Aberdeen only from August 1965 until March 1966 when she moved to Fleetwood. *[Aberdeen City Libraries]*

Grampian Explorer, returning to Aberdeen 2nd June 1979, continued to serve as an offshore standby vessel until 1992. *[J. and M. Clarkson]*

UNION-CASTLE'S BLACK SHIPS
Alan Mallett

PART ONE: 1893-1914

From the outset cargo was an essential part of the Union-Castle Line's service to South Africa. Initially this, for the most part, comprised imports by Cape and Natal colonies, and the two Boer republics to their north, and such cargoes as the Union and Castle Line mail ships, sailing weekly from 1876, could not carry were transported by casual sailing craft and, from the late 1870s, other steamship companies, of which the Clan Line and predecessors of the Ellerman empire were to become increasingly important. The discovery of diamonds in the late 1860s, followed by gold twenty years later, and the development of the agricultural industry all made for improved two-way trade, as did technical advances such as sophisticated mining and railway equipment, all of which had to be imported from Europe and America.

Initially Union and Castle provided additional 'extra' sailings, sometimes using superannuated mail ships, sometimes chartered tonnage, and as often as not these catered only for cargo. From time to time elderly former mail ships were relegated to cargo only service, and Union's *Durban* (2,875/1877) and Castle's *Conway Castle* (2,966/1877) both became marine casualties whilst operating in this capacity within a month of each other, the former on 11th June 1893 off Tenerife, the latter a month earlier on 10th May off Madagascar.

Conway Castle of 1877. *[Ships in Focus]*

Coincidentally, in 1893 Castle Line established a new service jointly with Bucknall Brothers (The British and Colonial Steam Navigation Company, later to form part of the Ellerman group) for a joint United States to South Africa service entitled American and African Line, whilst Union Line collaborated with Clan Line for a similar service. Initially, so far as the mail companies were concerned, the service was operated with chartered tonnage and, with minimal South African exports to North America, vessels generally loaded for Europe on the return leg, thereafter proceeding to the United States in ballast.

Castle Line did not allocate any of their fleet to this service, but Union Line negotiated to purchase four 'slightly used' vessels, one in 1895, and the other three in 1898. The first of these, *Mariposa*, presents something of an enigma. Completed in 1891, measuring 5,305 grt, she was a twin-screw vessel capable of 12 knots and catering for 12 first

class passengers and was engaged on the Liverpool to Canada service under Elder, Dempster auspices, with the capability of carrying emigrants. The possibility that she was intended for the Union Line fortnightly Intermediate Service, which largely catered for emigrants, cannot be excluded, enhanced by the choice of *Gascon* as her intended name. Union Line had recently built four vessels for the Intermediate Service of similar size, all being given names commencing with the letter G. In the event it is academic, because *Mariposa* was wrecked prior to handover. The name *Gascon* was soon afterwards bestowed upon one of a larger trio completed in 1897 for the Intermediate Service.

Mariposa (5,305/1891), ex *Ruthenia*, in the Thames off Gravesend, whilst on charter to the Atlantic Transport Company. *[J. and M. Clarkson]*

Gascon (6,278/1897) of 1897. *[J. and M. Clarkson]*

The other three purchases, all in 1898, were a different matter and were given names with American connotations. *Sandusky*, of similar size and layout to *Mariposa*, was soon found to be unsuitable and sold on within a year. The other two, *Sabine* and *Susquehanna*, smaller at around 3,800 grt, single-screw and nine knots speed, served initially on the American route. Later, between 1904-1910, they were frequently engaged in ferrying coal from the company-owned mines in Natal to the Cape. They were disposed of shortly after the 1918 Armistice.

The Castle Line acquired the assets and liabilities of the Union Line early in 1900 and, with an early end to the Anglo-Boer War and a consequent boom in emigration and trade expected, hastily ordered or purchased on the stocks four cargo vessels, ordering a further six larger twin-screw vessels for the emigrant trade. The four purely cargo vessels measured 4,500 to 5,300 grt, about 7,000 to 8,000 deadweight and nine knots speed, and were predominantly engaged on the United States service until the First World War, during which they were variously engaged on government service, after which the three survivors returned to the company service, either from the United States or increasingly on the East African routes. Unlike the passenger ships, they were given black-painted hulls, hence the soubriquet 'black ships' which, barring the period 1946-1954, distinguished all the Union-Castle general cargo ships. After the war the three surviving vessels continued on the United States or, increasingly, on the East African service introduced in 1910 until retired in the mid twenties.

The six twin-screw vessels were in a different category. Predominantly cargo carriers, with accommodation for up to 80 first, second and third class and around 240 steerage passengers, they fell into two distinct groups, the first four being flush deckers averaging 6,000 grt, the last pair three island vessels of around 5,300 grt. Unlike other cargo vessels they wore the lavender grey hulls. Their employment was problematic as the end of hostilities prompted a depression rather than a boom, and ultimately they were allocated to a new monthly service to Mauritius, hardly an exacting schedule. The loss in 1908 of *Newark Castle*, the newest of the flush deckers, may well have been perceived as a silver-lined curse. The remaining three were no luckier, one being torpedoed in 1917, another burning out in 1919, and the third, *Cawdor Castle*, after some years operating as a 'black ship' being wrecked in mid-1926.

The smaller pair were more fortunate, both surviving the war, until they were laid up in 1922 and transferred two years later to a newly acquired subsidiary Bullard King and Co. (Natal Line) whom they continued to serve well into the thirties.

SABINE 1898-1921
O.N. 104458 3,819g 3,002n 6,015d.
371.0 x 43.2 x 27.5/24.9 feet.
T. 3-cyl. (24, 40, 66 x 42 inches) by Muir and Houston Ltd. Glasgow; 1,750 IHP, 9 knots.
10.11.1894: Launched by Harland and Wolff Ltd., Belfast (Yard No. 290) for T. Dixon and Sons, Belfast as MARINO.
2.1895: Completed.
10.1895: Sold to Ocean Transport Co. (Elder, Dempster and Co., managers), for a Liverpoo to Canada service.
8.1898: Acquired by The Union Steam Ship Co. Ltd., Southampton for their United States to South Africa service and renamed SABINE.
2.1900: Owners became The Union-Castle Mail Steamship Co. Ltd. (Donald Currie and Co., managers), London.
1906-1909: Engaged in moving coal from Durban to Cape Town.
9.1909: Chartered by William Lund and Sons, managers of The Blue Anchor Line Ltd., to search on behalf of families and others aboard for their steamer WARATAH (9,339/1908) which had failed to arrive at Cape Town as expected in July 1909.
11.9.1909: Departed Cape Town under command of Captain Stanley H. Owen with one officer and four seamen from HMS HERMES and steamed 14,000 miles on a zig-zag course based on the previous drifting of the steamer WAIKATO (4,767/1892) after she was disabled.
7.12.1909: Returned to Cape Town having made no discovery of importance. A similar search in 1910 by the steamer WAKEFIELD (117/1877) proved equally fruitless.

12.1909: Returned to owners' service.
4.1912: Management vested in owners.
9.2.1921: Sold to the owners' newly acquired subsidiary Bullard, King and Co. Ltd. (The Natal Line), London for £40,000 and renamed UMZINTO.
7.1925: Sold to Dutch shipbreakers.
11.1925: Resold to Italian shipbreakers.
12.1925: Arrived Venice for breaking up.

Captain Stanley Howard Owen was born in Islington, London in 1865 and went to sea in 1880. His first command, in 1908, was *Sabine* and he went on to command 27 further vessels of the Union-Castle Line. His first passenger ship was *Braemar Castle* in 1911, and in August 1914 he commanded *Carisbrook Castle* and, a month later *Dunvegan Castle*, both being engaged in transporting the British Expeditionary Force (the 'Old Contemptibles') across the Channel. His first mail ship command came in 1920 when he was appointed to *Saxon*. His final appointment was RMS *Arundel Castle* from which he retired in 1929, subsequently becoming a local councillor in Kingston-on-Thames, Surrey. He died in 1935.

Sabine. [J. and M. Clarkson]

SUSQUEHANNA 1898-1921
O.N.106000 3,702g 2,389n 6,080d.
350.0 x 45.3 x 17.9/23.7 feet.
T. 3-cyl. (25, 41, 67 x 45 inches) by Barclay, Curle and Co. Ltd., Glasgow; 350 NHP, 2,000 IHP, 9.5 knots.
14.4.1896: Launched by Barclay, Curle and Co. Ltd., Glasgow (Yard No. 407) for John Smith and William Service, Glasgow as MOUNT SEPHAR.
5.1896: Completed.
10.6.1898: Acquired by the Union Steamship Co. Ltd., Southampton.
18.8.1898: Renamed SUSQUEHANNA
14.5.1900: Transferred to Union-Castle Mail Steamship Co. Ltd. (Donald Currie and Co., managers), London.
4.1912: Management vested in owners.
21.2.1917: Government requisition as a transport carrying munitions from the United States to Great Britain and Russia and stores to Basra.
5.1917: Captain Albert Barron in command until early 1918.
21.6.1921: Sold to Denaby Shipping and Commercial Co. Ltd. (Henry J. Tremellen, manager), London.
20.5.1922: Renamed LONDON CITY
1922: Reduced to a coal hulk at Brixham, but not deleted from 'Lloyd's Register' until 1930.
28.12.1923: Transferred to Denaby and Cadeby Main Collieries Ltd., London.
31.12.1929: Transferred to the Torbay and Brixham Coaling Co. Ltd., London.

15.7.1940: Sunk during an air raid at Brixham. Later raised.
31.3.1942: Partially sunk during an air raid at Brixham.
15.9.1942: Register closed.
Wreck demolished after the war.

Captain Albert Barron subsequently commanded 30 of the company's ships culminating in his appointment as Commodore in January 1937. He retired at the end of 1938 and was tragically killed in September 1940, aged 66, whilst fire-watching during the London Blitz; a request to return to active service afloat having been turned down. One of the characters of the Union-Castle Line, his idiosyncrasies became legendary, the best being the time when, commanding one of the old coal-burning mail ships, he steamed into the centre of a Royal Navy exercise involving the Atlantic and Mediterranean Fleets under the irascible Admiral Sir John (Joe) Kelly. On being signalled to remove his ship as he was impeding the exercise of His Majesty's ships of war, Barron promptly replied 'and you, Sir, are impeding the carriage of His Majesty's Mails'. The exercise was delayed to let the mail ship through.

Susquehanna. [Ships in Focus]

SANDUSKY 1898-1899
O.N. 99359 5,504g 3,574n.
430.0 x 47.0 x 22.4 feet.
T. 6-cyl. (19, 31, 52 x 42 inches) by Harland and Wolff Ltd., Belfast; 2,200 IHP, 11 knots.
31.10.1891: Launched by Harland and Wolff Ltd., Belfast (Yard No. 242) for the City of Liverpool Steam Navigation Ltd. (D. and C. Maciver, managers), Liverpool as IONIA.
1.1892: Completed.
10.1892: Management transferred to Elder, Dempster and Co. Ltd., Liverpool following purchase of the owners by Ocean Transport Co. Ltd., Belfast, renamed MONTEZUMA and chartered to the Atlantic Transport Co. Ltd., London (6,357g 4,863n).
7.1898: Sold to the Union Steam Ship Co. Ltd., Southampton and renamed SANDUSKY for their United States to South Africa service.
6.6.1899: Sold to Harland and Wolff Ltd. in part payment for new tonnage under construction, subsequently resold to Mississippi and Dominion Steamship Co. Ltd. (Richard Mills and Co., managers), Liverpool and renamed ENGLISHMAN.
17.10.1899: Chartered to the British Government as Infantry Transport No 60 for the Boer War.
3.11.1902: Returned to owners.
24.3.1916: Captured by the German submarine U 43 (Kaptain-Leutnant Hellmutt Jurst) 30 miles north east of Malin Head whilst on a voyage from Avonmouth to Portland, Maine, and sunk by torpedo after being abandoned by her crew.

Union-Castle ships
YORK CASTLE 1901-1925
O.N. 112849 5,310g 3,467n 8,400d.
408.0 x 50.3 x 32.0 feet (draft 25.5 feet).
T.3-cyl. (27, 43, 72 x 51 inches) by George Clark Ltd., Sunderland; 2,400 IHP, 9 knots.
5.3.1901: Launched by Sir James Laing and Sons Ltd., Sunderland (Yard No. 582) for The Union-Castle Mail Steamship Co. Ltd. (Donald Currie and Co., managers), London, having been ordered in January 1900 by Wright, Graham and Co., Glasgow, and sold by them in January 1901.
5.1901: Completed for the United States to South Africa service and named YORK CASTLE.
1 to 4 1919: Captain Albert Barron in command.
6.1919: Ashore for two days in the Rovuma Channel off the Mozambique coast. During the Third Officer's watch (Jack Trayner) he noted that the ship was apparently heading straight for the shore. Captain Barron duly appraised the situation and set a course east north east and then retired. Not long afterwards Trayner observed much broken white water but no discernible motion. A kedge anchor was run out and at high water the ship was refloated by alternately going full ahead and full astern on the engines for half an hour, then heaving on the kedge with the crew 'rolling ship', she was refloated. A subsequent inquiry allotted blame to 'an ill-lit coast, faulty charts, and an unknown current'.
27.11.1925: Sold to B. Bibolini, Genoa, Italy for £15,000 and renamed SAN TERENZO.
10.1932: Broken up at Genoa

Mr Jack Trayner became a mail ship master in 1948, retiring late in 1959 after six years in command of *Capetown Castle.*

York Castle passing Woolwich 9th August 1913. [F. W. Hawks]

GORDON CASTLE 1901-1924
O.N. 114677 4,408g 2,824n 7,010d.
385.0 x 50.2 x 26.5 feet (draft 23.9 feet).
T.3-cyl. (23, 42, 72 x 48 inches) by Dunsmuir and Jackson Ltd., Glasgow; 2,200 IHP, 9.5 knots.
1.5.1901: Launched by Charles Connell and Co. Ltd. Glasgow (Yard No. 260) for The Union-Castle Mail Steamship Co. Ltd. as GORDON CASTLE, having been ordered by John Warrack and Co., Leith, as GORDON.
6.1901: Completed for the United States to South Africa service.
15.5.1918: Damaged in air attack on Calais.
5.5.1924: Sold for £10,250 to German shipbreakers and broken up from October.

Gordon Castle. [Author]

AROS CASTLE 1901-1917
O.N. 114732 4,459g 2,870n 7,080d.
392.4 x 48.6 x 29.2 feet (draft 24.0 feet).
T. 3-cyl. (27, 43, 72 x 48 inches) by Barclay, Curle and Co. Ltd., Glasgow; 2,500 IHP, 9.5 knots.
4.7.1901: Launched by Barclay, Curle and Co. Ltd., Glasgow (Yard No. 427) for The Union-Castle Mail Steamship Co. Ltd., London as AROS CASTLE.
8.1901: Completed for the United States to South Africa service.
9.1907: Captain E.W. Day in command.
21.11.1917: Torpedoed by the German submarine U 50 (Kapitan-Leutnant Walter Remy) whilst in convoy 300 miles south west of Bishop Rock in position 47.19 north, 12.45 west and sank with the loss of two lives. She was on a voyage from London to Baltimore in ballast.

Captain Day subsequently commanded three further ships before taking command of *Galician* (6,757/1900) in December 1913. On 15.8.1914 she was stopped by SMS *Kaiser Wilhelm Der Grosse*, a former Norddeutscher Lloyd Blue Riband holder now serving as an armed merchant cruiser. Two military passengers were removed and on 16.8.1914 *Galician* was released to continue her voyage 'on account of the women and children aboard'. In September 1922 whilst Day was commanding *Kinfauns Castle* (9,664/1899) passengers and crew of the foundering HAPAG liner *Hammonia* (7,291/1909) were rescued. He retired in 1924 and died in 1930.

Aros Castle. [J. and M. Clarkson]

CORFE CASTLE 1901-1927
O.N 114773 4592g 2958n 7010d.
401.7 x 48.6 x 29.9 feet (draft 24.1 feet).
T. 3-cyl. (27, 43, 72 x 48 inches) by Barclay, Curle and Co. Ltd., Glasgow; 2,500 IHP, 9 knots.
12.9.1901: Launched by Barclay, Curle and Co. Ltd.,

Glasgow (Yard No. 428) for The Union-Castle Mail Steamship Co. Ltd., London as CORFE CASTLE.
10.1901: Completed for the United States to South Africa service.
4.9.1927: Sold to W. Schumann, Bremerhaven, Germany for £12,000 and renamed OSTSEE.
1932: Sold for breaking up by Flenderwerke A.G.
3.11.1932: Arrived Lubeck.
1.1933: Demolition commenced.

Corfe Castle. [J. and M. Clarkson]

Emigrant cargo ships
ALNWICK CASTLE
O.N. 114784 5,893g 3,796n 7,630d.
400.4 x 50.2 x 26.8 feet (draft 26.3 feet).
Passengers: 12 first, 16 second, 42 third, 230 steerage/open.
Two T. 3-cyl. (21.5, 35, 58 x 48 inches) by William Beardmore and Co. Ltd., Glasgow; 3,400 IHP, 11.5 knots.
27.9.1901: Launched by William Beardmore and Co. Ltd., Glasgow (Yard No. 475) for The Union-Castle Mail Steamship Co. Ltd., London as ALNWICK CASTLE.
11.1901: Completed and principally employed on the London to Mauritius service, Captain B. Burt in command.
1908-1909: Laid up. Subsequently engaged on the London to Mauritius service.
1915-1916: Trooping between Great Britain and the Mediterranean.
9.1915: Captain B. Chave in command.
18.3.1917: Rescued 25 survivors from TREVOSE (3,112/1896) which had been torpedoed a day previously.
19.3.1917: Became the owners' first war loss when torpedoed and sunk by the German submarine U 81 (Kapitan-Leutnant Raimund Reisbach) 310 miles west by half south from Bishop Rock in position 47.38 north, 13.24 west whilst on voyage London to Cape Town with passengers and general cargo. She sank 40 minutes later, U 81 having surfaced to observe. All 14 passengers, including a mother and her three-month-old baby and the 100 crew and 25 survivors boarded the lifeboats which hoisted sail and set course eastwards. The weather deteriorated and the Captain's boat became separated.
24.3.1917: The 24 survivors of the 29 in the Captain's boat were rescued by the French steamer VENEZIA (6,827/1907), including Captain Chave and Cadet John Oakley, making his first voyage. The Chief Officer's boat with the mother, child, and sole stewardess reached the Spanish coast on 27.3.1917, the other two boats were never found, 40 dying. Captain Chave was later knighted in recognition of his hydrological

and surveying work for the Admiralty and retired as a mail ship master in the 1920s. U 81 was torpedoed and sunk by HM Submarine E 54 (Lieutenant-Commander Robert Raikes) on 1.5.1917. The seven survivors of the 38 strong crew included Kapitan-Leutnant Reisbach.

Captain Burt lost his life in the sinking of H.M. Hospital Ship *Glenart Castle*, formerly *Galician* (6,757/1900), in July 1918. John Oakley achieved the rank of commodore in the early 1960s.

Alnwick Castle. [J. and M. Clarkson]

BERWICK CASTLE 1901-1920

O.N. 114822 5,883g 3,788n 7,630d.
398.2 x 50 x 26.8 feet (draft 26.2 feet).
Passengers: 12 first, 16 second, 42 third, 230 steerage/open.
After 1912: to eight first, 24 second, 42 third.
Two T. 3-cyl. (21.5, 35, 58 x 48 inches) by William Beardmore and Co. Ltd., Glasgow; 3,400 IHP, 11.5 knots.
7.12.1901: Launched by William Beardmore and Co. Ltd., Glasgow (Yard No. 476) for The Union-Castle Mail Steamship Co. Ltd., London as BERWICK CASTLE.
1.1902: Completed and principally engaged on the London to Mauritius service.
18.3.1904: Rammed and sank H.M. Submarine A-1 with the loss of all 18 of the submarine's crew off the Nab Lightship whilst on a voyage from Southampton to Hamburg.
19.3.1907: Captain J.T. Robinson in command, ran aground off Mozambique whilst under charge of a pilot, but successfully refloated.
27.5.1907: Sailed for South African ports and then to Brisbane, Sydney, and Adelaide loading wool and other cargo for the United Kingdom, returning in November. This charter reflected the difficult trading conditions as BERWICK CASTLE, along with ALNWICK CASTLE, was subsequently laid up in July 1908 for some months, and Captain Robinson retired.
1915: Transported Nigerian troops from Lagos to Mombasa in connection with the campaign in East Africa.
16.10.1919: Fire broke out in a bunker whilst at Port Reitz, Kilindini whilst on voyage from Beira to Mombasa. The fire rapidly became uncontrollable. Beached at Mombasa where the fire was allowed to burn out.
19.10.1919: Fire extinguished.
4.1920: Refloated and steamed to Durban for laying up.
15.12.1920: Sold for £16,000 to Andorra Société Anonyme de Construzione Imprese Navale, Genoa, Italy.
6.1921: Renamed ANDORRA CASTLE and arrived Porto Maurizio, Italy for conversion to emigrant ship, but laid up.
3.1925: Arrived at La Spezia for breaking up.

Berwick Castle. [Author's collection]

CAWDOR CASTLE 1901-1926

O.N. 114823 6,235g 4,052n 8,150d.
404.2 x 51.2 x 28.0 feet (draft 27.0 feet).
Passengers: 12 first, 16 second, 42 third, 230 steerage/open.
After 1912: to eight first, 24 second, 42 third.
Two T. 3-cyl. (21.5, 35, 58 x 48 inches) by Barclay, Curle and Co. Ltd., Glasgow 3,400 IHP, 11.5 knots.
7.12.1901: Launched by Barclay, Curle and Co. Ltd., Glasgow (Yard No. 429) for The Union-Castle Mail

Cawdor Castle as a transport (top and middle) and in peacetime colours. [Top and bottom: Author, middle: Ships in Focus]

29

Steamship Co. Ltd., London as CAWDOR CASTLE.

1.1902: Completed and principally engaged on the London to Mauritius service.

8.1914: Requisitioned as a transport.

13.12.1915: Attacked by an enemy submarine in Mediterranean but escaped.

1923: Laid up.

1924: Returned to service as a cargo ship. The hull was probably painted black at this time.

30.7.1926: Captain J. Attwood in command, ran aground in Conception Bay, South West Africa (Namibia) whilst on a voyage Hamburg and London to Mauritius with general cargo. Despite efforts to salvage, including sending the new tug T.S. MCEWAN (793/1925) from Cape Town, became a total loss.

Captain Attwood subsequently commanded two mail ships and retired in 1934.

NEWARK CASTLE 1902-1908

O.N. 115806 6,253g 4,066n 8,150d.

414.1 x 51.2 x 28.0 feet (draft 27.0 feet).

Passengers: 12 first, 16 second, 42 third, 230 steerage/open.

Two T. 3-cyl. (21.5, 35, 58 x 48 inches) by Barclay, Curle and Co. Ltd., Glasgow; 3,400 IHP, 11.5 knots.

22.3.1902: Launched by Barclay, Curle and Co. Ltd., Glasgow (Yard No. 430) for The Union-Castle Mail Steamship Co. Ltd., London as NEWARK CASTLE.

4.1902: Completed and placed on the United Kingdom to Mauritius service.

12.3.1908: Captain N.R. Neilson in command, ran ashore on an uncharted rock four miles off the coast near Port Durnford, Natal, having sailed from Durban six hours earlier with troops for the Mauritius garrison, general cargo and paper money. She was abandoned with the loss of three lives when one of the lifeboats capsized. The wreck subsequently refloated and drifted seven miles to ground off Richards Bay, and became a total loss.

Captain Neilson, a former Union Line Master, continued in command until retiring from RMS WALMER CASTLE at the end of 1921, then being 67 years old.

Newark Castle. [J. and M. Clarkson]

CLUNY CASTLE 1903-1924

O.N. 118323 5,147 g 3,303 n 7,270d.

409.1 x 50.2 x 28.2 feet (draft 24.6 feet).

Passengers: six first, 24 second, 52 third, 230 steerage/open.

After 1912: six first, 24 second, 110 third.

Two T. 3-cyl. (19, 31, 52 x 48 inches) by Barclay, Curle and Co. Ltd., Glasgow; 2,900 IHP, 11.5 knots.

10.8.1903: Launched by Barclay, Curle and Co. Ltd.,

Glasgow (Yard No. 441) for The Union-Castle Mail Steamship Co. Ltd., London as CLUNY CASTLE.

9.1903: Completed and placed on the United Kingdom to Mauritius service.

1909-1910: Laid up.

1915: Transferred to the East African coastal service.

7.1917: Requisitioned as a transport until 1919.

1922: Laid up for sale.

12.1924: Sold, with COMRIE CASTLE, to Bullard, King and Co. Ltd. (Natal Line), London for their London to South Africa service. Refitted to carry 100 passengers in one class.

2.1925: Renamed UMKUZI.

7.1938: Sold to Hughes Bolckow Shipbreaking, Blyth for £8,750, and broken up.

Cluny Castle. [J. and M. Clarkson]

COMRIE CASTLE 1903-1918

O.N. 118342 5,167g 3,311n 7,270d.

419.3 x 50.2 x 28.3 feet (draft 24.6 feet).

Passengers: six first, 24 second, 52 third, 230 steerage/open.

1912: six first, 24 second, 126 third.

Two T. 3-cyl. (19, 31, 52 x 48 inches) by Barclay, Curle and Co. Ltd., Glasgow; 2,900 IHP, 11.5 knots.

5.10.1903: Launched by Barclay, Curle and Co. Ltd., Glasgow (Yard No. 442) for The Union-Castle Mail Steamship Co. Ltd., London as COMRIE CASTLE.

11.1903: Completed and entered the London to Mauritius service.

1909: Laid up but resumed service at end of year.

8.1914: Requisitioned as a troopship.

14.3.1918: Captain G. Owens in command. Torpedoed in the English Channel whilst on a voyage from London to New York with the loss of nine lives. Beached on the Horse Tail Bank, subsequently refloated and towed to Netley for repairs which were completed in mid-1919.

8.1922: Laid up.

12.1924: Sold, with CLUNY CASTLE, to Bullard, King and Co. Ltd. (The Natal Line), London. Accommodation revised to carry 100 first class passengers.

Comrie Castle. [J. and M. Clarkson]

2.1925: Renamed UMVOTI.
8.1925: Took a homeward-bound Royal Mail sailing from Cape Town due to the regular mail ships being strikebound.
6.1940: Requisitioned by the British Government.
29.7.1940: Sunk as a blockship at Folkestone.
1943: Wreck raised and broken up on the beach by Thomas W. Ward and Co. Ltd.

Umvoti. [Ships in Focus]

PART TWO: MANAGED SHIPS AND 1915-1917 PURCHASES

Between 1915 and 1917 four further vessels were added, three acquired from other owners and one, *Carlow Castle*, specifically built for the company. The motivation for these acquisitions is not apparent from available records, but in the case of the three second-hand ships one possible reason, apart from a shortage of tonnage due to Government requisition, was the fact that the Blue Book rates of charter differentiated between liner and tramp tonnage, the former rates being significantly higher than the latter. Classification was based solely on ownership rather than the ships. Thus John Latta's Nitrate Producers Steamship Co.Ltd. sold three of its newer vessels two to Cunard and *Anglo Brazilian* to Union-Castle. Renamed *Chepstow Castle*, she had cost £87,000 to build in 1913, and Union-Castle paid £200,000 for her, and her charter rate immediately increased to the liner scale. The other two purchases were from F.S. Holland, London, and the first, renamed *Carlisle Castle* in 1916 (torpedoed 1918), and the second, *Hova*, in 1917, after her owner ceased trading, renamed *Crawford Castle* in 1920.

The new build was *Carlow Castle*, prototype of the F1 Standard design of which a further 10 vessels were ordered for the British Government. The designer was the managing director of the shipyard. They were particularly distinguished for their fine lines, fitted with 'tween decks and facilities for rapid cargo handling. The three survivors were principally engaged on the UK to South and East Africa services throughout the 1920s, barring a few United States voyages by *Chepstow Castle* and *Carlow Castle*. *Carlow Castle* and *Crawford Castle* were sold to other owners in 1930 as the Depression and financial pressures continued to bite, while *Chepstow Castle*, which had been the model for two further new buildings in 1921 and 1922, might have been retained had she not drifted ashore early in 1932.

CHEPSTOW CASTLE 1915-1932
O.N. 135294 7,486g 4,668n 11,300d.
425.5 x 56.3 x 28.3 feet (draft 30.5 feet).
Q. 4-cyl. (25.5, 36.5, 52.5, 76 x 54 inches) by North Eastern Marine Engineering Co. Ltd., Newcastle-upon-Tyne; 3,000 IHP, 11 knots.

2.10.1913: Launched by Short Brothers Ltd., Sunderland (Yard No. 381) for the Nitrate Producers Steamship Co. Ltd. (Lawther, Latta and Co., managers), London as ANGLO BRAZILIAN.
12.1913: Completed at a cost of £87,000.
21.10.1915: Acquired by The Union-Castle Mail Steamship Co. Ltd., London for £200,000 and renamed CHEPSTOW CASTLE.
4.1916: Captain G.J. Whitfield in command.
1.1917: Armed with one 4.7 inch gun, sailed from Cape Town to Boston, United States with gold bullion, 6,000 tons of chrome ore, and general cargo.
23-24.2.1917: Weathered a hurricane in the North Atlantic which reduced the lifeboats to matchsticks and swept much deck cargo including grapefruit and cooped chickens overboard. Captain Whitfield went on to command several of the mail ships and retired in the mid-1930s.
1919: Engaged on United Kingdom to South Africa and United States services.
1927: Opened the new berth alongside at Walvis Bay, South West Africa (Namibia).
5.7.1930: Laid up in East India Dock, London, and subsequently Middlesbrough.
10.2.1931: Recommissioned for voyages United Kingdom to South Africa and New York to South Africa.
30.12.1931: Laid up in Rothesay Bay.
7.4.1932: During a strong gale anchor cable parted and ship grounded at Toward Point. Refloated with damage assessed at £10,000 of which £2,700 was recoverable from insurers.
10.5.1932: Sold to Douglas and Ramsey, Glasgow for £3,300 for breaking up.

Chepstow Castle docking at Avonmouth (top) and aground near Toward Point on the Clyde in April 1932 after dragging her anchors. *[Top: J. and M. Clarkson, bottom: Author]*

CARLISLE CASTLE 1915-1918

O.N. 135264 4,325g 2,709n 8,400d.
400.0 x 53.0 x 23.8 feet (draft 23.8 feet).
T. 3-cyl. (26.5, 44, 72 x 48 inches) by Blair and Co. Ltd.,
Stockton-on-Tees; 2,200 IIIP, 9knots.
19.7.1913: Launched by the Northumberland Shipbuilding
Co. Ltd., Newcastle-upon-Tyne (Yard No. 209) for F.S.
Holland, London as HOLTYE.
9.1913: Completed.
29.1.1915: Purchased by The Union-Castle Mail Steamship
Co. Ltd., London for £151,000 and renamed CARLISLE
CASTLE.
12.1917: Captain C.J. Duncan in command.
14.2.1918: Torpedoed and sunk by the German submarine
UB 57 (Oberleutnant zur See J. Lohs) in the English Channel
eight miles east by north of the Royal Sovereign Lightship
whilst on a voyage from Portland, Maine to London with
general cargo and grain. One life lost. UB 57 succumbed to
a mine on 14.8.1918 off the Flanders coast with the loss of all
her crew.

Captain Duncan took command of YORK CASTLE in April
1918 but died at the end of that year aged 46.

When less than two years old the *Holtye* became *Carlisle
Castle* in 1915. *[Author's collection]*

CRAWFORD CASTLE 1917-1930

O.N. 129150 4,253g 2,753n 7,525d.
380.0 x 49.0 x 26.4 feet (draft 23.8 feet).
T. 3-cyl. (25, 41, 69 x 48 inches) by North Eastern Marine
Engineering Co. Ltd., Newcastle-upon-Tyne; 1,800 IHP, 8.5
knots.
11.1910: Completed by Northumberland Shipbuilding Co.
Ltd. (Yard No. 175) for F.S. Holland, London as HOVA.
7.11.1917: Acquired by The Union-Castle Mail Steamship
Co. Ltd., London when F.S. Holland ceased trading.
1918: Poop and deckhouse added, now 4,383g, 2,820n.
11.2.1920: Renamed CRAWFORD CASTLE.
10.1926: With Captain A.O. Morgan in command, became
the first Union-Castle ship to dock at the new quay at
Kilindini, Mombasa.
25.12.1927: At 21.00 hours Haisbro' Lightship off the
north Norfolk coast reported to Cromer Coastguard that
CRAWFORD CASTLE, steaming in ballast in heavy seas
and an east north east gale, had collided with them. An
hour later the lightship reported slight damage but that
CRAWFORD CASTLE, now two miles to the north west was
showing out of control lights and in danger of drifting ashore.
26.12.1927: At 11.10 hours CRAWFORD CASTLE
reported being out of control 30 miles further north, near

the East Dudgeon Lightship, and in need of lifeboat and tug
assistance. If anything the weather was now worse. The
Cromer Lifeboat, under their renowned Coxswain Henry
Blogg, raced down the slip into massive seas. Shortly
afterwards CRAWFORD CASTLE signalled that she was
now out of danger, but owing to the heavy seas Blogg did
not see the recall posted by the coastguard and pressed on to
the search area. Meanwhile CRAWFORD CASTLE, having
narrowly missed the East Dudgeon Lightship at about 06.00
hours, had now proceeded on her way. Blogg, having fought
his way through 30 miles of stormy seas to no avail,
had perforce to continue to Grimsby, partly because beaching
at Cromer was out of the question, and also because
Grimsby, to the north, presented an easier passage than Great
Yarmouth. Despite his never having visited Grimsby and
having no charts, he duly reached the Humber and, recalling
charts he had seen in a Nautical Almanac back home, reached
Grimsby about midnight after the longest voyage (65 miles)
the Cromer lifeboat had ever made. Only some hours later,
because the storm had brought the telephone lines down, did
the families of the crew learn that their menfolk were safe
and on the way back, by train. At that time Blogg, then 51,
had already twice been awarded the RNLI Gold Medal, and
he subsequently received it a third time, as well as four Silver
Medals, the George Cross, and the British Empire Medal. He
retired after the war and died in 1954. Unsurprisingly there is
no mention of this episode in the official Union-Castle Line
records.
19.2.1930: Sold to W. Kunstmann, Stettin, Germany for
£21,500 and renamed VICTORIA W. KUNSTMANN.
9.1936: Sold to Emder Dampferkompagnie A.G. (Wilhelm
Nübel), Emden, Germany and renamed RADBOD.
5.12.1944: Bombed and sunk by Allied aircraft of Squadrons
455 and 389 at Selbervik near Aalesund, in Örstenfjord,
Norway.

Captain Morgan retired as Commodore and Captain of
STIRLING CASTLE at the end of 1937.

Crawford Castle. [Ships in Focus]

CARLOW CASTLE 1916-1930

O.N. 129199 5,833g 3,708n 9,150d.
400.0 x 53.0 x 32.8 feet (draft 26.2 feet).
T. 3-cyl. (27, 45, 74 x 48 inches) by Richardson, Westgarth
and Co. Ltd., Sunderland; 3.650 IHP, 11.5 knots.
9.11.1916: Launched by the Northumberland Shipbuilding
Co. Ltd., Newcastle-upon-Tyne (Yard No. 230) for The
Union-Castle Mail Steamship Co. Ltd., London as CARLOW
CASTLE, having been laid down by the shipbuilder and
purchased for £157,500 on the stocks.
2.1917: Completed.

25.4.1930: Sold to Sun Shipping Co. Ltd. (Mitchell, Cotts and Co. Ltd., managers), London for £26,750 and subsequently renamed CAPE ST COLUMBA.
15.2.1935: Sold to M.J. Carras, Chios, Greece and renamed ADELFOTIS.
1.5.1943: Torpedoed and sunk by the German submarine U 182 (Kapitanleutnant N. Clausen) in the South Atlantic in position 03 32 south, 21 33 west (German records claim 02 40 south, 21 20 west) whilst on a voyage from San Lorenzo and Buenos Aires to the United Kingdom with a cargo of linseed. U 182 was sunk with all hands on 16.5.1943 by USS MACKENZIE, north west of Madeira whilst attacking convoy UGL 4.

Carlow Castle. [J. and M. Clarkson]

First World War managed cargo ships

During and immediately after the war Union-Castle, like many other British ship owners, undertook the management of various ex-enemy vessels as well as several others. In the case of Union-Castle the majority were either passenger or hospital ships, or coastal craft and tugs in East African waters. The three cargo vessels are recorded below.

POLGLASS CASTLE 1915-1921
O.N. 139080 4,762g 2,968n 7,023d.
390 x 51.5 x 27.5 feet.
Q. 4-cyl. (23, 32, 48, 72 x 54 inches) by Swan, Hunter and Wigham Richardson Ltd., Newcastle-upon-Tyne; 2,400 IHP, 10 knots.
7.9.1903: Launched by Swan, Hunter and Wigham Richardson Ltd., Newcastle-upon-Tyne (Yard No. 406) for Deutsche Dampfschiffahrts-Gesellschaft Hansa, Bremen, Germany as REICHENFELS.
10.1903: Completed.
5.8.1914: Seized as a prize at Colombo. Requisitioned by the Admiralty and placed under the management of Graham and Co.
1915: Served as a seaplane tender.
8.1915: Registered in the ownership of The Union-Castle Mail Steamship Co. Ltd., London as POLGLASS CASTLE.
2.9.1915-20.11.1920: Transporting various cargoes between the United States and France.
1918: Owner became The Shipping Controller (The Union-Castle Mail Steamship Co. Ltd., managers), London.
12.1921: Sold back to former owners and renamed REICHENFELS.
1934: Sold for breaking up by A.G. Weser.

Polglass Castle never traded on Union-Castle Line account.

HUNTSCLIFF 1916-1918
O.N. 139110 5,442g 3,393n.
419.8 x 54.5 x 28.2 feet.
Q. 4-cyl. (24, $34^5/_8$, $50^3/_8$, $70^7/_8$ x $53\frac{1}{4}$ inches) by Bremer Vulkan, Vegesack, Germany; 3,500 IHP, 11.5 knots.
Passengers: 12.
29.9.1911: Launched by Bremer Vulkan, Vegesack (Yard No. 553) for Deutsche Ost-Afrika Linie, Hamburg, Germany as RUFIDJI.
11.1911: Completed and placed on Hamburg to Tanganyika service.
18.8.1914: Intercepted by H.M. Torpedo Boat 060 off Cape Point and taken to Simonstown. Requisitioned by the British Government.
25.1.1916: Renamed HUNTSCLIFF, placed under management of The Union-Castle Mail Steamship Co. Ltd., London and engaged as Expeditionary Force Transport on the East African coast until January 1918, Captain K. Macdonald in command.
29.9.1918: Sailed in convoy from Montreal to Bantry Bay with a cargo of binned oats and oil, escorted by the Armed Merchant Cruiser HMS TEUTONIC.
5.10.1918: Developed list to port in heavy weather. Convoy ordered to heave to while attempts were made to compensate by shifting the cargo, but in the deteriorating weather list had increased to 25 degrees, rolling to 50 degrees by 8.10.1918 when crew were taken off by TEUTONIC.
9-11.10.1918: Unsuccessful attempts were made to pass a tow from HMS TEUTONIC.
12.10.1918: United States tug JENESEE arrived and officers of HUNTSCLIFF and 20 volunteers from TEUTONIC boarded, but further work was aborted when a submarine was reported.
14.10.1918: Towing commenced at a speed of five knots.
17.10.1918: With the weather again deteriorating and the list increasing HUNTSCLIFF was abandoned and sank at 06.00 hours having been towed 280 miles and only 120 miles short of her destination. This epic salvage attempt bears comparison with that of FLYING ENTERPRISE in January 1953.

Rufidji (above) became *Huntscliff* in 1916. *[Author's collection]*

HUNTSCRAFT 1917-1920
O.N. 136793 5,113g 3,176n.
450.0 x 54.1 x 26.3 feet.
T. 3-cyl (27, $44\frac{1}{2}$, 75 x 54 inches) by William Doxford and Son Ltd., Sunderland 1,864 IHP, 10 knots.
3.6.1913: Launched by William Doxford and Son Ltd., Sunderland (Yard No. 455) for Hamburg-Amerikanische-Packetfahrt A.G., Hamburg as SUDMARK.
7.1913: Completed and placed on Far East service.

15.8.1914: Captured by HMS BLACK PRINCE in the Red Sea whilst on a voyage from Yokohama to Hamburg and taken by British Government as a prize (Harrison and Dixon, London, managers).

23.9.1915: Renamed HUNTSCRAFT as Expeditionary Force Transport No. E 216.

20.5.1917: Management transferred to The Union-Castle Mail Steamship Co. Ltd., London.

6.7.1918: Torpedoed by submarine 10 miles off St. Catherine's Point, Isle of Wight whilst on a voyage from Le Havre to Southampton in ballast. Subsequently towed to St. Helen's, Isle of Wight and repaired.

7.1.1920: Sold to Clan Line Steamers Ltd. (Cayzer, Irvine and Co. Ltd., managers), Glasgow.

24.1.1920: Renamed CLAN MACKAY.

19.10.1934: Ran ashore at Carpenter Rock, Sierra Leone whilst on a voyage from Cairns to Montreal and became a total loss.

Clan MacKay (above), the former *Huntscraft*. [B. and A. Feilden/J. and M. Clarkson]

HUNSLET 1917-1921

O.N. 137678 5,632g 3,567n 8,000d.

418.0 x 54.0 x 20.1 feet.

Q. 4-cyl. (24, 34, 51, 74 x 54 inches) by Wigham, Richardson and Co. Ltd., Newcastle-upon-Tyne; 2,900 IHP, 11 knots.

23.3.1898: Launched by Wigham, Richardson and Co. Ltd., Newcastle-upon-Tyne (Yard No. 336) for Deutsche Dampfschiffahrts-Gesellschaft Hansa, Bremen, Germany as TANNENFELS.

4.1898: Completed.

8.10.1914: Captured in Basilan Strait, Philippines, and taken to Hong Kong. Requisitioned by the British Government.

19.1.1915: Renamed BASILAN.

23.7.1915: Renamed HUNSLET.

1915-2.1916: Served as a hospital ship.

2.1916: Placed under the registered ownership and management of Oceanic Steam Navigation Co. Ltd. (White Star Line), Liverpool and employed as Expeditionary Force Transport No. E 1086.

17.5.1917: Registered under ownership of The Shipping Controller (The Union-Castle Mail Steamship Co. Ltd., managers), London.

21.9.1921: Sold to Woermann-Linie, Hamburg, Germany and renamed USUMBARA.

1922: Renamed WAGANDA.

1932: Sold to shipbreakers.

1933: broken up at Hamburg by Deutsche Werft A.G.

PART THREE: ACQUISITIONS 1918-1922

In the aftermath of the First World War the British Government was left with a substantial quantity of former enemy tonnage as well as many standard design vessels either completed or under construction and, in 1919 Sir Owen Philipps and Lord Inchape, Chairman of P and O, undertook to sell off this surplus as best they could, and retain the remainder in their own fleets. Depressed trading conditions quickly ensured that supply exceeded demand and both had to absorb many of these vessels within their own fleets. Consequently Philipps' Royal Mail Group took 75 vessels, of which seven were allocated to Union-Castle. Few survived the 1930s under the British flag, most being slow and uneconomical, to the extent that, in the late 1930s when Harland and Wolff offered to build two new cargo ships using engines removed from mail ships, Union-Castle declined on the grounds that their three surviving cargo ships were losing enough money already. More surprisingly, despite this addition of extra tonnage, two large turbine-powered (but coal-fired) steamers were ordered for delivery in 1921 and 1922. Arguably the greatest merit of these additions was the continuance of the habit; introduced by the Union Line G intermediates and more recently continued in the C group of cargo ships, of maintaining the initial letter basis of nomenclature. Thus the two vessels, very different, built abroad took names commencing with R, the three N class fabricated ships (confusingly) took B names whilst the two B type vessels took D as their initial. The new turbine steamers used the letter S. Uncertainty as to the outcome of the 1919 Versailles Conference probably explained why two of the N ships were not laid down until well into 1919, and built from material accumulated at the yard.

The company's services were, until 1922, in a state of flux, other than the mail service, but in that year the Intermediate/East Africa services were re-organised, with an Intermediate steamer taking a sailing from London to Cape Town fortnightly, two of which, over a 12-week period, would continue their voyage from Beira up the coast and return via Suez. Meantime, two further Intermediates would be despatched out via Suez over the same 12-week period to return via the Cape. The four-weekly service was completed by a cargo vessel sailing at appropriate intervals. Generally these sailings were taken by *Ripley Castle* and the three B class ships until 1931 when, with the departure of most of the cargo ships, and increased emphasis on economy, further passenger ships were allocated, providing a four-weekly service in each direction that lasted, bar the 1939 to 1946 period, until the early 1960s.

The United States to South Africa service required outward sailings from New York at approximately four-weekly intervals. Other ports featuring included Philadelphia and Charleston, South Carolina and on occasions calls were made at Trinidad, St. Vincent, and, nearer their destination, St. Helena, Luderitz, and Walvis Bay. Voyage times were less than scintillating; a 28-day New York to Cape Town passage in 1936 by *Dundrum Castle* was well above the 30 to 31 day average, whilst a 24-day passage by the new refrigerated ship *Rothesay Castle* was a record for the company. Generally, the two B type standard *Dromore Castle* and *Dundrum Castle*, and the turbine S ships *Sandown Castle* and *Sandgate Castle* were the regular vessels although others did join in from time to time. Roughly one in four outward voyages returned to New York, the rest mainly returning to Britain via the West Coast, and then proceeding in ballast from the United Kingdom to load in the USA.

The onset of the Great Depression saw the cargo fleet whittled down until by 1932 only five remained, one of which, *Chepstow Castle*, was sold in May of that year after being blown ashore in heavy weather whilst laid up, and another, *Sandgate Castle* succumbed to fire at sea in 1937. The two standard ships were lost, one in 1941 to mine, the other two years later to fire, leaving *Sandown Castle* to soldier on post-war until early 1950.

The ships themselves were a motley crew. The two overseas buildings were *Rosyth Castle*, built in Canada, and *Ripley Castle*, twin-screw and built in Japan, the only Union-Castle ships built outside the UK. Within a year the former was transferred to the newly-acquired subsidiary Bullard King and Co. Ltd., whom she served until 1937 when sold to Japanese owners. Somehow surviving the carnage of the Pacific war, she remained on the register until 1966. *Ripley Castle*, after a short lay-up, went to breakers at the end of 1931. The three B type fabricated ships were sold on to Greek owners, one being broken up a few years later, one succumbing to torpedo attack, and the third sunk by the Luftwaffe. *Dundrum Castle* and *Dromore Castle* were ordered as standard B types but modified with an additional pair of kingposts forward and additional 'tween deck space, and served the company throughout their careers. Whilst the cargo fleet generally was fully employed until the end of the 1920s, it has to be added that it is highly unlikely that they were profitable, and the sale of most of them at knock-down prices reflected the need to save money, indeed get money, in the aftermath of the Royal Mail group collapse. Probably their greatest merit was that they provided future captains with early experience.

ROSYTH CASTLE 1919-1921

O.N. 142724 4,328g 2,580n 7,211d.
380.4 x 49.2 x 26.7 feet (draft 24.5 feet).
T. 3-cyl. (27, 44, 73 x 48 inches) by Canadian Vickers Ltd., Montreal, Canada; 2,400 IHP, 10 knots.
8.1918: Completed by Canadian Vickers Ltd., Montreal, Canada (Yard No. 19), for the Imperial Munitions Board, Canada, and transferred to The Shipping Controller (Harris and Dixon Ltd., managers), London and named WAR EARL.
4.11.1919: Acquired by The Union-Castle Mail Steamship Co. Ltd., London.
11.2.1920: Renamed ROSYTH CASTLE.
25.4.1921: Sold to Bullard, King and Co. Ltd., London for £90,000 and renamed UMLAZI.
10.6.1936: Sold to Tramp Shipping Development Co. Ltd., London.
25.9.1936: Transferred to Campden Hill Steamship Co. Ltd. (Counties Ship Management Co. Ltd., managers), London and subsequently renamed CAMPDEN HILL.
3.11.1937: Sold to Kitagawa Asikichi, Osaka, Japan and subsequently renamed HOKUJU MARU.
1938: Name now spelt HOKUZYU MARU.
1950: Name reverted to HOKUJU MARU.
1954: Owners restyled Kitigawa Sangyo Kaiun K.K.
1955: Sold to Osaka Zoshenska K.K.
1966: Reported broken up at Osaka.

No photograph has been located showing this ship in Union-Castle colours.

RIPLEY CASTLE 1919-1931

O.N. 140379 7,591g 4,636n 10,449d.
445.5 x 58.4 x 31.3 feet (draft 26.5 feet).
Two T. 3-cyl. (21, 35, 59 x 48 inches)

Umlazi, formerly *Rosyth Castle*, of which no photographs have been located. *[Ships in Focus]*

Ripley Castle at Cape Town. *[Ships in Focus]*

by Kawasaki Dockyard Co. Ltd., Kobe, Japan 3,200 IHP, 9 knots
6.1917: Completed by Kawasaki Dockyard Co. Ltd., Kobe, Japan (Yard No. 389) for the Shipping Controller, (Furness, Withy and Co. Ltd., managers), London as WAR SOLDIER.
23.12.1919: Acquired by The Union-Castle Mail Steamship Co. Ltd., London.

16.6.1920: Renamed RIPLEY CASTLE.
1926: On a voyage from New York to Cape Town a trimmer was reported missing, have last been seen at about 12.30 am. Captain G. Sinclair ordered the ship to put about and steam back on her course. At about 01.50, when the ship had steamed approximately eight miles, a faint cry was heard by

the lookout on the port quarter. Chief Officer J.C. Brown (Commodore, 1947 to 1950) launched a boat and the man was duly recovered, having apparently fainted due to the heat in the boiler room, waking up afloat 350 miles from land, and suffered attack by a sea bird and a fish. Brown, a deeply religious man, attributed the success of the rescue to divine answering of his prayers. Curiously, in the 1960s two passengers, one off WINDSOR CASTLE the other off S.A. VAAL, were similarly rescued after falling overboard and floating for up to 12 hours.

5.4.1931: Laid up at Netley.

2.12.1931: Sold for £4,500 to Balla and Nervloet S.A., Genoa for breaking up at Savona.

DROMORE CASTLE 1919-1941
Modified B-type

O.N. 143826 5,242g 3,199n 7,930d. 400.3 x 52.3 x 28.5 feet (draft 25.2 feet).
T. 3-cyl. (27, 44, 73 x 48 inches) by Harland and Wolff Ltd., Greenock; 2,500 IHP, 9.5 knots.

28.8.1919: Launched by Harland and Wolff Ltd., Greenock (Yard No. 539) for The Shipping Controller, London as WAR POPLAR.

Acquired by The Union-Castle Mail Steamship Co. Ltd. for £190,000.

17.11.1919: Completed as DROMORE CASTLE.

6.1936: On a voyage from London to Philadelphia in ballast ran into severe weather, hove to, and to keep head to wind Captain C.F. Marriner ordered both anchors to be lowered (in mid Atlantic!). On the weather improving lack of steam power precluded both recovery of the anchors and progress, so DROMORE CASTLE duly arrived minus both anchors. The owners were not amused, and on arrival at Port Elizabeth he was relieved by H.A. Causton (Chief Officer of WARWICK CASTLE, killed in January 1940 when DUNBAR CASTLE was mined off Deal). Captain Marriner was then appointed to command SANDOWN CASTLE on a similar voyage, but despite not losing his anchors he was again relieved, at Cape Town, by another Chief Officer of WARWICK CASTLE, Captain J. Lecky. He then resigned.

26.4.1940: Sailed Glasgow with 151 vehicles and trailers and 30 motor cycles for Norway.

28.4.1940: Arrived Scapa Flow.

Ripley Castle. [Ships in Focus]

Dromore Castle. [Ships in Focus]

5.5.1940: Withdrawal from her designated destination of Andalsnes having been ordered, she returned to Glasgow to discharge cargo and load nine AA guns, 55 vehicles and trailers, 12 motorcycles, and sundry items of airport construction equipment.

11.5.1940: Departed Glasgow arriving 19.5.1940 at Harstad staying until 29.5.1940 when she sailed south with 150 French troops and other stores and munitions, arriving 3.6.1940 at Scapa and finally 14.6.1940 at Glasgow.

12.12.1941: Under Captain R. Hodgson mined and sunk 20 miles south south east of the Humber in position 53.29 north, 00.52 east whilst on a voyage from London to Leith in ballast to load for Russia. No lives were lost

DUNDRUM CASTLE 1919-1943
Modified B type steamer

O.N. 144207 5,259g 3,214n 7,930d.

400.3 x 52.3 x 28.5 feet (draft 25.2 feet).
T. 3-cyl. (27, 44, 73 x 48 inches) by Harland and Wolff Ltd., Greenock; 2,500 IHP, 9.5 knots.

23.10.1919: Launched by Harland and Wolff Ltd., Greenock (Yard No. 572) for The Shipping Controller as WAR OAK.

12.1919: Acquired by The Union-Castle Mail Steamship Co. Ltd., London; completed, and renamed DUNDRUM CASTLE.

17.6.1940: Under Captain M.H. Dhobi Williams, whilst trying to depart St Nazaire German aircraft bombed and sunk H.M. Transport LANCASTRIA (16,243/1922). Lifeboats from DUNDRUM CASTLE were launched and some 120 survivors taken aboard. Total loss of life on LANCASTRIA is unknown but believed to be in excess of 3,000.

2.4.1943: Under Captain S. Aldous,

cargo caught fire and ship abandoned in the Red Sea in position 14.37 north, 42.33 east whilst on a voyage from Liverpool to Suez with general cargo. No lives were lost.

BRATTON CASTLE 1919-1932
Modified N type prefabricated steamer

O.N. 144603 6,696g 4,154n 10,515d. 412.2 x 55.8 x 34.4 feet (draft 28.1 feet).
T. 3-cyl. (27, 44, 73 x 48 inches) by North Eastern Marine Engineering Co. Ltd., Newcastle-upon-Tyne; 2,500 IHP; 9 knots.
1919: Laid down by Armstrong, Whitworth and Co. Ltd., Newcastle-upon-Tyne (Yard No. 951) for The Shipping Controller, London. No name officially allocated.
Acquired on the stocks by The Union-Castle Mail Steamship Co. Ltd., London.
8.12.1919: Launched.
5.1920: Completed to a modified design with cruiser rather than V transom stern and named BRATTON CASTLE.
29.1.1932: Sold for £7,250 to the Tramp Shipping Development Co. Ltd., London, and resold to Atlanticos Shipping Co. Ltd., Syra, Greece (Rethymnis and Kulukundis, Piraeus, Greece, managers,) and renamed PROTEUS.
1932: Renamed MOUNT TAURUS and registered in Panama.
17.11.1942: Torpedoed and sunk by the German submarine U 264 in position 54.30 north, 37.30 west whilst on a voyage from London to Halifax, Nova Scotia.

BAMPTON CASTLE 1920-1931
Modified N type steamer

O.N. 144603 6,698g 4,154 n 10,840d. 412.2 x 55.8 x 34.4 feet (draft 28.1 feet).
T. 3-cyl. (27, 44, 73 x 48 inches) by North East Marine Engineering Co. Ltd., Newcastle-upon-Tyne; 2,500 IHP, 9.5 knots.
1919: Laid down by Armstrong, Whitworth and Co. Ltd. Newcastle-upon-Tyne (Yard No. 957) for the Shipping Controller. No name officially allocated.
Acquired on the stocks by The Union-Castle Mail Steamship Co. Ltd., London.
4.3.1920: Launched.
5.1920: Completed to a modified design with cruiser rather than V transom stern

Dundrum Castle at Beira in December 1937. *[Ships in Focus]*

A builder's photograph of the new *Bratton Castle.* *[Author's collection]*

Bampton Castle. [J. and M. Clarkson]

and named BAMPTON CASTLE.
31.12.1931: Sold for £6,500 to The Tramp Shipping Development Co. Ltd., London, resold to Atlanticos Steamship Co. Ltd., Syra, Greece (Rethymnis and Kulukundis, Piraeus, Greece, managers), renamed MOUNT TAYGETUS and registered in Panama.

28.2.1933: Fouled WARWICK CASTLE at anchor at Madeira, costing £1,843 for that vessel's lost anchor and cable.
23.12.1933: Stranded on English Rocks, Memphis Channel, Chile whilst on a voyage from San Antonio to London with a cargo of grain.

1.1.1934: Refloated and beached.
13.1.1934: Towed to Magallenes Roads and abandoned to salvors.
Taken to Europe and sold to Metal Industries Ltd. in July.
19.7.1934: Arrived Rosyth for breaking up.

Note. No names were officially allocated to the two Modified N type vessels above but the names WAR DUTY, WAR FERVOUR, WAR HONOUR and WAR VALOUR were allocated to this class by The Shipping Controller

BANBURY CASTLE 1921-1931
N type fabricated steamer
O.N. 142647 6,429g 4,002 n 10,750d. 412.4 x 55.8 x 34.4 feet (draft 28.2 feet).
T. 3-cyl. Tyne (27, 44, 73 x 48 inches) by Swan Hunter and Wigham Richardson Ltd., Newcastle-upon-Tyne; 2,500 IHP, 9.5 knots.
8.8.1918: Launched by Swan Hunter and Wigham Richardson Ltd., Newcastle-upon-Tyne (Yard No. 1089) for The Shipping Controller, London (Lowden, Connell and Co., Liverpool, managers) as WAR CLIMAX.
9.1918: Completed.
23.9.1919: Sold to Glen Line Steamers Ltd., London and renamed GLENSTRAE.
24.1.1921: Acquired by The Union-Castle Mail Steamship Co. Ltd., London and renamed BANBURY CASTLE.
1.9.1931: Sold to G. Vergottis, Argostoli, Greece for £6,000 and subsequently renamed ROKOS.
1933: Tonnages 4,781g, 2,783n.
1935: Owners S.G. Razos, Argostoli, Greece; tonnages 6,429g, 4,002n.
1936: Owners Ionian Steamship Co. Ltd., Argostoli (Vergottis, Ltd., London).
26.5.1941: Bombed by German aircraft whilst at Suda Bay, Crete during a voyage from Calcutta to Piraeus with a cargo of coal. Driven ashore and became a total loss.

The two new buildings below were the only cargo ships Union-Castle ordered to be fitted with steam turbines. The design was based on that of *Chepstow Castle* (above). There is photographic evidence that one or both were painted with grey hulls at some point in the 1930s, but this colour scheme did not last long.

Banbury Castle of 1918 (upper) and as *Rokos* (lower). *[Upper: Nautical Photo Agency; lower: J. and M. Clarkson]*

SANDOWN CASTLE 1920-1950
O.N. 1146147 7,607g 4,707n 11,500d. 425.5 x 56.3 x 36.4 feet (draft 30.5 feet).
Three direct-reduction geared turbines by North Eastern Marine Engineering Co. Ltd., Newcastle-upon-Tyne; 3,200 SHP, 10.5 knots, trials 12.61 knots.
Passengers: fitted for 12 but accommodation not used commercially.
12.10.1920: Launched by Short Brothers Ltd., Sunderland (Yard No. 407) for The Union-Castle Mail Steamship Co. Ltd., London as SANDOWN CASTLE.
4.1921: Completed at a cost of £399,463.
1924: Carried 330 cattle to Birkenhead in an unsuccessful attempt to rival the South American trade.
21.3.1930 to 29.4.1930: Converted to burn oil fuel and also fitted with Oertz Rudder.
11.1936: Commenced voyage London

to United States ports in ballast, Captain Marriner in command.
1.2.1937: Arrived Cape Town with Captain J. Lecky in command. After proceeding to Beira and returning to Cape Town, Captain R.T. Smailes, Chief Officer of ATHLONE CASTLE, took command for the return voyage to United States ports.
12.1941: Captain J. Trayner (subsequently a mail ship master) on his first command sailed for Alexandria via the Cape with 7,000 tons of Eighth Army stores. Fired on by Luftwaffe aircraft at Port Said during raids. Proceeded to Haifa when fire broke out in copra loaded at Zanzibar. After it was extinguished a number of 6 x 1 inch diameter capsules containing inflammable liquid were found, indicating the possibility of sabotage. Returned to South Africa, loading 10,000 tons of raw materials, including copper, wool and lead and proceeded

independently to Freetown. Became Vice-Commodore ship of a 48-ship convoy which was subjected to heavy attack and suffered a number of losses before arriving at Liverpool 27.7.1942.

8.1942: Sailed for Durban non-stop with stores, vehicles, and boom defence equipment for Mauritius.

1.1943: Sailed from Mauritius for Glasgow via Cape Town, Walvis Bay, Brazil, Trinidad, New York, Boston and Halifax; 13,000 miles in 100 days, cargo 10,000 tons sugar (sufficient for five pounds for every man, woman and child in Great Britain).

1946: Hull painted lavender. Engaged on South and East African service.

11.1947: Captain C.G. Cuthbertson RNR in command.

31.5.1950: Arrived London from East Africa.

13.6.1950: Sailed for Sunderland and lay-up pending survey which indicated repairs costing £80,000 were necessary.

30.8.1950: Sold for £17,000 to British Iron and Steel Corporation as lies and delivered to Clayton and Davie Ltd.

21.9.1950: Demolition commenced.

Captain Lecky rose to command *Llangibby Castle* until his death in July 1941. Captain Smailes subsequently commanded HM Hospital Ship *Llandovery Castle* and the troopships *Arundel Castle*, *Athlone Castle* and *Carnarvon Castle* until April 1947, when he was appointed back to *Athlone Castle* on completion of her post-war refit, but unable to take command owing to ill health.

Captain C.G. Cuthbertson RNR in August 1941 was in command of the corvette HMS *Zinnia* escorting Convoy OG 71 to Gibraltar. The convoy suffered the loss of a number of ships, and many lives when, on 23.8.1941, *Zinnia* was torpedoed and sunk. Cuthbertson survived, one of only 15 of the 100 complement, despite swallowing much oil and water. Taken to Gibraltar, he met Nicholas Montserrat, First Lieutenant of another corvette, HMS *Campanula*, also escorting Convoy OG 71. Over a gin and tonic or three Montserrat questioned him closely on his experiences after the sinking. Subsequently, Montserrat recorded in his memoirs that the character of Lieutenant Commander Ericson, one of the lead characters in his novel 'The Cruel Sea', was based on Cuthbertson. Born in 1906, Cuthbertson died at the age of 87.

Sandown Castle in May 1939 with black hull (top), in wartime grey (middle) and at Cape Town in October 1948 with her hull painted lavender (bottom). *[Top and bottom: J. and M. Clarkson, middle: Author's collection]*

SANDGATE CASTLE 1920-1937

O.N. 146633 7,634g 4,725n 11,500d.
425.5 x 56.3 x 36.4 feet (draft 30.5 feet).
Three direct-reduction geared turbines by North Eastern Marine Engineering Co. Ltd., Newcastle-upon-Tyne; 3,200 SHP, 10.5 knots, trials 12.735 knots. Passengers: fitted for 12 but accommodation not used commercially.
19.3.1919: Ordered.
23.12.1920: Launched by Short Brothers Ltd., Sunderland (Yard No. 408) for The Union-Castle Mail Steamship Co. Ltd., London as SANDGATE CASTLE.
1921: Work ceased on account of economic conditions and towed to Tyne and laid up.
2.1922: Towed to Sunderland.
9.1922: Completed.
2.10.1926: With Captain C.R. Bickford in command collided with the steamers STESSO (2,290/1922) and MEXICANO (3,694/1911) whilst outward bound in Gravesend Reach.

9.10.1926: Continued voyage.
7.12.1929 to 9.1.1930: Became the first Union-Castle steamer to burn oil after her furnaces were modified. Oertz rudder also fitted.
29.6.1937: With Captain H. Berger in command caught fire off Cape Hatteras

in position 36.51 north, 60.05 west whilst on a voyage from New York to Cape Town. The crew were rescued by the steamer PRESIDENT PIERCE (12,579/1921).
30.6.1937: Last sighted by the steamer CONTE DE SAVOIA (48,502/1932).

Sandgate Castle. [Author's collection]

PART FOUR: MANAGED AND CHARTERED VESSELS, 1939-1949

From an early stage in the Second World War, Union-Castle, in common with virtually all other significant British ship owners, were required to manage various vessels on behalf of the British Government. Initially nine were allocated to Union-Castle being, French, and Italian and Dutch ships of various sorts, of which those not catering for passengers fall within the scope of this article. Some at least were of questionable value to the Allied war effort. In December 1943 five Liberty type vessels were allocated to Union-Castle. The French and other ships were returned to their former owners by the end of 1945, but the Liberties continued to be operated until 1947 or 1948. They were, for the main part, engaged on Allied operations and had scant impact on Union-Castle services. In 1946 two further vessels were taken on charter until 1949, the Canadian-built *Fort Carillon* and the British *Empire Duchess*, the latter being purchased when her charter expired and is dealt with in the following section.

EMPIRE SUCCESS

O.N. 167430 6.009g 3.646n 9,440d.
451.5 x 58.2 x 26.8 feet.
T. 3-cyl. (31½, 52$^{5}/_{16}$, 84¼ x 59$^{13}/_{16}$) by A.G. Vulcan, Hamburg, Germany; 3,500 IHP; 11.5 knots.
1928: Low-pressure turbine added to engines; 5,000 IHP; 13 knots.
21.2.1921: Launched by A.G. Vulcan, Hamburg (Yard No. 636) for A.G. Deutsche-Australische Dampfschiffs Gesellschaft, Hamburg and named HAGEN.
5.1921: Completed.
1926: Owners acquired by Hamburg-Amerikanische Packetfahrt Gesellschaft, Hamburg.
8.9.1939: Seized by South African forces at Durban and renamed IXIA. Following seizure evidence of sabotage to the engines, damaging several components, was discovered.
30.1.1940: Transferred to the Ministry of Shipping (The

Empire Success at Cardiff 14th May 1946. [National Museums and Galleries of Wales 1524/1617]

Union-Castle Mail Steamship Co. Ltd., managers), London and renamed EMPIRE SUCCESS.
30.9.1940: Severely damaged by bombing five miles east of Peterhead.
1940 to 1942: Engaged on voyages

between United Kingdom and South and East Africa.
1.1948: Laid up at Liverpool with engine trouble
22.8.1948: Scuttled in the Bay of Biscay with poison gas shells.

BOSKOOP 1940-1945

5,538 g 3,320n 9,000d.

400.6 x 58.3 x 26.4 feet (draft 26.6 feet).

C. 4-cyl. (2 x 29, 47¼ x 47¼ inches) by Rotterdam Dry Dock Co., Rotterdam, Netherlands; 2,500 IHP; 11 knots.

7.1927: Completed by Van der Giessen & Zonen N.V., Krimpen (Yard No. 575) for Koninklijke Nederlandse Stoomboot Maatschappij, Amsterdam, Netherlands as BOSKOOP.

22.7.1940: Chartered by the Ministry of Shipping (The Union-Castle Mail Steamship Co. Ltd., managers), London

3.7.1945: Returned to owners.

1960: Sold to Desguaces y Salvamentos S.A. for demolition.

21.6.1960: Arrived Avila.

30.11960: Demolition commenced.

EMPIRE ARUN 1941-1946

O.N. 159353 5,490g 3,417n 8,599d.

391 x 54 x 29.0 feet (draft 25.3 feet).

Two steam turbines by Franco Tosi, Legnano, Italy geared to a single screw shaft; 3,500 SHP, 11 knots.

8.1952: C. 4-cyl. (2 x 11⁷/₁₆, 20½ x 13¾ inches) and direct-reduction geared low pressure turbine by Uraga Dock Co., Yokosuka, Japan; 1,750 SHP, 10 knots.

11.1922: Completed by Stabilimento Tecnico, Triestino, Trieste, Italy (Yard No. 736) for Navigazione Libera Triestino, Trieste as SAVOIA.

1936: Owners became Lloyd Triestino Societa Anonima di Navigazione, Trieste, following reorganisation of the shipping industry by the Italian Government.

11.2.1941: Captured by HMS HAWKINS at Kismaya whilst on voyage to Diego Suarez.

6.3.1941: Requisitioned by Ministry of War Transport (The Union-Castle Mail Steamship Co. Ltd., managers), London.

5.1.1942: Renamed EMPIRE ARUN. Made 14 voyages under Union-Castle management, mainly to North America but also South America and South Africa.

26.8.1946: Sold to Ormos Shipping Co. Ltd. (Goulandris Brothers, managers), London.

24.11.1947: Renamed GRANLAKE.

14.2.1949: Transferred to Compania Maritima del Este S.A., Panama, and renamed DRYAD.

1951: Sold to Hikari Kisen K.K., Tokyo, Japan and others and renamed SHIRANESAN MARU.

8.1952: Re-engined.

1954: Sold to Mitsui Kinkai Kusen

Boskoop in the Mersey in the 1930s. *[B. and A. Feilden/J. and M. Clarkson]*

K.K. and others, Tokyo.

9.1955: Converted to burn oil fuel.

1956: Sold to Hokuyo Suisan K.K., Tokyo and subsequently converted into a crab cannery.

1962: Sold to Nichiro Gyogyo K.K., Tokyo and renamed TAINICHI MARU.

1969: Sold for demolition.

9.8.1969: Demolition commenced by Utsumi, Shodio-gun, Kagawa.

CHARLES L.D. 1941-1942

O.N. 135620 5,267g 3,126n.

426.2 x 56.6 x 25.7 feet.

4SCSA 8-cyl. (29¹/₈ x 59¹/₁₆) oil engine by Götaverken A/B, Gothenburg, Sweden; 3,600 BHP, 13 knots.

1.1934: Completed by Götaverken A/B, Gothenburg (Yard No. 475) for Louis Dreyfus and Compagnie, Paris as CHARLES L.D.

1940: Confiscated with the entire Louis Dreyfus fleet by the Vichy Government (the Dreyfus family were Jewish) and allocated to the newly-formed Compagnie Marseillage de Navigation Coloniale, Marseilles, and renamed PROCYON

24.3.1941: Captured by HMS LEANDER, 200 miles off Mauritius.

1941: Requisitioned by The Ministry of Shipping (The Union-Castle Mail Steamship Co. Ltd., managers), London and renamed CHARLES D.

9.12.1942: Torpedoed and sunk by the German submarine U 553 (Korvetten-Kapitan Karl Thurmann) 500 miles east of Cape Farewell, Greenland in position 59.02 north, 30.45 west whilst on a voyage from Karachi and New York to the Clyde in convoy HX 217 with general cargo. 36 lives were lost.

Charles LD in Australian waters. *[A.C.Green/States Library of Victoria, Australia]*

JEAN L.D. 1941-1945

O.N. 168690 5,795g 3,333n 9,130d.
446.9 x 57.1 x 25.8 feet.
2SCSA 8-cyl. (25⁵/₈ x 47¼ inches) oil
engine by Compagnie de Construction
Mecaniques Sulzer, St. Denis, France;
3,300 BHP, 13 knots.
25.3.1936: Launched by Société de
Ateliers et Chantiers de France, Dunkirk
(Yard No. 157) for Louis Dreyfus and
Compagnie, Paris as JEAN L.D.
1940: Confiscated by the Vichy
Government, allocated to Compagnie
Marseillage de Navigation
Coloniale, Marseilles, and renamed
BETELGEUSE.
21.1.1941: Intercepted 200 miles off
Mauritius by HMS LEANDER when
sailing in convoy from Dakar.
17.2.1941: Requisitioned by the
Ministry of Shipping (The Union-Castle
Mail Steamship Co. Ltd., managers),
London and renamed JEAN L.D.
16.3.1945: Returned to Compagnie
Marseillage de Navigation Coloniale
and renamed BETELGEUSE. Engaged
in transporting military equipment to
Vietnam, during which time she was

Jean L.D. with neutrality markings at Cape Town in 1941. *[Ian Farquhar collection]*

attacked by the Vietnamese, killing and
injuring a number of the crew.
1947: Owning company wound up,
ship returned to Louis Dreyfus and
Compagnie and renamed JEAN LD.
1954: Transferred to Buries Markes
Ltd., London and renamed LA
LAGUNA.
1958: Sold to Alma Shipping Co. S.A.,
Panama and renamed ACHEAN under
the Greek flag.
1960: Owners Transfruit Shipping Co.

Ltd., Chios (S.M. Frangos, Athens),
Greece.
1965: Sold to Transropodi S.A.
Geneva, Switzerland and renamed
TRANSROPODI under the Haitian flag.
1.1966: Transferred to the Greek flag.
1968: Sold to Navigation Maritime
Bulgare, Varna, Bulgaria and renamed
ALPHECCA.
3.6.1968: Arrived at Mihara for
demolition by Seibu Kogyo K.K.
8.1968: Work completed.

The Liberties

At the end of 1943 Union-Castle were allocated five Liberty
types then under construction, and delivered over the turn of
1943/1944. For the most part they were engaged on voyages
on Government account either in the Mediterranean or Far

East, some of considerable duration, although there were
occasional voyages on company account (see voyages 5
and 6 of *Frank A. Vanderlip*, 6 and 7 of *Sampan*). All were
returned in late 1947/early 1948, after which only *Samflora*
went to sea again.

SAMSTEEL 1943-1947

O.N. 169643 7,219g 4,380n 10,000d.
422.8 x 57 x 34.8 feet.
T. 3-cyl (24, 37, 72 x 48 inches) by
Iron Fireman Manufacturing Company,
Portland; 2,500 IHP; 11knots.
31.7.1943: Launched by California
Shipbuilding Corporation, Los Angeles
(Yard No. 233) for the United States War
Shipping Administration, Washington as
JAMES H ROBINSON.
15.8.1943: Completed and delivered
on bareboat charter to the Ministry of
War Transport (The Union-Castle Mail
Steamship Co. Ltd., managers), London
and renamed SAMSTEEL.
29.8.1943: Departed San Pedro for
Hobart, Tasmania via Indian ports
(Voyage 1).
21.1.1944: Arrived Manchester.
22.2.1944: Left Liverpool for
Mediterranean (Voyage 2).
22.1.1945: Arrived Hull.
18.5.1945: Sailed Cardiff (Voyage 4)
for Baltimore, Suez, calling several
times in India, Burma, Singapore, Hong
Kong, Batavia, and returning via South
African ports, Buenos Aires and St
Vincent.

Samsteel. [Ships in Focus]

13.1.1947: Arrived Liverpool after a
voyage of 605 days, 12 hours, 3 minutes
covering 63,680 miles.
18.4.1947: War service completed.
9.1947: Returned to United States and
renamed JAMES H. ROBINSON.
11.1961: Sold for demolition to Union
Minerals and Alloys Corporation and
broken up at Panama City

SAMPAN 1943-1947

O.N. 169802 7,219g 4,380n 10,000d.
422.8 x 57 x 34.8 feet.
T. 3-cyl (24, 37, 72 x 48 inches) by
Iron Fireman Manufacturing Company,

Portland; 2,500 IHP; 11knots.
4.8.1943: Launched by California
Shipbuilding Corporation, Los
Angeles (Yard No. 234) for the United
States War Shipping Administration,
Washington as WILLIAM I. KIP.
17.8.1943: Delivered on bareboat
charter to the Ministry of War Transport
(The Union-Castle Mail Steamship Co.
Ltd., managers), London and renamed
SAMPAN.
29.8.1943: Left Willington for Hobart in
company with SAMSTEEL
29.2.1944: Arrived Hull.
12.12.1945: Voyage 6 was on a Union-

Castle berth to South Africa and Beira, returning to Southampton 19.3.1946.
28.4.1946 to 24.8.1946: Voyage 7 was on the Round Africa service out via Suez.
24.10.1947: Returned to United States and renamed WILLIAM I. KIP.
1962: Broken up at New Orleans by Southern Scrap Material Co. Ltd.

SAMFLORA 1943-1947

O.N. 169577 7,219g 4,380n 10,000d.
422.8 x 57 x 34.8 feet.
T. 3-cyl (24, 37, 72 x 48 inches) by General Machinery Corporation, Hamilton, Ohio, 2,500 IHP; 11 knots.
9.11.1943: Launched by Bethlehem-Fairfield Shipyard Inc., Baltimore, Maryland (Yard No. 2268) for United States War Shipping Administration, Washington and named ISRAEL J. MERRITT.
11.1943: Delivered to the Ministry of War Transport (The Union-Castle Mail Steamship Co. Ltd., managers), London and renamed SAMFLORA.
1.12.1943: Departed Baltimore for New York and Alexandria.
4.11.1944: Departed Manchester.
1.11. 1946: Arrived Ellesmere Port after 747 days, 10 hours, 20 minutes covering 75,207 miles, a record voyage for Union-Castle.
4.1947: Sold to Putney Hill Steam Ship Co. Ltd. (Counties Ship Management Ltd., managers), London and renamed PRIMROSE HILL.
2.1949: Transferred to London and Overseas Freighters Ltd., London.
1950: Renamed LONDON VENDOR.
1.1952: Sold to Arequipa Compania Naviera S.A. (Dimitrios L. Condylis, manager), Panama, and renamed CABANOS.
1963: Sold to Compania Santa Helle S.A., Panama (D.J. Papadimitriou Sons, London, managers), and renamed THEBEAN under Greek registry.
1964: Transferred to Compania Santa Roberta S.A., Panama (D.J. Papadimitriou Sons, London, managers), remaining Greek registered.
1968: Sold to Koshin Sangyo K.K., Japan.
14.3.1968: Arrived Onomichi for demolition

SAMBUFF/FRANK A. VANDERLIP 1943-1948

O.N. 169700 7,219g 4,380n 10,000d.
422.8 x 57 x 34.8 feet.
T. 3-cyl (24, 37, 72 x 48 inches) by

Samflora on15th February 1944. *[Ian Farquhar collection]*

General Machinery Corporation, Hamilton, Ohio, 2,500 IHP; 11 knots.
13.11.1943: Launched by Bethlehem-Fairfield Shipyard Inc., Baltimore, Maryland (Yard No. 2269) for United States War Shipping Administration, Washington and named FRANK A. VANDERLIP.
20.11.1943: 36 days after keel laying, delivered on bareboat charter to the Ministry of War Transport (The Union-Castle Mail Steamship Co. Ltd., managers), London and renamed SAMBUFF.
12.12.1943: Left Baltimore for Port Said, returning to St John's, New Brunswick, 2.1944.
1944: Following representations by the widow of banker Frank Vanderlip, renamed FRANK A.VANDERLIP.
Voyage 2: St John's to Port Said and back to New York.
Voyage 3: Left New York 20.6.1944

for Trinidad, Cape Town, Durban, Mombasa, Suez, Gibraltar and Glasgow, arriving 25.11.1944.
Voyage 4: Left Glasgow 1.1945 sailing initially between numerous Mediterranean ports until 2.1946 when course was set for Colombo, Singapore, Japan and Vancouver, thereafter down the west coast of the United States to the Panama Canal, arriving Liverpool 10.7.1946.
Voyage 5: Left Liverpool 1.8.1946 for Workington, Middlesbrough, London, Southampton to South and East African ports, Malta, Trieste, Venice, Gibraltar and arriving Hull 2.1947. In command during this voyage were two future Commodores, H. Dellar who was relieved by W.S. Byles in January.
4.1948: Returned to the United States.
5.1967: Demolition commenced by Lipsett Division, Luria Brothers and Co. Inc., Kearney, New Jersey.

Frank A. Vanderlip. [World Ship Photo Library]

43

SAMTRENT 1943-1947

O.N. 169724 7,219g 4,380n 10,000d.
422.8 x 57 x 34.8 feet.
T. 3-cyl (24, 37, 72 x 48 inches) by
General Machinery Corporation,
Hamilton, Ohio, 2,500 IHP; 11 knots.
1.11.1943: Keel laid.
24.11.1943: Launched by New England
Shipbuilding Corporation, South Portland,
Maine (Yard No. 2199) for United States
War Shipping Administration, Washington
and named PERCY D. HAUGHTON.
30.11.1943: Delivered to the Ministry of
War Transport (The Union-Castle Mail
Steamship Co. Ltd., managers), London
and renamed SAMTRENT.
1.12.1943: Sailed South Portland for
|New York and Suez.
10.1947: Returned to United States and
renamed PERCY D. HAUGHTON and
laid up in Mobile Reserve Fleet.
4.1962: Demolition began by Pinto Island
Metal Co, Mobile, Alabama.

PART FIVE: POST-WAR TIME CHARTERS

FORT CARILLON 1946-1949

O.N. 168482 7,129g 4,344n 10,000d.
424.6 x57.2 x 34.9 feet /26.8.
T. 3-cyl. (24, 37, 72 by 48 inches) by
Dominion Engineering Works Ltd.,
Montreal, Canada; 2,500 IHP. 10 knots.
5.5.1943: Completed by Davie
Shipbuilding and Repairing Co. Ltd.,
Lauzon, Quebec, Canada (Yard No.
542) for The Dominion of Canada and
bareboat chartered to the Ministry of
War Transport (Dodd Thomson and
Co. Ltd., managers), London as FORT
CARILLON.
9.1946: Bareboat chartered to The
Union-Castle Mail Steamship Co. Ltd.,
London as supplementary cargo vessel
for their United States, and South and
East African services.
9.1949: On conclusion of charter

management transferred to Maclay and
McIntyre Ltd., Glasgow.
1950: Sold to Fort Carillon Shipping
Co. Ltd. (J.P. Hadoulis Ltd., managers)
London and renamed MOUNT
ROYAL.
1956: Sold to Callao Compania
Naviera S.A., Panama (Giannis A.
Kairis) and renamed MONTE RICO
under Liberian registry.
1960: Transferred to Greek registry
and renamed LAMYRIS.
1963: Sold to Stamle Compania
Naviera S.A. (Franco Shipping
Co.), Andros, Greece and renamed
BARBARINO.
7.1.1968: Driven ashore during severe
weather whilst in ballast outside
Novorissisk, Black Sea and abandoned
as a constructive total loss.

EMPIRE DUCHESS
See BRAEMAR CASTLE

Fort Carillon sailing from Cardiff on 11th November 1947. *[National Museums and Galleries of Wales , 1788/1872]*

The Ministry Ships

As the Second World War drew to a close the management were conscious of the need to enhance the available cargo carrying capacity, with particular reference to the USA to South and East Africa trade. Accordingly bids were submitted for three of the Fast Standard 15-knot cargo ships completed towards the end of hostilities or then under construction. Additionally, application was made to the British Government to acquire one or two of the United States C2-type standard vessels but this was refused.

Known as the Ministry ships, and for the first seven years of service wearing the traditional lavender hull, they initially proceeded to New York, the first voyage being that of *Drakensberg Castle*, sailing on 16th April and, after a brief overnight call at Trinidad to embark passengers, arrived 23 days later at Cape Town. As a matter of interest an earlier, similar, voyage by *Sandown Castle* had taken 35 days. The voyage continued to Beira and back to Cape Town, where her registry was transferred to South Africa, and on to London, the Cape to London voyage taking 17 days, the fastest yet by one of the company's dry cargo ships. *Good Hope Castle*'s service started in like fashion with a 22-day passage from New York and she too was registered in Cape Town

on the return leg, but returned to New York for her second voyage. *Kenilworth Castle* did even better on her second voyage, reaching Cape Town 23 days after leaving New York, inclusive of a three-day post-Christmas stopover at Trinidad. The Trinidad call was necessary to circumvent United States regulations regarding passenger embarkation.

In addition to the United States service the trio carried out many United Kingdom to South and East Africa voyages, and these assumed greater importance as the United States trade withered, largely on account of intense United States government support of the indigenous lines, Farrell, Robin, and Lykes, as well as the newly-formed South African Marine Corporation. By the mid-1950s this service had ceased. The original spartan passenger accommodation, imposed on orders from the Ministry, was reduced in 1952 and eliminated totally seven years later.

The trio served their owners well albeit for a relatively short time; indeed in the early 1950s they were described as the best revenue earners, for their size, in the fleet. However the 50 tons daily consumption of oil by the two steamers saw their withdrawal and replacement by Clan Line tonnage in 1959, *Kenilworth Castle* continuing in service until mid-1967.

DRAKENSBERG CASTLE 1946-1959

O.N. 180157 9,904g 7,186n 12,058d.
475.4 (500.3 loa) x 64.1 x 40.0 feet
(draft 29.7 feet).
Two double-reduction geared steam
turbines by C.A. Parsons and Co. Ltd.,
Newcastle-upon-Tyne; 6,800 SHP, 15
knots.
Passengers: 54.

18.10.1944: Launched by J.L.
Thompson and Sons Ltd., Sunderland
(Yard No. 633) for the Ministry of War
Transport (Prince Line Ltd., managers),
London as EMPIRE ALLENBY.
6.1945: Completed.
7.8.1945: Radio Officer John Coundley
intercepted a message in which the
Japanese authorities declared their
wish to discuss surrender terms. This
was the day after the Hiroshima
bombing. His Captain dismissed it as
a hoax and refused permission to break
radio silence and relay the message to
London. Later, realising his mistake,
the Captain ordered the Australian
transport authorities in Perth to seal
Coundley's radio book (quoted in the
'Daily Telegraph' obituary of John
Coundley, who died 1.1.2016).
3.1946: Acquired for £460,500 by The
Union-Castle Mail Steamship Co. Ltd.,
London and renamed DRAKENSBERG
CASTLE. Hull painted Lavender grey.
6.1946: Registered in Cape Town, South
Africa.
11.1946: Whilst on a voyage from
Port Said to Genoa the Fourth Officer

The hull of *Drakensberg Castle* was repainted from lavender grey (upper) to black
(lower) in October 1953 *[Author's collection]*

observed a small boat on the crest of a
wave in foul weather. Captain Trayner
turned his vessel and poured oil to calm
the seas bringing the ship alongside at
the second attempt whereupon crew
members scrambled down nets and
brought the seven terrified occupants
aboard. The survivors proved to be
the captain and crew of an Italian
steamer reported as ELENA which
had sunk some hours earlier off Ponza.
None could speak English. Captain
Trayner subsequently received a letter
of appreciation from the owner, G.
Forzinetti.
4.1947: Docked in London with cargo
including £1,000,000 in gold and a

menagerie of six poisonous snakes, a
cheetah, two giraffes and 50 assorted
monkeys, three of which escaped in
Port Said and shinned up the jigger mast
where they stayed for two days until,
smoke blackened from the funnel, they
were lured down by bananas.
1952: Passenger accommodation
reduced to 12.
10.1953: Hull reverted to black.
1957: Passenger accommodation
removed.
7.1959: Sold to Mollers (China) Ltd.,
Hong Kong for demolition.
5.8.1959: Arrived Hong Kong for
demolition by Hong Kong Salvage and
Towage Ltd.

GOOD HOPE CASTLE 1946-1959

O.N. 166620 9,879g 7,054n 11,775d.
475.8 (494.5 loa) x 64.4 x 40.0 feet.
Two double-reduction steam turbines by
Richardsons, Westgarth and Co. Ltd.,
Hartlepool; 6,800 SHP, 15 knots.
Passengers: 54.

12.1.1945: Launched by Caledon
Shipbuilding and Engineering Co. Ltd.,
Dundee (Yard No. 407) for the Ministry
of War Transport, London (T. and J.
Harrison Ltd., Liverpool, managers) as
EMPIRE LIFE.

5.1945: Completed.

3.1946: Acquired for £493,600 by The
Union-Castle Mail Steamship Co. Ltd.,
London and renamed GOOD HOPE
CASTLE. Hull painted lavender grey.

14.7.1946: Registered in Cape Town,
South Africa.

3.1950: Funnel heightened by 10 feet.

18.6.1951 to 22.6.1951: Engine disabled
in Gulf of Aden. Subsequently her
engineer officers were awarded additional
three months pay in recognition of their
efforts to repair the engines.

1952: Passenger accommodation reduced
to 12.

1954: Hull painted black.

1957: Passenger accommodation
removed.

3.1959: Chartered to Springbok Lines
Ltd., Cape Town for round voyage United
Kingdom to Africa, funnel repainted in
charterer's colours.

7.1959: Sold for £85,000 to Hong Kong
Salvage and Towage Co. Ltd.

14.7.1959: Arrived Hong Kong.

8.1959: Demolition began.

Empire Life (top), and *Good Hope Castle*, the latter in lavender grey but still with wartime floats mounted aft (middle) and in black with a white line (below). In 1950 her funnel was substantially increased in height. *[Author's collection]*

KENILWORTH CASTLE
1946-1967

O.N. 161498 9,916g 7,118n
11,943d.
475.4 (497.4 loa) x 64.3 x
40.0 feet.
2SCSA 6-cyl. Doxford-type
oil engine by Barclay, Curle
and Co. Ltd., Glasgow; 6,800
BHP, 15 knots.
Passengers: 36.
18.8.1944: Launched by
Charles Connell and Co. Ltd.,
Glasgow (Yard No. 446) for
the Ministry of War Transport
(Stanley and John Thompson
Ltd., managers), London as
EMPIRE WILSON.
12.1944: Completed.
4.1946: Acquired by The
Union-Castle Mail Steamship
Co. Ltd., London for £482,500
and renamed KENILWORTH
CASTLE. Hull painted
lavender grey.
1952: Passenger
accommodation removed.
1954: Hull painted black.
10.1957: Arrived London
with what was believed to be
the largest, most varied and
most valuable collection of
wild life ever to leave East
Africa. Destined for the
London and Dudley Zoos
the manifest included two
full-grown hippopotami, a
lion, lioness and cub, two
leopards, four cheetahs, two
buffalo, two hyenas, four
giant rats, four crested rats,
a rhinoceros, three zebras,
two eland, two jackals, one
onyx, one wildebeeste or gnu,
two warthogs, two skunks,
three blue monkeys, five giant
tortoises (some believed to be
150-years old), nine leopard
tortoises and a vast collection
of exotic birds.
1958: Passenger (human)
accommodation removed.
1.1.1966: Managers became
Cayzer, Irvine and Co. Ltd.
4.4.1967: Sold to Hong Kong
Chip Hua Manufactory Co.
(1947) Ltd. for demolition.
4.6.1967: Arrived Hong Kong.
Resold to Taiwanese breakers.
31.7.1967: Arrived Kaohsiung
in tow.
12.1967: Demolition
commenced.

Kenilworth Castle at three stages of her Union-Castle career: in lavender grey prior to 1954 (top), black with white line leaving Cape Town (middle), and arriving at a South African port with a less than pristine hull (bottom). [Top: Author's collection, middle; Ships in Focus, bottom; Ian Shiffman]

1946-1977

Until 1950 the dry cargo fleet comprised the three Ministry ships, *Sandown Castle*, and the two chartered vessels, plus other charters, many from the King Line (acquired 1948 and 1949) as and when required. The first of the chartered vessels, *Fort Carillon*, was returned in 1949 while the other, *Empire Duchess*, noteworthy only for being the owners' final coal-burner, was purchased in that year but sold in 1950 to King Line. Finally the ageing *Sandown Castle* was laid up in the Tyne early in 1950 after a troubled voyage and sold for breaking up a few weeks later rather than undergoing an £80,000 survey.

Nevertheless there remained a perceived need for further tonnage and accordingly in mid-1952 the Chairman, Sir Vernon Thomson, ordered what turned out to be his final ships, *Tantallon Castle* and *Tintagel Castle*, the first dry

cargo freighters ordered since 1919. Completed in 1954, and capable of moving 10,000 tons cargo at 15 to 16 knots, they served for 17 years, mainly on the United Kingdom to South and East Africa routes but also on outside charter until rationalisation of services to South Africa was effectively imposed by the South African Government as a precursor of containerisation. In 1962, following reductions in the Round Africa passenger fleet, two former Clan Line cargo vessels were added, *Kinnaird Castle* and *Kinpurnie Castle*, having previously been transferred to The South African Marine Corporation but deemed surplus to requirements. Interestingly, they did not come under Union-Castle ownership, thereby enabling them to operate with less expensive non-white crews. The former lasted until 1975; the latter was sold in 1968.

BRAEMAR CASTLE 1949-1950
O.N. 180051 7,067g 4,879n 10,080d.
431.0 x 56.3 x 35.2 feet
(draft 26.8 feet).
T. 3-cyl. (24.5 x 39.0 x 70.0 x 48.0 inches) by John Dickinson and Sons Ltd., Sunderland; 2,500 IHP, 10 knots.
14.8.1943: Launched by Short Brothers Ltd. Sunderland (Yard No. 478) for the Ministry of War Transport, London (H. Hogarth and Sons Ltd., Glasgow, managers) as EMPIRE DUCHESS.
13.12.1943: Completed
7.8.1946: Management transferred to The Union-Castle Mail Steamship Co. Ltd., London on a three-year bareboat charter as supplementary cargo vessel.
1949: Acquired by The Union-Castle Mail Steamship Co. Ltd., London and renamed BRAEMAR CASTLE.
1950: Transferred to King Line Ltd., London and renamed KING JAMES. Converted to burn oil instead of coal. She was the last coal-fired Union-Castle ship.
1958: Sold to the Cambay Prince Steamship Co. Ltd. (John Manners and Co. Ltd., managers), Hong Kong and renamed TYNE BREEZE.
1963: Sold to the Cathay Trader Steamship Co. Ltd., Hong Kong and renamed CATHAY TRADER.
1964: Sold to Pacific Pearl Navigation Co. Ltd., Hong Kong and renamed HABIB MARIKAR.
4.11.1967: Ran aground on Lincoln Island, Paracels, 400 miles south south west of Hong Kong in position 16.38 north, 112.45 east following an engine breakdown and became a total loss. One life was lost. She was on a voyage to Hong Kong with a cargo of cement.

TANTALLON CASTLE 1954-1971
O.N. 186029 7,448g 4,369n 10,835d.
477.2 (494.6 loa) x 65.1 x 29.2 feet
(draft 27.7 feet).

Braemar Castle passing Erith on 8th October 1949 (above). *[J. and M. Clarkson]*
Tantallon Castle at London (below). *[J. and M. Clarkson]*

2SCDA 8-cyl. ($24^1/_{16}$ x $55^1/_8$) Burmeister & Wain-type oil engine by Harland and Wolff Ltd., Belfast; 8,500 BHP, 16 knots.
Passengers: 12.
22.10.1953: Launched fifteen days after the centenary of the registration of The Union Steam Collier Co. Ltd.
3.1954: Completed by Harland and Wolff Ltd., Belfast (Yard No. 1499) for the Union-Castle Mail Steamship Co. Ltd., London as TANTALLON CASTLE.

1963: Passenger accommodation closed.
1.1.1966: Managers became Cayzer, Irvine and Co. Ltd.
1971: Sold (with TINTAGEL CASTLE) to Aria Shipping Co. Ltd., Famagusta, Cyprus (Pateras Brothers Ltd., Piraeus, Greece) and renamed ARIS II.
1972: Renamed ARIS.
1973: Tonnage openings closed, now 9,561g, 5,468n.
1978: Sold to Ishikawajima Kogyo K.K., Japan, for demolition and arrived Aioi prior to 3.8.1978.

TINTAGEL CASTLE 1954-1971

ON186074 7,447g 4,368n 10,854d.
477.2 (494.6 loa) x 65.8 x 29.2 feet
(draft 27.7 feet).
2SCDA 8-cyl. ($24\frac{1}{16}$ x $55\frac{1}{8}$) Burmeister
& Wain-type oil engine by Harland and
Wolff Ltd., Belfast; 8,500 BHP, 16 knots.
Passengers: 12.
4.2.1954: Launched by Harland and
Wolff Ltd., Belfast (Yard No. 1500) for
The Union-Castle Mail Steamship Co.
Ltd., London as TINTAGEL CASTLE.
6.1954: Completed.
1963: Passenger accommodation closed.
1.1.1966: Managers became Cayzer,
Irvine and Co. Ltd.
1971: Sold (with TANTALLON
CASTLE) to Armar Shipping Co. Ltd.,
Cyprus (Pateras Brothers Ltd., Piraeus,
Greece) and renamed ARMAR.
1973: Tonnage openings closed,
tonnages now 9,559g, 5,466n.
27.6.1978: Arrived Kaohsiung to be
broken up by Nan Enge Steel Enterprise
Co. Ltd.
2.8.1978: Demolition commenced.

Three views of *Tintagel Castle*, the top
photograph leaving Cape Town, and
the middle view on the Thames with
the white hull line, which had been
overpainted by the time the bottom
shot was taken. Neither she nor sister
Tintagel Castle ever carried the lavender
grey hull. *[Top: Ian Shiffman; middle and
bottom: J. and M. Clarkson]*

KINNAIRD CASTLE 1962-1975

O.N. 185040 7,698g 4,263n 10,075d.
502.8 x 65.7 x 27.3 feet.
Three steam turbines double-reduction
geared to single screw shaft by Parsons
Marine Steam Turbine Co. Ltd., Wallsend-
on-Tyne; 10,340 SHP, 17 knots.
17.1.1956: Launched by the Greenock
Dockyard Co. Ltd., Greenock (Yard No.
487).
4.1956: Completed for The Clan Line
Steamers Ltd. (Cayzer, Irvine and Co.
Ltd., managers), London as CLAN ROSS.
7.1961: Transferred to the South African
Marine Corporation, Cape Town, South
Africa for £883,000 and renamed
SOUTH AFRICAN SCIENTIST.
9.4.1962: Transferred to The Clan Line
Steamers Ltd. (Cayzer, Irvine and Co.
Ltd., managers), London and renamed
KINNAIRD CASTLE.
1966: Transferred to King Line Ltd.
(Cayzer, Irvine and Co. Ltd., managers),
London.
1.10.1974: Arrived Lobito and obliged
to lie at anchor for 129 days owing to
severe congestion, eventually docking
on 1.2.1975.
1975: Sold to Dasonab Compania
Naviera S.A., Panama (Monnoo
Overseas Ltd., Dubai) and renamed
NAZEER.
26.4.1978: Arrived at Gadani Beach for
demolition.
5.1978: Demolition began.

KINPURNIE CASTLE 1962-1968

O.N. 185001 8,163g 4,587n 11,070d.
488.9 (512.6 loa) x 66.3 x 28.0 feet.
Three steam turbines double-reduction
geared to single screw shaft by Parsons
Marine Steam Turbines Co. Ltd.,
Wallsend-on-Tyne; 10,340 SHP, 17 knots.
20.10.1953: Launched by the Greenock
Dockyard Co. Ltd., Greenock (Yard No.
481).
20.1.1954: Registered in the ownership
of The Clan Line Steamers Ltd. (Cayzer,
Irvine and Co. Ltd., managers), London
as CLAN STEWART.
24.2.1954: Completed.
6.1961: Transferred to Springbok
Shipping Co. Ltd., London. It was
intended to rename her SPRINGBOK.
5.8.1961: Transferred to the South
African Marine Corporation, Cape
Town, South Africa for £650,000
and renamed SOUTH AFRICAN
SCULPTOR.
18.4.1962: Transferred to The Clan Line
Steamers Ltd. (Cayzer, Irvine and Co.
Ltd., managers), London and renamed
KINPURNIE CASTLE.

Union-Castle's two former Clan Line ships were from different batches. *Kinnaird
Castle,* which was never formally transferred to the company, was from a group
of two which had accommodation trunked around the fourth hatch, ensuring
disturbance for anyone trying to sleep in these cabins during cargo handling (top
and middle).
In *Kinpurnie Castle,* seen on the Thames in October 1965, this accommodation was
omitted (bottom). *[Top and middle: Ian Shiffman; bottom; J. and M. Clarkson]*

1967: Transferred to King Line Ltd. (Cayzer, Irvine and Co. Ltd., managers), London.
1968: Sold to Astro Firme Compania Naviera S.A., Panama (D. Th. Petropoulos, London) and renamed HELLENIC MED under the Greek flag.
15.4.1978: Arrived at Gadani Beach for demolition.
5.1978: Demolition complete.

Right: *Kinpurnie Castle* as *South African Sculptor.* [Ships in Focus]

Below: *Southampton Castle* in the full glory of the lavender grey hull, by now reserved for mail ships (bottom). *[Ian Shiffman]*

THE FINAL MAIL SHIPS

The years 1965 and 1966 saw the introduction of two cargo-only mail ships, *Southampton Castle* and *Good Hope Castle.* Capable of 25 knots, they were designed for the new 11½-day schedule and at the time of completion were the fastest and most powerful cargo vessels afloat. From late 1967 they added calls at Ascension and St Helena which required them to maintain 26 knots between the two islands to keep to the 11½-day mail schedule. Their capacity included 60,000 gallon wine tanks for South Africa's burgeoning wine trade. But the rundown of services was inexorable. Withdrawal of *Pendennis Castle* (28,582/1958) in 1976 saw a 12-month charter of Blue Star's *Andalucia Star*, duly repainted in Union-Castle colours. *Southampton Castle* took the final Union-Castle mail sailing in September 1977.

SOUTHAMPTON CASTLE 1964-1978

O.N. 307788 13.152g 7,336n 11,211d.
1967: 10,538 g 4,235n.
545.0 (592.8 loa) x 77.5 x 31.1 feet.
Two 2SCSA 8-cyl. (35³/₈ x 61 inches) Sulzer-type oil engines by Wallsend Shipbuilding and Engineering Co. Ltd., Wallsend (port) and Barclay, Curle and Co. Ltd., Glasgow (starboard); 34,720 BHP, 25 knots.
Refrigerated capacity: 380,310 cubic feet.
Wine capacity: 60,000 gallons.
Total capacity: 606,006 cubic feet.
20.10.1964: Launched by Princess Alexandra of Kent.
5.1965: Completed by Swan, Hunter and Wigham Richardson Ltd., Wallsend (Yard No. 2010) for The Union-Castle Mail Steamship Co. Ltd., London as SOUTHAMPTON CASTLE.
1.1 1966: Managers became Cayzer, Irvine and Co. Ltd.
7.1966: Embarked three yachts in Cape Town for the Australian Admirals' Cup Races Team at Cowes regatta from a Norwegian vessel, thereby enabling them

to compete by arriving Southampton 17.7.1966, three days before the event started and 12 days before the Norwegian vessel, diverted owing to the closure of the Suez Canal, would have arrived.
11.1967: Cabin accommodation and additional lifeboats for 12 passengers added by Cammell, Laird and Co. Ltd., Birkenhead to enable her to replace CAPETOWN CASTLE (27,000/1938)

on the Ascension and St Helena service.
1971: Passenger accommodation opened for Cape Town to Durban voyages.
9.1977: Left Southampton on final Royal Mail sailing, 120 years and one day after the first Union Steamship Co. Ltd. sailing by DANE.
11.10.1977: Final departure from Cape Town arriving Southampton 24.10.1977.
11.1977: Laid up pending sale.

2.1978: Sold (with GOOD HOPE CASTLE) to Costa Armatori S.p.A., Genoa, Italy and renamed FRANCA C to ship fruit from South America to Italy.
1983: Sold for breaking up to Court Shipping Co. Ltd., Valetta and renamed FRANCA. Resold to China National Metals and Minerals.
16.1.1984: Arrived Dalian for demolition.

Franca C, the former *Southampton Castle,* on the New Waterway. *[Hans Kreyenbosch/Nigel Jones]*

Good Hope Castle off Cape Town in November 1977. *[Ian Shiffman]*

GOOD HOPE CASTLE (2) 1965-1978
O.N. 307986 13,152g 7,336n 11,211d.
1967: 10,538g 4,235n.
545.0 (592.8 loa) x 77.5 x 31.1 feet 31 ft
Two 2SCSA 8-cyl. (35³/₈ x 61 inches)
Sulzer-type oil engines by Wallsend
Shipbuilding and Engineering Co. Ltd.,
Wallsend (port) and Barclay, Curle and
Co. Ltd., Glasgow (starboard); 34,720
BHP, 25 knots.
Refrigerated capacity: 380,313 cubic feet.
Wine capacity: 60,000 gallons.
Total capacity: 606,006 cubic feet
16.2.1965: Launched by Swan, Hunter
and Wigham Richardson Ltd., Wallsend
(Yard No. 2011) for The Union Castle
Mail Steamship Co. Ltd., London and

named GOOD HOPE CASTLE.
12.1965: Completed.
1.1 1966: Managers became Cayzer,
Irvine and Co. Ltd.
10.1966: Cabin accommodation for
12 passengers and additional lifeboats
added by Cammell, Laird and Co. Ltd.,
Birkenhead to enable her to replace
CAPETOWN CASTLE on the Ascension
and St. Helena service.
29.6.1973: Caught fire 35 miles south east
of Ascension Island on a voyage from
Ascension to St Helena and abandoned.
10.7.1973: Taken in tow by tug
ALBATROSS.
18.8.1973: Arrived Antwerp for survey.
29.9.1973: Departed for Bilbao towed

by tug HEROS and arrived 9.10.1973.
24.1.1974: Towed to Santander for
repairs by Astilleros Espanoles.
31.5.1974: Resumed Royal Mail
service.
8.1977: Final Royal Mail sailing.
9.1977: Laid up.
2.1978: Sold (with SOUTHAMPTON
CASTLE) to Costa Armatori S.p.A.,
Genoa, Italy and renamed PAOLA C to
ship fruit from South America to Italy.
1984: Sold for demolition to Court
Shipping Co. Ltd., Valetta, Malta and
renamed PAOLA. Resold to China
National Metals and Minerals.
27.7.1984: Arrived Shanghai for
demolition.

Above: Now looking very
sorry for herself, *Good Hope
Castle* arrives at Antwerp on
18th August 1973 following
a fire and abandonment in
the South Atlantic at the end
of June. After survey she
was towed back to Bilbao
and later Santander for
repairs. She was returned
to Union-Castle service in
May 1974 (top and above,
left and right). *[All three: Jan
Anderiesse]*

Right: *Paola* on the
New Waterway. *[Hans
Krayenbosch/Nigel Jones]*

ANDALUCIA STAR 1976-1977

O.N. 365848 IMO 7342976.

9,784g 5,428n 11,092d.

1987: 9,981g 3,218n 11,092d.

155.81 (b.b.) x 21.49 x 8.56 metres.

2SCSA 9-cyl. Burmeister & Wain 9K74EF-type oil engine by J.G. Kincaid and Co. Ltd., Greenock; 17,400 BHP, 21 knots.

Refrigerated capacity: 466,266 cubic feet.

21.6.1974: Keel laid.

14.1.1975: Named but not launched because of high winds.

15.1.1975: Launched by Smith's Dock Co. Ltd., South Bank, Middlesbrough (Yard No. 1329) for Blue Star Line Ltd. (Blue Star Ship Management Ltd., managers), London as ANDALUCIA STAR.

17.6.1975: Delivered.

6.1976: Chartered by The Union-Castle Mail Steamship Co. Ltd. (Cayzer, Irvine and Co. Ltd., managers), London for one year to replace PENDENNIS CASTLE on the Royal Mail service.

7.1977: Returned to owners.

4.1983: Chartered by Department of Trade as a storage and supply vessel for the Falklands garrison. Fitted with a helicopter pad aft.

6.1984: Ministry of Defence charter ended.

14.11.1984: Transferred to Hong Kong registry.

23.11.1984: Transferred to Highvale Ltd. (Wallem Shipmanagement (Hong

Andalucia Star, seen in November 1976, repainted in 1976 for her one-year charter to Union-Castle to replace *Pendennis Castle* on Royal Mail sailings. *[Trevor Jones]*

Kong) Ltd., managers), Hong Kong and renamed FIFE.

16.10.1986: Sold to Atlanship S.A. (V. Pavesic), Lausanne, Switzerland and subsequently renamed ORANGE STAR under the Liberian flag.

31.10.1986: Transferred to Adriatic Reefer Corporation Inc., Monrovia, Liberia (Atlanship S.A., Lausanne) (Suisse-Outremer Reederei A.G., Zurich, Switzerland, managers).

16.12.1986: Arrived at Vegesack, West Gemany for conversion to a bulk orange juice carrier by Bremer Vulkan A.G. Schiffbau und Maschinenfabrik. This involved installation of six stainless steel

tanks for the carriage of orange juice in holds number 2, 3 and 4, with number 1 hold for general cargo and hold number 5 converted for ballast and fuel oil

22.6.1987: Re-delivered to owners, some ten weeks late, with Atlanship S.A, Lausanne, managers.

10.2010: Sold to NKD Maritime BVI Ltd., Chelmsford for $3,385,800 and renamed STAR IV under the St. Kitts and Nevis flag.

13.11.2010: Arrived at Alang, India for demolition by Sachdeva Steel Products, having been sold for $2,905,575.

20.11.2010: Work began.

Southampton Castle dressed for her last call at Cape Town. *[Ian Shiffman]*

WHITWILL, COLE – BRISTOL-BASED, SWEDISH-OWNED
Malcolm Cranfield

In 1912 the Bristol ship owner Mark Whitwill took into partnership Commander William Cole to run his Baltic ship agency business under the name of Whitwill, Cole and Co. Ltd. After the First World War Mark Whitwill sold all of his shares in this company to Commander Cole, so Whitwill, Cole became a separate entity. Mark Whitwill and Son Ltd., in addition to acting as shipping agents until 1975, was also sporadically involved in ship owning. 'Record' 61 showed a photograph of what was their last ship, *Avon Venturer* (8,140/1931), undergoing conversion from a tanker to bulk carrier in 1955.

Whitwill, Cole also operated as colliery agents and coal merchants, chartered shipbrokers, freight contractors, stevedores and forwarding agents. Acting as the Swedish and Norwegian consulates in Bristol, Whitwill, Cole became the main agency for the Scandinavian wood pulp and paper trades, handling the ships of both the Danish-owned J. Lauritzen and Swedish-owned Adolf Bratt. This article traces the often complex story of Whitwill, Cole as a subsidiary of Swedish owners.

Swedish ownership.
Adolf Bratt & Co A/B had begun business in 1877 as coal importers and merchants and in 1905 started a regular service from Gothenburg to Swansea and Bristol. In 1944 they acquired the Götha Line, founded in 1873, which ran a passenger service between Gothenburg and Antwerp and in 1948 took a majority shareholding in their Bristol agents, Whitwill, Cole.

Under the management of Erik Kekonius, Adolf Bratt & Co. A/B and Götha Line continued to operate their services, employing until 1967 the Belgian-built sister ships *Gertrud Bratt* (1,530/1957) and *Belgia* (1,496/1957) (which was Belgian-flagged) and (until sold in 1965) Götha's similar but older *Reine Astrid* (1,599/1953) and smaller *Monica Bratt*

(499/1960) plus Götha's *Patria* (499/1960) (sold in 1968). From 1967 their business was taken over by the new TOR Line. It is understood that Bratt had a joint venture in Belgium with their agents, A.M. De Keyser Thornton, so that they could access cheap loans available for Belgian-built vessels.

TOR Line and Salénrederierna.
In 1964 Lennart Parkfelt's Rederi A/B Transoil, a tanker operator formed in 1924, had joined with Ragnar Källström's Rederi A/B Rex of Stockholm to start roll-on/roll-off services to the United Kingdom and the Netherlands under the name of TOR Line (TO for Transoil and R for Rex). The first ship owned was the *Tor Anglia* (7,388/1966). This development followed the untimely death in 1963 of Gustaf B. Thordén, when Rederi A/B Rex, historically a tramp operator, acquired the Uddevalla-based Thordén Lines. TOR Line was joined in mid-1965 by Bratt and Götha and also by KNSM of Holland.

Rederi A/B Rex soon acquired Transoil, Bratt and Götha, but this rapid expansion placed Rex in financial difficulties and the group, together with its ships and interest in TOR Line, was acquired in 1967 by Salénrederierna. The share capital of Whitwill, Cole, by then owned by Götha as a subsidiary of Transoil, thereby became a Salén investment and in 1974 was formally transferred to the family-owned Rederi A/B Salénia. It is understood that Salén had commenced flagging ships in the United Kingdom in order to avoid the high costs of operating under the Swedish flag.

Whitwill, Cole as ship owners
In 1969 the ore carrier *Sheaf Wear* (10,867/1959) was acquired by Whitwill, Cole and registered at Bristol as *Baltic Ore* with her former owner W.A. Souter and Co. Ltd. of Newcastle-upon-Tyne continuing as manager. This ship was renamed *Irish Wasa* in 1971.

Monica Bratt berthed in Bristol City Docks. Built in Sweden in 1960 as *Shaka* and purchased by Bratt in 1962, she was sold in 1965 to Marseille Fret to trade as *Mejean II* until 1977. She was wrecked in 1981 as the Italian *Adelconcita*.
[Richard Parsons courtesy of John D. Hill]

At much the same time the 1963-built bulk carrier *Argo* (12,275/1963), acquired by Salén in 1969 from Lennart Parkfelt's Rederi A/B Tankoil but not immediately renamed, was renamed *Baltic Wasa* but still under the Swedish flag.

Also in 1971 Salén acquired from Erik O. Brodin of Stockholm two old-established companies, Rederi A/B Disa and Rederi A/B Poseidon. Of the several ships thus acquired, two were given names ending Wasa, thus *Lisa Brodin* (17,278/1968) became *Nordic Wasa* and *Eva Brodin* (12,985/1963) the *Scandic Wasa*. The name Wasa is understood to derive from the name of the Wasa family who had ruled Sweden between 1523 and 1654 and whose coat of arms showed a vase, an old Swedish word for sheaf. It is unclear whether the Wasa naming policy had derived from the purchase of *Sheaf Wear* or was coincidental.

Irish Wasa, the former *Sheaf Wear*, sailing from Birkenhead on 2nd July 1976 after discharging a cargo of iron ore from Sept-Îles, Quebec. *[Paul Boot]*

The 1963 Gothenburg-built, Stockholm-registered, bulk carrier *Baltic Wasa*, seen sailing from Avonmouth on 17th February 1974, was acquired by Salén in 1969 as *Argo* and renamed in 1971. She was sold in 1975 to Slobodna Plovidba of Šibenik to trade as *Skradin* for further ten years until broken up at nearby Split. *[Author]*

In 1970 and 1971, two other second-hand ships, the bulk carrier *British Wasa* (11,495/1969) and ore carrier *Scottish Wasa* (11,125/1961), were acquired by Whitwill, Cole and placed under Souter management. *British Wasa* had been built in Japan as the Philippine-owned *Belo* *Mundo* while *Scottish Wasa* had been built at Greenock as *Iron Crown* for Vallum Shipping Co. Ltd., a joint venture between British Iron and Steel Corporation, Matheson Ltd. and Common Brothers Ltd. of Newcastle who had acted as manager (see 'Record' 23).

Above: The 1969-built *British Wasa*, the former *Belo Mundo*, outbound from Rotterdam in August 1976. *[Dave Salisbury]*
Below: *Scottish Wasa*, the former *Iron Crown*. *[Fotoflite incorporating Skyfotos, 276810]*

.In 1972 two more second-hand ships, the bulk carriers *Cornish Wasa* (12,835/1966) and *Finnish Wasa* (14,921/1966), were acquired by Whitwill, Cole and placed under the management of its newly-created, London-based subsidiary, Whitco Marine Services Ltd. *Cornish Wasa* had been completed by John Brown and Co. Ltd. (Clydebank) for their ship owning subsidiary William Dennison Ltd. and bareboat chartered to Lyle Shipping Co. Ltd. as *Cape St.Vincent*. She was handed over to Whitwill, Cole (Salén) at Gothenburg in November 1972 and converted into a cement carrier. *Cornish Wasa* had called at Port Everglades several times in 1974 with cement loaded at the Norcem facility at Brevik near Porsgrunn, Norway. *Finnish Wasa* was completed at Uraga, Japan, as *General Aguinaldo* for the Philippine Government and was purchased in December 1972.

In 1973 Salén had placed an order for three new bulk carriers from Spanish yards. Two of these, *Spanish Wasa* (15,505/1974) and *Swedish Wasa* (15,505/1975), were delivered at Seville in 1974/5 to Whitwill, Cole while it is understood

that the third contract was sold at a good profit. Early in 1976 *British Wasa*, *Scottish Wasa*, *Finnish Wasa* and *Swedish Wasa* were all transferred from Whitwill, Cole to the nominal ownership of the newly-created Spanocean Line, a subsidiary of Spanocean Trading Ltd., a company set up by Salén in London to conduct shipbroking, trading and agency operations.

This move left just *Irish Wasa*, *Cornish Wasa* and *Spanish Wasa* in the ownership of Whitwill, Cole and these ships were all sold in 1977 and 1978 to become *Christina*, *Casparia* and *Annalock* respectively. On 14th February 1977 the Greek-owned *Christina*, time chartered back to Salén for two years, suffered a fire and explosions, and was abandoned by her crew during the ballast leg of her first round voyage between Ferrol and Glasgow. She was towed to Bilbao for breaking up.

Two ro-ros named *Tor Caledonia* were also brought into Whitwill, Cole ownership. However, the 1975 Kristiansand-built ship of that name (4,128/1975) was sold to VEB Deutsche Seereederi of East Germany and completed as *Fichtelberg*.

Left: *Cornish Wasa* at Port Everglades on 6th February 1974 discharging a cargo of cement loaded at Brevik. *[Author's collection]*

Below: The 1977-built *Tor Caledonia* outbound from Rotterdam in July 1980. *[Dave Salisbury]*

The larger Fredrikstad-built *Tor Caledonia* (5,056/1977), completed at Sandefjord, was delivered to Whitwill, Cole on 7th July 1977 but traded between North Europe and the Middle East for over two years before returning to the North Sea and was subsequently chartered to the British Government in 1982 to supply the Falklands Islands. At this time her ownership was transferred to Spanocean and Whitwill, Cole ceased to be a ship owner. On her return to Europe early in 1984 the ship was renamed *Gothic Wasa* and chartered to Grimaldi Lines. Laid up at Le Havre early in October 1984, two months later she proceeded to Rotterdam to load cargo for Apapa/Lagos but was instead detained and sold following the bankruptcy of Saléninvest.

Spanocean Line
As mentioned, the Salén family had in 1975 created a new British company called Spanocean Line Ltd. This company was associated with Geo.W. Thacker Ltd. of Newcastle, the owner from 1964 of the *Kingham* (1,978/1949), which had been damaged by fire at Oskarshamn in 1972 and was subsequently used as a barge at Gothenburg.

Spanocean's first vessel was the reefer *Cayman* (6,682/1971), formerly the *Greenland* of Maritime Fruit Carriers which, although sold in 1976 to Union Maritime Morocco-Scandinave ('Unimar') of Casablanca to become *Smara*, continued in Spanocean management until 1979. Similarly her sister *Lapland* (6,671/1972), was acquired by Salén in 1976 and renamed *Kungshamn*, but under the nominal ownership of Mentary Ltd. and managed by Whitco Marine Services Ltd, until sold to Unimar in 1977 to trade as *Sijilmassa*.

The 1969-built *Scottish Wasa* was sold in 1977 to be replaced by the former *Eva Brodin* which had previously been operated under the Swedish flag as *Scandic Wasa*. The *Swedish Wasa*, *Finnish Wasa* and *British Wasa* were all sold to Greece at the end of 1979 to trade as *Skyros*, *Georgios* and *Emma Methinitis*, respectively. Meanwhile in 1977 the *Nordic Wasa*, the former *Lisa Brodin*, was also transferred to the British flag, but into the nominal ownership of a new subsidiary of Spanocean named Mainquill Ltd. and renamed *Irish Wasa*, also registered in Bristol. This *Irish Wasa* was transferred to Spanocean in 1981 only to be almost immediately resold and renamed *Flores*.

Above: The Glasgow-registered *Kungshamn*, the former *Lapland*, outbound from London's West India Dock in April 1977. *[Dave Salisbury]*

Left: *Irish Wasa*, the former *Lisa Brodin*, arriving at Cape Town in April 1980 on voyage from Rosario to China. *[Ian Shiffman/ Author's collection]*

The 1972 built *Pacific Wasa* was similarly transferred to Mainquill in 1978 but was sold to Furness, Withy in 1980 to become *Rounton Grange*. Mainquill was also the recorded owner of the reefer *King Egbert* (6,680/1974) between 1976 and 1978. She had been built in 1974 as *Liverpool Clipper* for Maritime Fruit Carriers of Israel, a company with which Salén had considerable involvement and which collapsed in 1976. Both *King Egbert* and sister *King Edmund* (6,680/1973), the former *Bristol Clipper,* were sold in 1977 to East Germany.

However, Salén continued to operate some new ships under the Swedish flag including the Wismar-built *Arctic Wasa* (15,966/1973), the Saiki-built *Atlantic Wasa* (19,203/1974), the Wismar-built *Baltic Wasa* (15,966/1976),

Celtic Wasa (16,230/1976), *Gothic Wasa* (16,032/1977) and *Delphic Wasa* (14,584/1977) plus the Hiroshima-built *Forest Wasa* (40,420/1977).

Intriguingly the general cargo ship *Korshamn* (9,080/1957), formerly *Axeline Brodin*, was also transferred into Spanocean ownership in 1977, and again registered at Bristol, but was sold in 1978.

In addition Spanocean had managed from 1977 until 1982 the *Condora* (8,185/1968), formerly the *Persimmoncore*, on behalf of her new lessor owner C.C. Leasing Corporation of Baltimore. Briefly managed directly by Salén her operation was transferred in 1985 to Shui Hua Shipping Co. of Hong Kong.

Above: The 1972, Rijeka-built *Pacific Wasa*, sold to Houlder Brothers in 1980 to become *Rounton Grange*. [Fotoflite incorporating Skyfotos, 261168]
Below: *Condora*, the former *Persimmoncore*, outbound from Rotterdam in July 1977. [Dave Salisbury]

Furthermore, in 1979/80, Salén had transferred the reefers *Snow Ball* (11,404/1973), and *Snow Hill* (11,403/1974) to Spanocean with, on her sale in 1981, *Snow Ball* being replaced by *Snow Storm* (11,422/1972). All were managed by Salén UK Ship Management Ltd. based at Avonmouth. The *Spring Delight* (12,783/1984) and *Spring Dream* (12,615/1984) followed for a short time until the bankruptcy of Saléninvest in December 1984 took full effect. *Snow Hill* and *Snow Storm* were consequently sold to the Irano-Hind Shipping Company of Tehran, and renamed *Noor* (5,727/1977) and *Hood* (5,168/1979) respectively.

The names *Nordic Wasa* and *Scandic Wasa* were also adopted for two second-hand ro-ros purchased by Salén in 1981 and 1983, although the former was chartered out to Wilhelmsen for two years as *Tana*.

Liquidation of Spanocean Line Ltd. began in January 1985 followed by Geo.W. Thacker Ltd. and Salén UK Ship Management Ltd. in December 1986.

Al-Salama (10,397/1976) and *Al-Zahra* (10,397/1975), the former *Loch Maree* and *Loch Lomond*, owned since 1981 by Salarab Ltd. of Sharjah, assumed to be a joint venture between Salén and local interests. Renamed *Langelle* and *Fastelle* and nominally owned in Hong Kong, their manager was changed in 1986 to Wallem and in 1987 to Geest who operated them as *Geesthaven* and *Geestcape* respectively until 1993. They were registered at Boston, Lincolnshire.

In order to separate the agency and ship owning businesses, and so protect the agency operation from takeover, a new limited company, Whitwill, Cole and Co. (Agency) Ltd., had been formed in August 1979 under the directorship of Brian Fletcher. A corporate restructuring in 1995 saw this company renamed Osprey Shipping Ltd. in order to facilitate business expansion under the management of Nigel and Peter Fletcher, sons of Brian Fletcher. Osprey specialise in land and marine heavy lifting and transport, with offices in Bristol and Newcastle-upon-Tyne.

Whitco Marine Services Ltd.

The management of the *Liverpool Clipper*, *Bristol Clipper* and many sister ships owned by Maritime Fruit Carriers had been awarded to Whitco Marine Services Ltd., a company jointly created by Salén and Whitwill, Cole in 1972. Following the collapse of Maritime Fruit Carriers a new company named Whitco (Marine Services) Ltd. was incorporated at Avonmouth in September 1976. In 1977 this company was awarded by Fyffes the management of the *Matina* (6,351/1969) and five similar ships built in Japan between 1969 and 1972. Also in 1977 the management of four bulk carriers owned by Lambert Brothers, *Temple Inn* (14,651/1972), *Temple Arch* (13,543/1969), *Temple Hall* (13,523/1971) and *Temple Bar* (13,545/1971), was transferred from Whitco (Marine) Services Ltd. to Salén U.K. Ship Management Ltd.

After the collapse of Saléninvest

Following the collapse of Saléninvest at the end of 1984 a new company named Whitwill Cole and Co. Ltd. was jointly created together with the Salén family, Sven Hampus Salén being appointed a director in 1992. The management of two reefers was then transferred from Salén UK Ship Management Ltd. to Whitwill, Cole. These were the

Snow Hill in Gallions Reach, London in March 1976. *[Dave Salisbury]*

Fastelle departing from Bluff, New Zealand, on 18th April 1985 for Bandar Abbas via Fremantle while under Whitwill, Cole management. Cool Shipmanagement briefly took over before Wallem Shipmanagement Services (Isle of Man) Ltd. assumed responsibility in 1986. After several name changes she was broken up in 2000 as *Patagonian Pride*, managed by Magnus Carriers Corporation of Athens. *[Chris Howell collection]*

BLUE STAR FOLLOW-UP

We have been delighted with the reception give to 'Blue Star: A Fleet History' by Tony Atkinson, and our ever-vigilant readership has reported very few corrections, although these include details of a small craft which was missed entirely. We take this opportunity to include corrections, updates and additions, plus a number of extra photos, and to thank readers who have expressed their satisfaction with the book. It is still available from Ships in Focus at £30 plus postage at £3.50 (UK) or £4.50 (elsewhere). Don't delay ordering, as stocks are dwindling and it is unlikely the book will be reprinted.

Extra vessel

Apparently Vesteys had just one vessel registered in their own name. This is the former Royal Mail West Indian feeder vessel *Tees*, 180 gt, built at Paisley in 1892 and sold off about 1915 when Royal Mail introduced some new feeders. She was sold locally and registered at Trinidad. Vestey bought her in 1918, keeping her registered in Trinidad – how they used her I have no idea and I suspect finding out what became of her will be a challenge. She drops out of 'Lloyd's Register' in 1934, but is still listed in the 1940 'Mercantile Navy List'. Looks likely to me she was discarded without a thought given to bothering to properly close her British register. Registered owner is Vestey Brothers Ltd., 13/16 West Smithfield, London EC.
WILLIAM SCHELL, 330 South Franklin Street, Holbrook, MA 02343, USA
Registration documents for Tees *are absent from file BT110 in the National Archives, indicating that her register was never formally closed, as Bill suggests. Ed.*

More on ANRO

Referred to on page 192, *Australia Star* (3) vessel was in fact chartered to the ANRO Consortium by Blue Star Line and was accordingly renamed *Anro Fremantle* and reflagged to the Bahamas on 20th May 1994.

Pacific International Lines, to the very best of my knowledge, had no involvement in ANRO services apart from their purchase of *Anro Fremantle* from Blue Star on 29th July 1994, the sale including the balance of the ANRO charter which expired in June 1995.

ANRO was a consortium consisting of the Australian National Line (ANL), Australian Straits Container Line and Nedlloyd (Singapore) Pte. Ltd. Initially they operated from Australia to Singapore and Malaysia and from 1978 also to Indonesia (Djakarta).
NIGEL KIRBY, 22 Randolph Terrace, Lyttelton 8082, New Zealand.

Willowbank later *California Star*

Author Tony Atkinson has discovered more about the service of *Willowbank* before she was sold to Blue Star (page 204).

A return service from Australia and New Zealand to the U.S. Gulf was started in 1977 with the creation of Bank and Savill Line for which the *Willowbank* and two near-sister ships were delivered in 1980. When this line was sold to the Shipping Corporation of New Zealand (SCONZ) in March 1984, *Willowbank* was chartered by SCONZ to operate on their ANCL, later ANZCL (Australia, New Zealand Container Line) or Boomerang service to California, until sold at Sydney in July 1988 to the Vestey Group. The sale had followed the 1988 merger of ANZCL with PAD (Pacific Australia Direct Line) to form ANZDL (Australia New Zealand Direct Line) and the subsequent sale of the SCONZ share in ANZDL to Sofrana Line (SOciété FRANçaise de Navigation). The Auckland-based shipping arm of the Sofrana Group, Sofrana Unilines (NZ) Ltd., continues to operate services in the South Pacific region.

Loss of former *Polar Uruguay*

On 5th May 2017, the *Uruguay Reefer*, formerly *Uruguay Star* and before that *Polar Uruguay* in the Star Reefers' fleet (see page 288), was badly holed when she hit an ice floe in the Southern Ocean about 75 miles north east of the South Shetland Islands and 75 miles north of the Antarctic Peninsula (position 60.28 south, 052.15 west). She made for the Falkland Islands, but it proved impossible to stop the leak, so that holds 1, 2 and 3 were flooded and she lost power. On 7th May 2017 her crew of 42 were taken off by the *Taganrogskiy Zaliv* (10,629/1993, the former *Polar Chile*; see page 288), whilst the *Frio Las Palmas* (9,070/1990) took over, the tow later passing to the Chilean tug *Otway* (428/2006). However, on 16th May she sank about 400 miles north east of the Falklands. Given the position of her sinking, it would seem that the authorities in the Falkland Islands insisted that, in view of the risk of pollution from her fuel tanks, she sank well outside the Falkland Islands Conservation Zone.

Uruguay Star had become *Uruguay Reefer* in August 2015 on sale for a reported $5,000,000 to Diamond Faith Shipping S.A. (Lavinia Corporation) (Baltmed Reefer Service Ltd., managers), Athens, Greece. All three reefers referred to above were under the Panama flag, all ultimately owned by Lavinia Corporation and managed by

Anro Fremantle at Singapore 19th April 1995. *[Nigel Kirby]*

the associated Baltmed Reefer Service Ltd. *Uruguay Reefer* had a cargo of frozen squid and krill, collected from vessels working around the South Shetland Islands.

Empire Javelin: a rethink

Data on Second World War losses is still subject to amendment, and the loss of *Empire Javelin* (page 273) is now attributed to a mine rather than to be being torpedoed, as no submarine was in the vicinity.

Updates of ships' histories

The number preceding the ship's name refers to its entry in the individual fleet list in 'Blue Star: A Fleet History', with the page number of the entry shown in brackets.

SMALL CRAFT

1. GENERAL PAU (page 216)
2013: Sold to Nathalie Tabaray, Madagascar and renamed MIRANDA.
8.2016: Reported sold abroad.

2. GENERAL MARKUS (page 216)
9.2013: Sold to unknown owners. Still operating as ZOULFECAR, running along the East African coast from Beira, in Mozambique to Dar-es-Salaam including islands of Madagascar, Comoros and Mayotte.

CHARTERED SHIPS

26. BRASIL STAR (2) (page 236)
24.12.2016: Left Singapore for India, subsequently renamed ELGI and registered in Moroni, Comoros.
6.1.2017: Arrived Alang, India.
11.1.2017: Beached for demolition by Rushil Industries.

32. BRASIL STAR (3) (page 239)
3.2012: Transferred to Liberian registry.
17.2.2015: Sold to Seafaith Maritime Co. (Element Shipmanagement S.A., Piraeus, Greece, managers), for $7,500,000 and renamed PANTHER under the Liberian flag.

STAR OFFSHORE SERVICES (SUPPLY BOATS) LTD.

9. STAR PISCES (page 257-8)
1.5.2017: Arrived Chittagong, Bangladesh as CENTURION, registered Alofi, Niue, having been sold for $854,250.
25.5.2017: Demolition began.

14. STAR POLARIS (2) (page 260)
4.2016: Transferred to Panama registry.
6.2016: Sold to Latinamerican Trading S.A., Panama and renamed BUZCADOR.

21. STAR AQUARIUS (2) (page 262)
Owners now FS Shipping Ltd., Aberdeen.

STAR OFFSHORE SERVICES (Tugs) LTD.

4. MOORSMAN (4) (page 263-4)
Noted as deleted from 'Lloyd's Register', MOORSMAN is currently operating from Valletta, Malta.

STAR REEFERS LTD.

3. CAP TRIUNFO (page 280)
1.2017: Transferred to Panama registry.

4. CAP VALIENTE (page 280)
20.11.2015: Managers became Favour Ship Management Co. Ltd., Hong Kong and transferred to Tarawa, Kiribati registry.
12.12.2015: Fire in engine room 35 miles east of Taizhou, China in the East China Sea in position 28.13.12 north, 122.11.20 east whilst on voyage from Beilun, Zhejiang to Singapore.
18.12.2015: Arrived Jintang, Zhoushan for repairs.
29.1.2016: Resumed trading.

5. CAP VERDE (page 281)
12:2016: Favour Ship Management Co. Ltd., Hong Kong became managers.

14. POLAR ECUADOR (page 286)
5.2016: Managers became Goldenking Shipping Co. Ltd., Nanjing, Jiangsu, China and transferred to Liberian registry.
1.2017: Managers became Zhong Xiang Shipping Ltd., Monrovia.

19. POLAR CHILE (page 288)
2.2015: Sold to Silver Sun Shipping S.A. (Lavinia Corporation Athens, Greece, managers), Panama for $5,000,000 and renamed CRYSTAL REEFER.
3.2017: Transferred to Merlin Marine Corporation, Panama (Lavinia Corporation, Athens, Greece) and renamed TAGANROGSKIY ZALIV.

Ship number 5, *Brodvale*, was illustrated under previous names, and as *Tudor Star* (page 30). This photograph of her as *Brodvale* has now turned up. *[Tony Atkinson collection]*

Drover (right) was in service with Blue Star for barely two months, so it is quite gratifying that a photograph of her under this name has now been found (page 141). It was taken 1st December 1954. *[Tony Atkinson collection]*

Malcolm Cranfield points out that Gulf Lines' plain green was the original funnel colour of *Hawkes Bay*, the former *Wellington Star* (page 130), and not black as the caption stated. This photograph (below) which Malcolm supplied shows her sailing on the same occasion from Melbourne, believed to be her first port of call following delivery at Sydney, and which shows the colour more clearly than in the published stern view.

A better photograph of the USSR's *Dnepr*, formerly *Brodhurst* and *Milton Star* (see page 32), on the Thames. *[Tony Atkinson collection]*

A photograph of Teneriffe shows two of the lengthened passenger liners in port together sometime between 1935 and 1939. There are three possibilities: *Almeda Star, Andalucia Star* and *Avelona Star*. *[Tony Atkinson collection]*

An additional photograph of *Brodfield* wrecked at St. Mary's, this time with her boats in the water (see page 37). *[C.J. King/ Tony Atkinson collection]*

A photograph of Majunga en fête. The vessel in the background could well be one of the four 'Generals' listed on page 216. *[Tony Atkinson collection]*

Corrientes (page 139) (top) was bought from Donaldson Line in August 1954 but sold in January 1955 before she could take her intended name *Oakland Star*. With much persistence, Tony Atkinson located this photograph of her at Vancouver in Blue Star colours. *[Vancouver Museum]*

Carmia (middle) was also bought from Donaldson Line, and in this photograph, also from Vancouver, she is in Blue Star colours but has yet to be renamed *Victoria Star*, dating it to between May and October 1954 (page 135). *[Vancouver Museum]*

A superb photograph of *Solent Star* (below) (page 240) arriving Lyttelton in the funnel markings of Federated Fruitcarriers, a joint venture between Nissui of Japan and Seatrade. *[Nigel Kirby]*

JOHN COCKERILL'S TILBURY SERVICE
Flor van Otterdyk

How it started

There has long been a strong maritime connection between Great Britain and Belgium. In addition to the services between regions of the British Isles and Antwerp, there was also a regular liner service between London and Oostende. A document from about 1870 mentions a number of British vessels plying between the British capital and the Belgian coastal port such as the *Holland* (383/1848) and *Belgium* (457/1848) with an additional vessel, the *Seine* (391/1849), joining between September and the end of February. These vessels were sometimes replaced by the *Moselle* (574/1852), *Leo* (569/1847) and *Cologne* (435/1858), but their masters were transferred from the regular vessels.

This article concerns the service between Tilbury and Ostend operated under the Belgian flag by John Cockerill's shipping company and which began in the 1890s and ran for almost three quarters of a century. The major promoter of the link was Jules Vandenpeereboom, the Belgian Minister of Railways, Mail and Telegraphy between 1884 and 1899. The Maritime Department of his Ministry was concerned mainly with the interests of Belgium's railways. Thus, the Minister's initiative aimed not so much to improve Belgium's participation in shipping, but to increase the tonnage operated by the Belgian State Railways. Vandenpeereboom expected the railways to acquire additional traffic through a shipping service which swiftly conveyed foodstuffs grown in Belgium and adjacent countries to lucrative markets in London. The Minister planned to create a cargo service between Belgium and Great Britain to complement the passenger service between Ostend and Dover which had been established half a century earlier, operated by the state-owned Ostend-Dover Line. When founded in 1845 (first sailing in 1846) this ferry service exclusively targeted passengers and mail.

The immediate predecessor on the Belgian service was a regular cargo service started in 1894 between Ostend and Tilbury. This service provided daily departures in each direction with modern steamers chartered from the fleet of William Robertson of Glasgow including *Citrine* (602/1894) *Girasol* (602/1895), *Opal* (599/1894), *Gem* (432/1887) and *Jacinth* (453/1888). Another vessel of which movements were noted was the *Hawk* (648/1876). The smaller vessels used initially were replaced when the rapid expansion of

Rubis (1) in the dazzle paint applied during the First World War. The maiden arrival at Tilbury on 18th May 1897 of Cockerill's first vessel under the Belgian flag to inaugurate the regular service from Ostend was rather unfortunate. Damage to the bow after a collision with the pier at Tilbury required repairs at the owner's yard in Hoboken which took a fortnight, meaning that the second voyage could only be undertaken in early June. Notwithstanding this mishap the *Rubis* served the company for almost 40 years with the exception of the First World War and was not broken up until 1936.

As can be expected over this long career the ship suffered some minor mechanical problems, the worst being the loss of a screw in early February 1911. She had a few mishaps which were inevitable in the busy shipping lanes in which she operated. For instance, she was involved in a collision with the Swedish steamer *Gustafberg* (1,156/1870) in the Thames on 7th August 1904 when both suffered considerable damage. A frightening moment for the crew was the very close encounter with a floating mine near the Westhinder Light Vessel on 7th February 1931. *[Author's collection]*

traffic called for ships with a larger capacity. This service ran in competition with that run by General Steam Navigation between London and Ostend with the paddle steamers *Swallow* (625/1875) and *Swift* (627/1875).

Although the Société Anonyme John Cockerill was at least partially involved in this initiative to operate a liner service between Ostend and Tilbury, it was only two years later, on the 15th of June 1896, that this regular service was formally established by the Belgian company.

The Cockerill Group

At the turn of the twentieth century Société Anonyme John Cockerill was an influential multinational group with its headquarters at Liège on the river Maas. It had been founded in 1817 by John and Charles James Cockerill, sons of a British immigrant who was formerly a Lancashire weaver. The company quickly grew into one of the major European industrial groups, with diverse interests which included iron and steel making and coal mining. It is claimed Cockerill was the first great industrialist on the European continent. In 1842, two years after John Cockerill's death, the Belgian government bought the company which had become a vital part of the country's economy. Renamed Société Anonyme pour l'Exploitation des Etablissements John Cockerill, the group became known simply as John Cockerill.

The first steps into maritime transport were taken in 1858 when the shipping company Société Cockerill was founded at Antwerp. The main reason for this initiative was to transport iron ore from their mines in the Iberian peninsula to Antwerp. But there were also plans to open liner services, initially concentrating to and from ports in the Mediterranean, and in 1891 the company built larger vessels to operate a liner service to Australia. The vessels of the Shipping Division were built at the group's own shipyard, first at Antwerp and later at Hoboken, to where the shipyard had moved in 1873 (the new yard was inaugurated on 15th January 1874).

Set-up and organisation

It is not surprising that Cockerill was favourable to the ideas of Minister Vandenpeerenboom and agreed to become involved with short sea traffic. Ships for this service remained a class apart in the group's fleet.

From the outset it was the intention of the initiators to use their own tonnage on this route, so that chartered tonnage would be replaced as soon as possible. On 2nd May 1896, even before the service had been established, three vessels were ordered from John Cockerill's yard at Hoboken. The contract price was 466,000 Belgian francs for each ship and the contracts were numbered 355, 356 and 357. Identical sisters, they were designed to transport 210 tons of cargo plus 40 tons of coal bunkers. This relatively small cargo capacity was sufficient as the main cargo was fruit and vegetables. To improve stability each vessel carried 50 tons of ballast. Two triple expansion engines provided a service speed of 16 knots. This speed was necessary to enable the ships to arrive at Tilbury in the evening to be able to unload merchandise so that it arrived on time at London markets which opened early in the morning. It was a tremendously fast speed for that time and these coasters were amongst the fastest pure cargo ships for a long period.

The new Belgian-flag vessels were delivered as the *Rubis, Topaze* and *Saphir* respectively in May, July and August 1897, replacing a chartered ship as each entered service. These first three units of the fleet were named after gems, setting a pattern for the naming of all further vessels of the fleet. Apart from the three mentioned there were the *Améthyste, Eméraude* and *Turquoise. Rubis* and *Topaze* were each used three times, *Diamant, Saphir* and *Turquoise* each twice with *Eméraude* and *Améthyste* once each.

The naming of the vessels followed the example set by the Robertson steamers which inaugurated the service in 1894. However, it can also be traced to a tradition started with the Ostend to Dover packets. They too were originally named after gemstones before the decision was made to name these passenger ferries after members of the Royal family (and cities).

Another indication that the 'Tilbury ships' were considered an addition to the popular Ostend to Dover packets is the fact they had the same funnel colours: yellow with black

tops. This distinguished them from the deep-sea ships of the Cockerill fleet which had a plain black funnel. The house flag of the company was a Belgian flag with, in the black section nearest to the hoist, the letter S in white and the white letter C in the red section to the fly. In the yellow middle sector was the shield of the Cockerill group with underneath the shield in a blue banderol the Latin motto of the group 'Courage to the last'. This house flag changed slightly in 1955 when Cockerill merged with Ougrée-Marihaye, another Belgian steel producer.

The office of the shipping company was set up at Ostend. However, the home port of the ships was Antwerp, except for the period 1910-1924 when Ostend became their homeport.

Reliability

This first trio of vessels gave the company valiant service for many decades but, as can be expected on such an express route in crowded waters, the vessels had their share of mishaps but also their moments of glory. In fact the start of the service with the Belgian vessels was rather unlucky, the maiden voyage of *Rubis*, the first Belgian vessel in service, not going well. Arriving at Tilbury under the command of Captain Renier, she collided with a pier and damaged her bows. However, overall the vessels were very reliable. During its existence the Ostend to Tilbury service had but two major interruptions, both during world wars, although there were also occasional stoppages due to strikes of stevedores.

As was the case with the passenger vessels of the Ostend-Dover Line, the Ostend-Tilbury cargo vessels acquired a reputation for clockwork regularity, sailing in all weathers. All sorts of perishables were transported, including fruit, vegetables, meat products, eggs and poultry. Early in the twentieth century new methods of cargo handling were introduced for certain refrigerated cargoes which can now be recognised as 'pre-container' systems. Indeed, in addition to employing fast ships, Cockerill developed specially designed containers measuring two metres square to speed up the

The *Saphir* (1), the last of the initial trio of Tilbury ships, had the longest service of any ship of the John Cockerill Line. In a career spanning 55 years she survived two world wars and proved a reliable unit in a very strenuous and demanding service.

She ran trials on 31st August 1897, just 58 days after her launch, a good performance for her builders at the time. During her trials the weather was so bad that the ship rolled up to 30 degrees, much to the discomfort of the guests on board. Two days later the *Saphir* left on her maiden voyage to Tilbury.

Saphir was not as fortunate as her predecessors as during her first seven years collision damage was reported six times. One occasion when *Saphir* was in the news was March 1898 when she towed the Ostend fishing vessel *Gustave Clemence* to safety. During the First World War, in which she served as ammunition carrier, she was in collision with a French torpedo boat, which was blamed for the accident. In July 1917 she had a 37 mm gun fitted. *[Author's collection]*

loading and discharge of cargo. Two types of containers were in use: closed for refrigerated cargo and open for vegetables and fruit.

Not only produce grown in Belgium was booked, but also perishable goods arriving by train from more distant parts of Europe such as Italy and Hungary. No effort was spared to ensure smooth transshipment of goods, and during the busy periods of the year - between October and March with a peak over the Christmas period - an agent of the company was dispatched to an office at the Belgian border to help with customs clearance.

The twin-screw vessels, sailing under the Belgian flag, provided a daily service with the exception of Saturday. Ships sailed from the berth in Ostend at 2.00 pm with arrival at Tilbury in the evening after a voyage of some seven hours. The cargo was unloaded into the vans of the London, Tilbury and Southend Railway for transfer to London where it arrived in time to be sold from 4.00 am in markets at Billingsgate, Haymarket and Covent Garden.

The day after arrival general cargo was loaded for the return trip to Ostend which departed Tilbury at 8.00 pm to arrive back at Ostend at about 4.00 am the next morning from where most of the cargo was delivered to the consignees on the same day.

In the spring of 1904 the Cockerill Line with its daily service to Tilbury and the General Steam Navigation Company with three sailings a week between Ostend and London agreed to both services being managed by the Cockerill enterprise.

Due to the huge expansion of its main steel manufacturing activity, the Cockerill group gradually became less interested in ship owning. The deep-sea fleet was run down and early in 1910 the last ocean-going vessels were sold so that Cockerill's shipping department was reduced to the sole but specialised Ostend to Tilbury service. The one major change in the latter's case was the alteration in the vessels' home port. On 25th June 1910 the *Rubis, Saphir* and *Topaze* were registered in Ostend instead of Antwerp. However, this process was reversed after the First World War when a twice-weekly service between Antwerp and Tilbury was introduced. From 1924 vessels of the enterprise were again registered with Antwerp as home port.

In 1911 it was planned to add an additional vessel when the company had to charter a vessel at short notice because two of the existing ships of the fleet were damaged. The general idea was for a vessel with the same dimensions as the existing trio but instead of steam engines the new ship would be powered by a diesel engine. It was hoped to put this fourth vessel into service in 1912. The project did not develop as expected and the ship, which eventually received steam engines, was ordered from the Cockerill shipyard at Hoboken only on 28th April 1915 to be delivered when hostilities were over. This vessel became the first *Diamant*.

But the success of the Cockerill Line attracted the attention of potential competitors. One such venture was announced in early April 1913 and was due to open in 1914. The London and Continental Steamship Company would initially use two turbine steamers of 4,200 tons deadweight and a length of 300 feet to offer a daily service - except on Sundays - between Ostend and Tilbury aimed at passengers and mail. The vessels were to be built by John Brown and Co. But this project came to nought.

First World War

Soon after the outbreak of the First World War in August 1914 the service was reduced to three sailings a week and in October 1914 it stopped altogether. The three vessels were placed in the service of the Belgian Army and ran mainly between British and French Channel ports with ammunition and other military supplies. A few trips were made to Rotterdam in the summer and autumn of 1917 to pick up young men who had earlier fled to the then neutral Netherlands in order to bring them to England where they were enrolled in the Belgian Army. The conditions on board the vessels on these trips were poor, especially when the vessels remained for a longer period in the Dutch port because the local authorities were not cooperative, fearing the neutral status of the Netherlands might be put in jeopardy.

During the First World War the shipping company gained the reputation of having one of the best organised and most regular services for military goods shipped from the U.K. to Le Havre, Calais, Dunkirk and Gravelines for the Belgian Army. Between October 1914 and early 1919 a total of 562 voyages were made with army goods whose total value exceeded over £100,000,000 without a single package being lost. It was testimony to the excellent service given by the three vessels involved.

On 14th October 1914 two Cockerill vessels were the last ships to leave the port of Ostend within view of the German troops nearing the city. They returned to Ostend only in January 1919 as the port was not opened by the British authorities until 17th January 1919 and even then vessels could enter or leave only at high tide.

While the first three vessels of the John Cockerill fleet were built in record time, eleven years elapsed between planning and delivery of the fourth, *Diamant* (1). At one point during this process, which began in 1908, it was proposed to install diesel engines but, when the order was signed with the group's shipyard at Hoboken on 28th April 1915, it was agreed she would have a steam engine.
In June 1928 she was badly damaged in a collision on the Scheldt with the Swedish steamer *Bellis* (422/1900) and the Belgian *Adour* (1,099/1898). To prevent her sinking the *Diamant* was run on to a sandbank and after temporary repairs towed to a dry dock to complete repairs. One crew member lost his live in this accident. Six years later the vessel was again damaged in a collision with the Dutch motor coaster *Grietje* (410/1919) on the Scheldt. *[Author's collection]*

While the city of Ostend sustained considerable damage, the offices of the Cockerill Line were unscathed except for the interior which had been used as a canteen by German troops.

Fleet renewal

The three vessels survived the conflict and were returned to their owners and resumed their regular trips across the Channel. They were joined in February 1920 by a new vessel, the *Diamant*, the first ship with that name in the Cockerill fleet. It was the 65-metre, twin-screw ship that had been ordered at the group's shipyard at Hoboken in 1915 and the first of four acquisitions made in the interwar period.

The second vessel to be commissioned in the early 1920s was the *Eméraude,* the company's first second-hand ship. As with so many other shipping companies, Cockerill was in desperate need of additional tonnage at the end of the First World War and took the opportunity to buy the former Brazilian cargo vessel *Rio Pardo*. This ship had been captured by a German torpedo boat in 1916, taken into Zeebrugge but scuttled by the retreating Germans in the canal to Bruges. Salvaged on behalf of the Belgian Government, it was bought by Cockerill. Taken to the shipyard at Hoboken in June it took some eight months to be thoroughly rebuilt and it was only in the spring of 1921 that the *Eméraude* could enter service.

In the meantime John Cockerill had expanded the Tilbury service with a call at Antwerp. As from 1920, and in addition to the daily service from Ostend, a departure from the main Belgian port was offered twice a week, on Wednesdays and Saturdays.

Commercially there was little change in the 1920s but the fleet suffered some mishaps with vessels badly damaged in collisions, and a number of repairs were needed which could be handled by the group's shipyard at Hoboken. The Tilbury service was fortunate to have the backing of this shipyard, part of the same industrial group. It enabled rapid repairs, smooth maintenance of the vessels and efficient conversions when necessary. Another post-war development was closer collaboration between Cockerill and General Steam, the two lines advertising their sailings jointly.

The three original ships, *Rubis, Topaze* and *Saphir,* were very sturdily-

A number of civilians can be seen on deck of *Topaze* (1). The picture was taken in Rotterdam during the First World War in either July or September 1917. On both these occasions *Topaze* under command of Captain Pedro de la Rue was in the Dutch port to embark Belgian citizens who had taken refuge in the neutral Netherlands but had volunteered or had been called up to serve in the Belgian army. They were transported to the United Kingdom and later via France to the Belgian front. As the Netherlands wished to maintain a strict neutrality there were difficulties before the *Topaze* was given permission to leave the port. In July the vessel embarked some 200 passengers and in September about 100.

In mid-July 1905 the *Topaze* was involved in a serious accident which fortunately did not prove fatal. In thick fog she collided with the Dutch ferry *Koningin Regentes* (3,618/1894) and both vessels were badly damaged. Some of the 120 passengers on the *Koningin Regentes* were transferred to the *Prins Hendrik* (3,528/1890) which had come to assist, before the *Koningin Regentes*, with a badly damaged bow, returned to Flushing. The *Topaze* was badly damaged on the port side near the engine room and had to be repaired at the group's shipyard at Hoboken. *[Martijn Lindenborn]*

Only three vessels of the Tilbury fleet were bought second hand, the first of these being *Eméraude*. Although the three original vessels survived the First World War, the company directors thought it wise to add a fourth to act as a reserve. After looking for some time, they seized the opportunity to purchase the former Brazilian *Rio Pardo* (ex *San Lorenzo*, ex *Gaucho*) which had been captured by the Germans in 1915. During the German retreat in October 1918 she was scuttled but was later salvaged and became the property of the Belgian Government, later being bought and slowly rebuilt by John Cockerill. In November 1923 she had to return to the shipyard to repair serious damage sustained in a collision with the Danish steamer *Primula* (1,531/1896).

The *Eméraude* experienced the same chaos that many vessels endured in French ports during May and June 1940 but fortunately was in British waters at the time of the Belgian armistice. Transferred to the Ministry of Shipping she remained laid up at Tilbury until October, and then worked on the British coast for the rest of the war.

The year 1941 was a bad one for the *Eméraude* as she was involved in three major incidents. On 20th April 1941 during a voyage from Newport to Liverpool she collided with and sank the steam trawler *Ben Aden* (203/1918). A fortnight later she was seriously damaged in Liverpool when the steamer *Malakand* (7,649/1919) blew up whilst loaded with 7,000 tons of ammunition. On 9th September 1941 she stranded in Uig Bay and could be refloated eight days later only after jettisoning part of her cargo of sugar. Her bad luck continued even after her return to Belgian control as on 2nd July 1945 she sank after hitting a submerged wreck some eight miles off Ostend. *[Author's collection]*

built and after more than 30 years of intense use on a demanding cross-channel route they were still bearing the brunt of the service. However, it was obvious that they could not last forever. The reduction in orders at the group's shipyard in Hoboken in the early 1930s was seized on as an opportunity to order new tonnage, ships which became the company's first motor ships. They were built side-by-side as yard numbers 646 and 647. The first to join the fleet was the *Améthyste*, first of the name, on the 12th of February 1933, followed in June by the *Turquoise*, also the first in the fleet with this name. Both had two Burmeister and Wain-type diesel engines of 600 BHP built at Cockerill's own engine works at Seraing, giving a speed of 12.5 knots. The reduction in speed did not affect the service as over the years the vessels had become general cargo-vessels transporting all types of merchandise. A year after their delivery, and soon after the *Prince Baudouin* (3,050/1936, then the fastest motor vessel in the world) had been handed over for the Ostend to Dover service, the yard closed down for lack of orders. It was re-opened officially on 31st March 1936 by King Leopold II.

When the motor ships entered service two of the original trio, the *Rubis* and the *Topaze*, were laid up in reserve to replace vessels in maintenance or repairs. In September 1936 they were sold for scrap and broken up at Hendrik-Ido-Ambacht in the Netherlands. With the exception of the First World War, they served exclusively on the route and under the house flag of the company for which they were built. It was also in the first half of the 1930s that the company had its largest fleet, seven ships: the *Diamant,* of 1919, the *Eméraude* of 1920, the new *Améthyste* and *Turquoise* and the original trio *Saphir, Rubis and Topaze.*

The *Saphir,* the second vessel to enter service in 1897, was spared and remained in service. She survived the Second World War and lasted until 1952 when scrapped by Van Heyghen Frères in Ghent. As such she became the longest serving vessel in the history of the John Cockerill Line. The only modification she underwent in that period was re-engining in 1933. Together with the two new motor vessels she maintained the sailings on the route between Ostend and Tilbury while the *Diamant* and *Eméraude* ran the regular service between Antwerp and Tilbury.

Seen on the left of her older sister, *Turquoise* (1) was launched on 20th February 1934 by Mrs. Smal, wife of a director of John Cockerill's shipyard.

The *Turquoise* made headlines in the local press when on 27th January 1937 she stranded spectacularly on a breakwater for a couple of hours after missing the entrance to Ostend.

She had very similar wartime experiences to her sister, leaving Ostend on 17th May 1940 with 85 refugees and arriving two days later at Dieppe where she was bombed, shot at and robbed. Later scuttled, she was raised by the German occupiers who intended to use her to supply the Channel Islands. However, on 18th June 1942 during her very first voyage she was wrecked on the Calvados Rocks near Port en Bessin when pursued by British motor torpedo boats. *[Heemkundige Kring Hoboken; Hobuechen 1135]*

The *Améthyste* was the first of two sisters which began a new chapter in the history of the company as the first units with diesel engines. The two ships were designed by G. Dufour, later director of Compagnie Maritime Belge, but at the time an engineer at the shipyard of John Cockerill at Hoboken.

Although the top speed reached during trials on 6th January 1933 was 15.25 knots, the service speed of these twin diesel-engined vessels was 12.5 knots, sufficient to cover the distance between Ostend and Tilbury in the required nine hours. The shape of the hull meant that this speed could be maintained even in the most adverse weather conditions. *[Author's collection]*

Second World War

It all changed in the late summer of 1939, when once again war was declared between the United Kingdom, France and Germany. Belgium at first remained neutral but the Cockerill service was affected nevertheless. That changed completely with the German invasion of Belgium. Two of the five Cockerill vessels, the *Saphir* and *Eméraude*, were able to escape to Great Britain, the former being the last Belgian vessel to leave Ostend in May 1940. During the war they were managed from the Cockerill office in London. This agency, a daughter of the group, also managed a number of other Belgian coasters which had escaped and were working around the British Isles. Among other things the *Saphir* was used as a transport at the landings in Normandy in June 1944. Both the *Saphir* and the *Eméraude* survived the war in the service of the British Ministry of War Transport. Unfortunately, the *Eméraude* was lost after the hostilities in Europe had ended in a collision with the submerged wreck of the *Empire Path* (6,140/1943) off Ostend. Three members of the crew died in this accident.

The three other vessels of the fleet fell under German control. The oldest of this trio, the *Diamant* was seized at Saint Malo by the Germans at the end of their campaign in France. The ship was used as a transport but was lost on 20th September 1942 when she struck rocks and was wrecked near St. Helier on a voyage to Guernsey with stores for the occupyimg German army. She was the second former Cockerill vessel in German service to be lost within a period of three months through war causes. The other was the *Turquoise* wrecked on 18th June 1942.

The 1933-built *Turquoise* escaped from her home port on 17th May in company with her sister *Améthyste* and three requisitioned Belgian patrol vessels with instructions to go to Dieppe. Both Cockerill vessels also had fugitives on board, the families of the crew members. Aboard the *Améthyste* was also the Director of the Ostend Office, Capitaine Miroir and his family. After a very adventurous voyage with many difficulties the vessels arrived at Dieppe where they were berthed in the dock behind the locks. They experienced several bombing raids and the ship was vandalised by thieves whilst the crew hid from the bombing. As they were blocked behind the locks in the port there was no escape. On 9th June 1940 the ships were scuttled by the retreating French troops in Dieppe. They were raised by the Germans in 1941 and declared prizes after which they were engaged in transport work for the Organisation Todt and in supplying the occupied Channel Islands. The *Turquoise* did not last long as she was stranded and wrecked off Port en Bessin when chased by British motor torpedo boats.

The *Améthyste* lasted longer. She was scuttled for a second time in August 1944 during the German retreat from Saint Malo. Salvaged in September 1945, the badly damaged vessel was towed in January 1946 to the Cockerill shipyard in Hoboken to be rebuilt. The decision to undertake this work on a vessel normally considered to be beyond economic repair was taken because the line was desperately in need of tonnage. Indeed, when peace returned in the second half of 1945, there was only one vessel available, the oldest of the five at the start of the war, the *Saphir*. Thus, in contrast to the First World War when no ships were lost, Cockerill lost three vessels out of its 1940 fleet, with a fourth barely surviving. Moreover, the office building and the sheds at Ostend were severely damaged by an explosion on 15th August 1940 when ammunition stored there exploded accidentally.

Second fleet renewal

The reconstruction of the *Améthyste* did not proceed as smoothly as hoped and planned. For various reasons rebuilding took over two years so that the rejuvenated vessel made its first trip only on 11th May 1948.

To overcome the shortage of tonnage, Cockerill chartered two Belgian coasters, the *Nellie* (492/1938) and the *Julia* (549/1907), for a period of one year. At the same time

they were desperately looking for additional tonnage. As no adequate ships were found, in 1946 John Cockerill bought two former Royal Navy warships, the 'Flower' class corvette HMS *Kingcup* and the sloop HMS *Speedwell*. With the expertise of Cockerill's own shipyard the two vessels, both of which had remarkable war careers, were converted at Hoboken. They were put into service in the spring and the winter of 1947 respectively as the second *Rubis* and the second *Topaze*, reviving the names of two of the Belgian vessels which had inaugurated the service half a century before.

In the early 1950s the commercial name The John Cockerill Line (TJCL) was adopted by the shipping company although it was generally still known as the 'Tilbury Line' with its 'Tilbury ships'.

An important reorganization in 1952 saw Captain R. Campana, a former master of Cockerill vessels, promoted to Director of the group's shipping business in succession of Captain Miroir. Captain Campana was one of numerous seamen who had given many years of faithful service to the shipping company. Several of these recorded more than one thousand voyages and their names were well known and respected in the maritime world. Later Captain Campana became General Manager of the three Cockerill offices, at London, Antwerp and Ostend.

Campana's main task was to make the maritime division profitable once more. It was a huge task. While the rebuilding of the fleet had demanded much investment, the ships were nevertheless not ideally suited to the traffic. The *Saphir*, *Rubis* and *Topaze* were simply stop-gaps in anticipation of the complete renewal of the fleet. This could not be achieved at the group's own shipyard at Hoboken. Since the latter part of the 1940s the shipyard's order book had included large tankers, passenger ships and ocean-going cargo vessels booked for years ahead. As Hoboken could not deliver the projected coasters quickly, other possibilities had to be examined.

The management of the Maritime Division of Cockerill was able to obtain a small budget from head office and approval to order a single-hold, 'tween deck ship. Built at the Husumer Schiffswerft in the north-east German town with the same name, she joined the fleet in June 1953 as the second *Diamant*. This new vessel, the first of a series of almost identical ships, was to replace the *Saphir* of 1897 which, after intense service over 55 years, had been sold for scrap in Ghent during April 1952.

As the results obtained with the new *Diamant* were excellent, approval was obtained to order two further sisters from the same German yard. These vessels, the second *Saphir* and the third *Topaze*, were delivered on 28th May 1954 and 1st September 1954 respectively. They differed slightly from the preceding Husumer vessel, being one metre longer and equipped with a MAK engine of 800 BHP. At one time there were plans to convert the *Topaze* into a cattle carrier for a liner service between Ireland and Ostend but this was not pursued.

The new ships made it possible to part with the two converted warships. The former sloop *Topaze* was sold for scrap in May 1954 while the former corvette *Rubis* was sold to the Seismograph Service Ltd., of Keston, Kent which had the ship rebuilt as a seismic survey vessel at a shipyard in Vlaardingen Oost.

The management was very satisfied with the new ships and a further pair were ordered, again at Husum.

Illustrating the difficulty of finding suitable tonnage immediately after the Second World War, the 549 grt steam coaster *Julia* was already 40-years-old when chartered by Cockerill in 1947(top). She had started life as *Klippan* on delivery by Göteborgs M/V, which built her as yard number 294. After 14 years sailing without a change of name for various Swedish owners – with the exception of the last few months when she was transferred to the Norwegian flag – she reverted to the Swedish flag becoming the *Snöfrid* in 1921, *Dana* in 1929 and *Haneström III* in 1933. After severe stranding damage she was bought by the Danish owner Hans Svenningsen who renamed her *Teddy*. In 1939 she was acquired by Armement Belgica and renamed *Julia* under the Belgian flag. During the Second World War she worked on the UK coast until taken up for the Normandy landings. Carrying ammunition, the *Julia* was one of the first coasters to arrive in the United States sector. Formally handed back to her Belgian owners on the 5th of January 1946 she remained under their house flag until the autumn of 1948, although she was laid up in mid-May 1948 following the end of her charter to Cockerill.

However, she had a third spell of life spanning 25 years. After sale to a Greek owner fell through she became the property of the Belgian company Le Commerce des Produits d'Afrique

which operated her, first as *Julia* and from 1951 as *Nadine*, on relatively long voyages. In 1953 her steam engine was replaced by a diesel, but in November 1954 the owner was declared bankrupt whilst the vessel was in Genoa. She was bought by an Italian and for the last 18 years of her career sailed as *Alcamo*. On 2nd February 1973 the 66-year-old vessel struck rocks off Cape Rosso, Corsica and sprang a leak. A survey declared her a constructive total loss and in November 1973 she was sold to breakers at Baia. *[Author's collection]*

Replacing an almost identical vessel with the same name which had sunk soon after she was put into service in 1937, *Nellie* was delivered by J. Boel et Fils of Temse at the end of May 1938 (lower). A motor vessel measuring 54.0 by 8.87 metres, she had a gross tonnage of 500 and a deadweight of 620 tons.

Nellie managed to leave the Gironde just before the capitulation of the France and arrived at Falmouth on 24th June 1940. In Allied service around the British coast throughout the war, she returned to Belgium in July 1945 to resume short sea trading for Armement Alexander, from whom Cockeril chartered her. Shortly after an autumn 1953 sale to Transport Maatschappij Vola of Rotterdam she was rebuilt as a reefer and renamed *Zeehaan*, first under the Dutch flag but from December 1963 under the South African flag. In May 1978 she sprang a leak while under tow and sank on the 12th of that month in position 20.42 south, 12.46 east. *[Author's collection]*

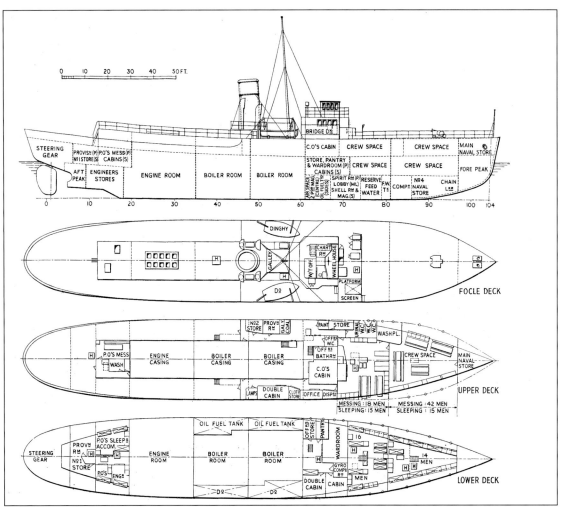

HMS *Kingcup*
(Roy Fenton
collection)

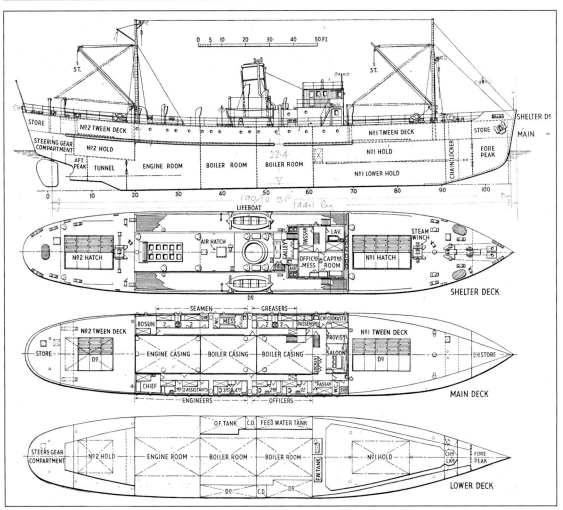

Rubis, formerly
HMS *Kingcup*.
[Roy Fenton
collection]

The *Topaze* (2) was also a former British warship, completed as HMS *Speedwell* in 1935 as one of the 'Halcyon' class minesweeping sloops. Originally based at Alexandria and attached to the Mediterranean fleet, she was later based at Devonport. In July 1938 she was placed in reserve at Sheerness but after the declaration of war resumed service and had a very busy and distinguished war career, being active in all theatres with the exception of the Far East. She initiated the sinking of *U 651*, and was one of the vessels which swept channels free of mines for ships participating in the invasion of Normandy.

At the end of 1945 she was again put into reserve and laid up at Harwich. She was acquired at the end of 1946 by John Cockerill, brought to the shipyard at Hoboken and converted into a merchant ship. After a year's work she entered the Tilbury service on 20th December 1947. A useful stopgap, but very expensive in operation, *Topaze* was sold for scrap in 1954 when new buildings for the company came on stream. *[Author's collection]*

The post-war modernisation of the Cockerill fleet began with the arrival of the second *Diamant* at Ostend on 23rd June 1953. Five days later she left the port on her maiden trip to Tilbury. This elegant coaster had been ordered from Husumer Schiffswerft because the group's own shipyard had a full order book and could not deliver on time. The first Cockerill vessel not built or converted at the group's own shipyard, she was also the first with accommodation aft. With just one hold the 'tween decker handled cargo with two derricks, one on the bow and another directly before the accommodation, each with a lifting capacity of two tons. She was the first of a series of five almost identical vessels, ordered in three batches. The *Diamant* was the only vessel of the first batch but the lead unit for the quintet.

Originally restricted to the services between Tilbury, Ostend and Antwerp, from 1956 *Diamant* served on the three regular services the company was operating and was also useful in one-off transport operations offered later in the company's existence. When the John Cockerill Line gave up its services in 1970, *Diamant* was laid up in the Demeydock in Ostend, becoming the first vessel to be sold on 20th August 1970. *[Author's collection]*

They were two metres longer than the *Diamant* and they had a refrigerated hold. The ships, the third *Rubis* and the second *Turquoise*, came into service at the end of November 1957 and July 1958. The latter was to be the last vessel to join the Cockerill fleet.

These last two fleet additions were registered after a major change in the group's structure had taken place. On 27th June 1955 the S.A. Société Cockerill merged with another important industrial group. S.A. Ougrée-Marihaye. to become Cockerill-Ougrée S.A. The immediate visible result was that the house flag changed slightly, with the C in the red panel changed to an O and, in the yellow panel the Cockerill logo replaced by that of the new group logo with underneath it the mottoes of both associated companies 'Courage to the last' and 'Summa Labore Summo'.

The modern ships provided an opportunity to broaden the range of cargoes carried. Whereas at the start of the service at the end of the nineteenth century, cargoes mainly comprised perishables and textiles, they became more varied as did the number of ports served: Volkswagen cars to the United Kingdom, wine from Rouen, British cars to the continent, steel from Antwerp to London, munitions from Zeebrugge to Felixstowe and Gravesend Reach to Zeebrugge. More ports were added to the schedule: London (Poplar Dock and Dagenham Dock for the Ford Factory), Shoreham, Sheerness, Rouen and later Rotterdam.

The ships were hard driven and the average distance sailed per year by these coasters was impressive.

1955: 23,980 miles per ship
1956: 24,402 miles per ship
1957: 25,482 miles per ship
1958: 25,811 miles per ship.

Although the ports served were not far apart, much of the navigation was at night and in all weathers. In this period some 83,000 tons of cargo were transported by this fleet of four (in 1958 five) vessels of which 27,000 tons were imported to Belgium and 56,000 tons exported.

The *Saphir* (2) was the lead ship
of the second batch ordered
from Husumer Schiffswerft. The
main differences from her older
sister ship were a MAK engine
of 800 BHP which gave her a
fraction more speed, an extra
metre in length and a higher
gross tonnage. Delivered on
28th May 1954 *Saphir* soon
settled into the daily routine
of the regular service, which
became more diverse when the
number of lines was increased
and the company's vessels
began to work on spot voyages.
　　　She had one major
mishap when she nearly sank
after a collision with an inland
waterway vessel in Antwerp.
Laid up in Ostend when the
company ceased trading on
30th June 1970, she was the
last to leave the fleet. *[Author's
collection]*

The third post-war new building,
Topaze (3) was the second of
the second batch from Husumer
Schiffswerft. After the Tilbury
service ceased she was also the
third to be sold, on 20th October
1970, after which she worked
mainly in the Mediterranean.
[Author's collection]

Named after the pioneer vessel
of the fleet, the *Rubis* (3) was
taken over from Husumer
Schiffswerft in November 1957
as the first of the third batch of
post-war orders. She differed
from the previous batch in being
one metre longer with an overall
length of 55.9 metres. The other
major modification was that
part of the hold was fitted to
transport cargo at temperatures
of -30°C. *[Author's collection]*

But the pace of development in shipping is fast and notwithstanding the new vessels it became more and more difficult to make a profit. A number of measures were taken including a reduction of the number of crew members in 1965, but a major expenditure, the maintenance of five teams, each of 17 dock workers, permanently employed at Tilbury was impossible to modify. Other initiatives taken were the opening of new liner services, such as a regular weekly link between Rouen and Shoreham in 1956.

If the service was only interrupted twice due to world wars, a third occasion must be added, for during the docker's strike at London in October 1954 the Cockerill vessels visited ports in the north of England and Scotland.

Plans to modify the structure of the fleet were not fulfilled because the management of the new group were not in favour. The Maritime Division was no longer considered part of their core business and this was reflected in the decision not to invest in new ships. Projects to have three larger vessels built at Husum were not acted on and nor did management positively consider ideas to have ro-ro or container feeder vessels built. The special Cockerill containers which the company had used for decades were not suited for feeder ships, and the line's vessels were not suited for modern, standard containers.

The five ships of the 1950s, *Diamant, Saphir, Topaze, Rubis* and *Turquoise*, were the last vessels of the company, which during its existence had owned a total of 14 ships.

The end of the line's existence was announced in June 1970. As from 1st July the 128 employees of the company (including crews of the vessels) were made redundant. But by June the ships were already laid up in Ostend awaiting sale. All were gradually disposed of in the second half of the year. The first to go was the *Diamant* on 20th August, 1970, followed on 18th September by the *Turquoise*, on 20th October by the *Topaze* and one day later by the *Rubis*. The last to be sold was the *Saphir* on 14th December 1970. All went for further trading which some of them did for another 20 years. So just before Christmas 1970 a story spanning 75 years had come to an end.

It seems strange that the last vessel to leave the Cockerill fleet was named after the second vessel which opened a regular daily service to Tilbury just short of three quarters of a century earlier. Over all these years the tradition of naming the vessels after gems was maintained for all vessels owned by The John Cockerill Line

The captain with the most recorded voyages on the Ostend/Antwerp-Tilbury service was Captain Pedro de la Rue, master of three vessels (*Topaze, Diamant* and again *Topaze*). Between 1st May 1897 and 28th February 1933 he made 2,794 voyages.

Between 1960 and 1970 the group – and as such the shipping division – had several names due to amalgamations but the shipping company was always known as The John Cockerill Line and the original motto of the Cockerill Group, 'Courage to the last', certainly applied.

The very last vessel to join the then 61-year-old Tilbury service, the *Turquoise* (2) is alongside the berth on the Scheldt which was used by the line until 1969. She was an exact sister ship to the *Rubis* (3) and used in the same trades and on the same regular services as the previous four vessels. As was the case 20 years earlier, it was again a *Turquoise* which gave the shipping division of Cockerill its fifth ship, the largest number in operation at one time. [*Author's collection*]

House flags
1897-1955: Belgian national flag – three vertical bands from hoist to fly black, yellow, red. In the black white letter S and in the red the white letter C. In the central yellow band the Cockerill shield with underneath the device 'Courage to the last'
1955-1970: Belgian national flag with in the black band the letter C in white and in the red the letter O in white. In the central yellow band the two shields of Cockerill and Ougrée, connected underneath by the devices of the two associated companies 'Courage to the last' and 'Summa Labore Summo'.

Funnel of Ostend services
Buff with black top.

Services operated
Ostend to Tilbury: daily except Saturday.
Antwerp to Tilbury: twice/three times a week, Wednesday and Saturdays, from 1920.
Rouen to Shoreham: weekly/twice weekly from November 1956.

The five vessels of the John Cockerill Line laid up in the Demeydock, Ostend after the company ceased operations on 30th June 1970. [Author's collection]

Fleet list

Note: the convention followed is not to note the ship's flag if it corresponds with the domicile of the owning company.

1. RUBIS (1) 1897-1936

633g 389n.
213.8 x 27.9 x 13.2 feet.
Two T. 3-cyl. by Société John Cockerill, Seraing driving twin screws; 142 NHP, 17 knots.
15.2.1897: Launched by Société John Cockerill, Hoboken (Yard No. 355) for John Cockerill, Antwerp as RUBIS.
18.5.1897: Maiden voyage to Tilbury under Captain Renier.
1910: Registered at Ostend.
1924: Register reverts to Antwerp.
9.1936: Sold via brokers Jacques Pierot & Zoon to N.V. Holland Scheepswerf en Machinehandel, Hendrik-Ido-Ambacht to be broken up, together with TOPAZE.

2. TOPAZE (1) 1897-1936

634g 389n.
213.8 x 27.9 x 13.2 feet.
Two T. 3-cyl. by Société John Cockerill, Seraing driving twin screws; 142 NHP, 17 knots.
1.5.1897: Launched by Société John Cockerill, Hoboken (Yard No. 356) for John Cockerill, Antwerp as TOPAZE.
13.7.1897: Arrived at Ostend from yard.
7. 1897: Maiden voyage to Tilbury under Captain P. De La Rue.
1897: Owner became S.A. John Cockerill, Antwerp
1910: Registered at Ostend.
1924: Register reverts to Antwerp.
9.1936: Sold via brokers Jacques Pierot & Zoon to N.V. Holland Scheepswerf en Machinehandel, Hendik-Ido-Ambacht to be broken up up together with RUBIS.

Rubis of 1897. [Roy Fenton collection]

Saphir (1). [World Ship Society Ltd.]

3. SAPHIR (1) 1897-1952

633g 389n 450d.
213.8 x 27.9 x 14.4 feet.
Two T. 3-cyl. by Société John Cockerill, Seraing driving twin screws; 139 NHP, 16 knots.
3.7.1897: Launched by Société John Cockerill, Hoboken (Yard No. 357).
2.9.1897: Maiden voyage to Tilbury.

1910: Registered at Ostend.
1924: Register reverts to Antwerp.
1933: Re-engined.
5.1940: Last vessel to leave Ostend.
1940-1945: In allied service for the Ministry of War Transport, London.
6.1944: Participated in Normandy landings.
31.3.1952: Sold for scrap.

4.4.1952: Left Ostend in tow of ZEELEEUW (163/1932) for Ghent to be broken up by Van Heyghen Frères.

4. DIAMANT (1) 1920-1940
715g 401n.
213.2 x 27.9 x 13.2 feet.
Two T. 3-cyl. by S.A. John Cockerill, Seraing; 71 NHP, 18.5 knots maximum, 16.5 knots service.
4.10.1919: Launched by S.A. John Cockerill, Hoboken (Yard No. 554).
1.1920: Maiden voyage to Tilbury.
1924: Registered at Antwerp.
25.5.1940: Left Tilbury on Admiralty orders.
4.6.1940: Arrived at Saint Malo.
18.6.1940: Abandoned by crew after they damaged the engines.
21.6.1940: Seized by the Germans.
20.8.1940: Declared a prize by German court. In service to Channel Islands.
20.9.1942: Struck rocks and wrecked near St. Hélier, Jersey in heavy weather whilst on a voyage from France to Guernsey with military stores. Five of the German crew were lost.

5. EMÉRAUDE 1920-1945
613g 297n.
195.4 x 28.9 x 13.0 feet.
T. 3-cyl. by North Eastern Marine Engineering Co. Ltd., Sunderland; 158 NHP, 9 knots.
18.11.1903: Launched by Craig, Taylor and Co., Stockton-on-Tees (Yard No. 99).
12.1903: Completed for L. Carsoglio & Co., Buenos Aires, Argentina as SAN LORENZO.
1909: Sold to Durisch & Co. Ltd., Rio de Janeiro, Brazil and renamed GAUCHO.
1912: Sold to Empreza Braziliara de Navegacion, Rio de Janeiro and renamed RIO PARDO.
1916: Sold to L. Lorentzen, Rio de Janeiro.
8.12.1916: Captured by a German torpedo boat whilst on a voyage from Rotterdam to London with general cargo. Taken to Zeebrugge and condemned by prize court.
5.10.1918: Scuttled by the retreating Germans at Zeebrugge.
1919: From February to September refloated by Smit & Co., Rotterdam and taken to Zeebrugge.
6.11.1919: Condemned as a prize, the Belgian Government became the owners despite a protest by a Norwegian insurance company on behalf of the previous owners.
19.7.1920: Acquired by S.A. John Cockerill, Ostend for 618,000 BF and subsequently sent to Hoboken for rebuilding.
4.1921: Renamed EMÉRAUDE.
1924: Registered in Antwerp.
7.6.1940: Arrived at Tilbury.
15.6.1940: Transferred to the Ministry of Transport (later Ministry of War Transport), London though only requisitioned on 24.6.1940. Remained idle at Tilbury until 20.10.1940 then put into the coastal service around Great Britain.
7.6.1945: Arrived at Ghent as first Belgian port after the war.
2.7.1945: Sunk in position 51.22 north, 02.50 east following a collision with the wreck of the EMPIRE PATH (6,140/1943) which had sunk after striking a mine on 24.12.1944. Two crew and one passenger were lost but 22 crew and four passengers were rescued by the United States steamer LAWRENCE J. BRENGLE (7,209/1944).
9.1960: Wreck dispersal began by Ackermans & van Haaren.
20.12.1960: Dispersal completed.

Bids for the salvaged RIO PARDO opened on 24.6.1920. The highest bid of 587,500 BF was put in by Jean Goossens of Armement Marcel Goossens & Co., Antwerp, but this was withdrawn on 5.7.1920.

6. AMÉTHYSTE 1933-1940/1948-1959
810g 448n.
178.4 x 35.6 x 15.5 feet.
Two 4SCSA 8-cyl. Burmeister & Wain-type oil engines by John Cockerill S.A., Seraing driving twin screws; 260 NHP, 15.2 knots on trials, 12.5 knots in service.
24.9.1932: Launched by S.A. John Cockerill, Hoboken (Yard No. 646) for John Cockerill Maritime Division, Ostend.
6.1.1933: Ran trials.
12.2.1933: Left on maiden voyage.
9.6.1940: Scuttled at Dieppe.
1941: Raised by the Germans and repaired by Société des Forges et Chantiers de la Méditerranée, Le Havre. Used to supply the Channel Islands.
7.8.1944: Scuttled in Bouvet Dock, Saint Servan-sur-Mer (near St. Malo).
26.8.1945: Raised and berthed.
2.1.1946: Left Saint Servan-sur-Mer in tow of ZEELEEUW (163/1932).
14.1.1946: Arrived at Hoboken to be rebuilt.
11.5.1948: Returned to service.
1.3.1959: Sold to Greek Atlantic Fishing (Constantin Diamantis), Piraeus, Greece and renamed ARKADIA.
1971: Broken up in Greece.

7. TURQUOISE (1) 1933-1942
810g 446n.
178.4 x 35.6 x 15.5 feet.
Two 4SCSA 8-cyl. Burmeister & Wain-type oil engines by S.A. John Cockerill, Seraing driving twin screws; 260 NHP, 12.5 knots service speed.
20.2.1933: Launched by S.A. John Cockerill, Hoboken (Yard No. 647) for John Cockerill Maritime Division, Ostend as TURQUOISE.
24.5.1933: Ran trials.
29.5.1933: Maiden arrival at Ostend.
27.1.1937: Stranded in dense fog off Ostend.
17.5.1940: Left Ostend with 85 refugees.

Améthyste on 7th June 1958. *[World Ship Society Ltd.]*

18.5.1940: Arrived Dieppe where she was later damaged on several occasions by gunfire and aircraft bombs.
9.6.1940: Scuttled in Dieppe by French armed forces.
1941/1942: Raised by Germans and repaired at the Société des Forges et Chantiers de la Méditerranée, Le Havre. Used to supply the Channel Islands.
18.6.1942: Stranded and wrecked six miles off Port en Bessin when chased by British motor torpedo boats.

8. RUBIS (2) 1947-1954
1,023g, 380n.
189.7 x 34.5 x 23.2 feet.
1954: 1,056g, 352n.
205.0 x 33.2 x 16.0 feet.
T. 4-cyl. by Harland and Wolff, Belfast; 2,700 IHP, 16 knots.
19.9.1939: Ordered
19.7.1940: Laid down.
31.10.1940: Launched.
30.12.1940: Commissioned.
3.1.1941: Completed by Harland and Wolff, Belfast (Yard No. 1076) for the Royal Navy as the 'Flower' class corvette HMS KINGCUP (K33).
31.7.1946: Sold.
1946: Acquired by John Cockerill Maritime Division and converted into a merchant ship by S.A. John Cockerill, Hoboken.
30.4.1947: Maiden arrival at Ostend as RUBIS.
28.8.1954: Belgian register closed on sale to Seismograph Services Ltd., Keston, Kent.
8.1954: Left Ostend for Vlaardingen-Oost where rebuilt as the seismic survey vessel SEISLIM.
5.1959: Towed to the Netherlands to be broken up.

9. TOPAZE (2) 1947-1954
1,032g 485n 1,532d.
53.77 x 8.20 x 3.57 metres.
C. 6-cyl.by William Beardmore and Co. Ltd., Dalmuir driving twin screws; 885 BHP, 1,747 IHP.
2.3.1934: Ordered.
20.6.1934: Laid down.
21.3.1935: Launched by William Hamilton and Co. Ltd., Port Glasgow (Yard No. 419).
30.9.1935: Completed for the Royal Navy as the 'Halcyon' class fast minesweeping sloop HMS SPEEDWELL (J87).
12.1946: Acquired by John Cockerill Maritime Division and converted by S.A. John Cockerill, Hoboken into a merchant ship.

20.12.1947: Entered service as TOPAZE under Belgian flag.
11. 5.1954: Sold to Arie Rijsdijk & Zonen, Alblasserdam, Netherlands.
14.11.1955: Demolition began.

10. DIAMANT (2) 1953-1970
565g 348n (British rules); 545g 404n (Belgian rules).
50.81 x 8.96 x 3.50 metres.
4SCSA 8-cyl. MAK by Maschinenbau Kiel A.G., Kiel, West Germany; 760 BHP, 11.5 knots.
16.5.1953: Launched by Husumer Schiffswerft, Husum, West Germany (Yard No. 1046) for John Cockerill Maritime Division, Ostend as DIAMANT.
22.6.1953: Ran trials.
26.6.1953: Arrived at Ostend from Husum.
28.6.1953: Left on maiden voyage.
20.8.1970: Sold to Continental Trading and Shipping (Liberia) Ltd., Monrovia, Liberia as GAETAN.
1971: Sold to Ship Investment Co. Inc, Panama (Fratelli Cosulich, Trieste, Italy) as SICADRIA.
1973: Renamed DAVID.
1974: Sold to Prudential Shipping Co., Famagusta, Cyprus and renamed MAPI.

1975: Sold to Cotransin Shipping Co., Limassol, Cyprus and renamed JOY.
1977: Sold to Rosalina Shipping Inc., Panama and renamed WHITE.
1979: Sold to Maligax S.A., Panama and renamed ARGO I.
1987: Renamed FLORIDA and transferred to Honduras flag.
1987: Sold to A. Fahel and H. Uamak (Fayza Shipping Co. Ltd.), San Lorenzo, Honduras and renamed REDA ALLAH.
1987: Renamed MAHLER.
1990: Sold to Amnah Abdul Rahman Douli and Khairieh Adul Kader Shehadad, Lattakia, Syria and renamed KHALED.
1992: Sold to Faten Mohamed Karroum and Abdelkarim Ahman Al Zaghir, Lattakia as AL AKRAMIN.
2001: Deleted from 'Lloyd's Register' as continued existence in doubt.

Diamant (2) on 22nd July 1953 (above) and on 12th July 1965 (below) by which time her derricks have been removed and her hatches raised (below). *[Above: L.A.Sawyer/ Roy Fenton collection, below: World Ship Society Ltd.]*

11. SAPHIR (2) 1954-1970
540g 382n 666d (summer).
54.70 x 8.20 x 3.56 metres.
4SCSA 8-cyl. oil engine by Maschinenbau Kiel A.G., Kiel, West Germany; 800 BHP, 12.75 knots (trials).
10.4.1954: Launched by Husumer Schiffswerft, Husum, West Germany (Yard No. 1060) for John Cockerill Maritime Division, Ostend as SAPHIR.
28.5.1954: Delivered.
31.5.1954: Maiden voyage.
14.12.1970: Sold to S.A. Godemar, Panama and renamed CHRISTINA K.
1980: Sold to Mohamed Benmoussa, Agadir, Morocco as SALAH EDDINE.
2002: Deleted from 'Lloyd's Register' as continued existence in doubt.

12. TOPAZE (3) 1954-1970
540g 384n 664d.
54.70 x 8.20 x 3.56 metres.
4SCSA 8-cyl. by Maschinenbau Kiel A.G., Kiel, West Germany; 800 BHP, 12 knots.
24.7.1954: Launched by Husumer Schiffswerft, Husum, West Germany (Yard No. 1061) for John Cockerill Maritime Division, Ostend as TOPAZE.
1.9.1954: Delivered.
3.9.1954: Maiden voyage.
20.10.1970: Sold to S.A. Godemar, Panama and renamed ANGELIKI K.
1972: Sold to Union de Transportes

Saphir (2). *[William A. Schell]*

Maritimes S.A., Panama and renamed FRANK.
1975: Sold to Fides Shipping Co. Ltd., Limassol, Cyprus and renamed STEPHY.
1996: Deleted from 'Lloyd's Register' as continued existence in doubt.

13. RUBIS (3) 1957-1970

560g 416n 620d (summer).
55.90 x 8.20 x 3.57 metres.
8-cyl. 4SCSA oil engine by Maschinenbau Kiel A.G., Kiel, West Germany; 800 BHP, 13 knots.
5.10.1957: Launched by Husumer Schiffswerft, Husum, West Germany (Yard No. 1114) for S.A. Cockerill-Ougrée, Antwerp as RUBIS
13.11.1957: In service.
20.10.1970: Sold to Compania Naviera Utrecht S.A., Panama and renamed VIRGO.
1971: Sold to P.T. Perusahaan Pelayaran Nusantara Kalimantan (Kalimantan Shipping Co.), Djakarta, Indonesia and renamed DINY.
5.2.1984: Arrived at Djakarta to be broken up.

14. TURQUOISE (2) 1958-1970

560g 416n 627d (summer).
55.90 x 8.20 x 3.57 metres.
4SCSA 8-cyl. oil engine by Maschinenbau Kiel A.G., Kiel, West Germany; 800 BHP, 13 knots.
3.5.1958: Launched by Husumer Schiffswerft, Husum, West Germany (Yard No. 1116) for S.A. Cockerill-Ougrée, Antwerp as TURQUOISE.
3.7.1958: Entered service
18.9.1970: Left Ostend following sale to Compania Naviera Utrecht S.A., Panama (Maritiem Bureau J.E. Brave, Amsterdam, Netherlands) and renamed TORO.
1973: Sold to P.T. Perusahaan Pelayaran Nusantara Kalimantan (Kalimantan Shipping Co.), Djakarta, Indonesia as FENNY.
1986: Renamed FEDI and transferred to Panama flag.
1988: Renamed JARRBT and transferred to Honduras flag.
1990: Renamed ANGKOR I.
1991: Renamed SOON LY.
10.9.1991: Reported sunk off the Vietnamese coast whilst on a voyage from Singapore to Phnom Penh.

Topaze (3). [William A. Schell]

Rubis (3). [William A. Schell]

Turquoise (2). [World Ship Society Ltd.]

THE TAXONOMY OF A CONVOY DISASTER: THE SHIPS OF SC.7, OCTOBER 1940

Malcolm Cooper

Merchant ship losses in the Battle of the Atlantic are a feature of most shipping company histories and fleet lists. The work of mercantile and naval historians, however, has not always overlapped, with the result that the losses have not always been placed in the wider context of the campaign. This piece seeks to provide colour for one part of this picture, its focus being the ships which sailed in convoy SC.7 in October 1940, a convoy which was destined to experience one of the highest loss rates of the entire Battle.

The Battle of the Atlantic in the autumn of 1940

Through the first year of the Second World War, U-boat operations in the North Atlantic were largely conducted against vessels sailing outside of the convoy system. Westbound, ships were only convoyed for the first four or five days after which they were deemed to be out of the main U-boat danger area. At this stage, the convoy itself dispersed and its escorts re-deployed to meet incoming eastbound convoys. U-boats generally attacked vessels too slow to meet the nine knots' speed requirement of these OB convoys, although there were occasions on which they picked off single ships soon after convoy dispersals. Eastbound ships were convoyed for the entire Atlantic passage, the first HX convoy sailing from Halifax, Nova Scotia on 16th September 1939. These too were restricted to vessels which could maintain the designated convoy speed of nine knots. Slower vessels were forced to sail independently, and losses were heavy, with the result that a separate series of slow eastward convoys was started in August 1940. These SC convoys, with an initial minimum speed of seven and a half knots sailed from Sydney, Cape Breton, except in the winter months when ice displaced them to Halifax.

By this time, the extent of the challenge facing the Allies on the ocean trade routes was becoming clear. British merchant shipping losses (excluding vessels commissioned in the Royal Navy) for the three months June through August had reached 776,000 gross tons. When Allied shipping losses were added, the figure grew to just over 1.2 million gross tons. To put this in context, the War Cabinet had been forced to reduce the annual domestic mercantile building target from 1.5 to 1.1 million tons due to a combination of steel and labour shortages, the loss of heavy machinery forgings from Scandinavian, Dutch and Belgian shipyards, the increased need for repair work, and the rapid acceleration of naval building. The addition of the mercantile marines of new Allies, particularly Norway and the Netherlands, and the seizure of a significant portion of Italian deep-sea tonnage did compensate for losses, but this was a one-time boost as on-going war losses could not be replaced at shipyards now in enemy hands. Finally, the combination of the closure of the Mediterranean and the Baltic, the necessity to seek new sources for imports far from Europe, the increase in imports to support war industries, and the delays inherent in the convoy system, meant that a far greater reservoir of merchant shipping was required to meet increased carrying requirements.

Although the frequency and effectiveness of individual enemy submarine attacks on convoys had both begun to increase in the summer, the first large-scale convoy battle did not take place until 21st to 22nd September 1940, when five U-boats sank 11 ships from convoy HX.72. There were only eight non-British ships in this convoy, but the balance was changing, with the proportion of Allied, Neutral and Ministry of Shipping acquisitions increasing, particularly in the slower SC convoys. SC.3, which was arriving in the U.K. just as the attack on HX.72 was developing, included no fewer than 18 Norwegian vessels, as well as six ex-foreign ships recently acquired by the Ministry of Shipping, and five Greek, one Dutch and one Finnish vessels. Two other trends, reflective of the need to muster tonnage from a wide range of sources, and of the extent to which more vulnerable vessels were concentrated in the new slow convoys, involved the size and age profiles of SC.3. Of the 48 ships assigned, 21 were vessels of less than 2,000 tons which would not normally have been involved in Atlantic trading; while no fewer than 25 ships were more than 20 years old, 10 of them having been built before the First World War. The first six SC convoys suffered steady attrition. SC.5 and SC.6 were not attacked, but the other four lost a total of 16 merchant ships, plus two naval escorts. These losses were the result of incursions by single U-boats. The picture was to change completely when SC.7 entered the eastern Atlantic.

SC.7 convoy composition – age, nationality and size

Exactly half of the ships involved with SC.7 (18 out of 36) had been built either during or before the First World War. Only four of the nine war-built ships had come from U.K. yards, the remainder coming from five different countries: Denmark, Germany, Japan, Norway and the United States. Of the nine pre-1914 vessels, the small Norwegian tanker *Thoroy* was easily the oldest, having originally been built on the Tyne as *Snowflake* for C.T. Bowring and Co. away back in 1893. The next oldest vessels, the tiny timber-carriers *Sneffield* of 1901 and *Havorn* of 1902, also flew the Norwegian flag. Due to their age, some of the older vessels had compiled decidedly convoluted career histories. Perhaps the most striking of these was that of the 1912-built *Creekirk*. Originally built on the Clyde as *Mariston* for William S. Miller of Glasgow, she was sold to Romanian owners after less than two years and entered the First World War as the *Milcovul*. Confined to the Black Sea by the war, she was requisitioned by the Imperial Russian Navy for service as a transport before being captured by advancing German forces at Sevastopol in 1918. Returned to her owners after the end of the war, she served them until 1933, when she changed owners, flag and name, re-emerging as the Greek *Hyphaestos*. In 1938, her career took its final and in some ways most peculiar twist, in the process reversing the common pattern of aged British vessels making their way to the Greek flag. Although she was now 26 years old, she returned to the British flag as *Creekirk* following purchase by Muir Young Ltd. of London.

Most of the remainder of the ships had been built in the 1920s, but three had been completed in 1930, and two British tramps in 1936. The newest, and arguably the most valuable, vessel in the convoy was the motor tanker *Languedoc* of 1937. Ocean-going tramps tended to be spread indiscriminately between HX and SC convoys; there were, for example, 17 British ones in the larger HX.79 which was crossing the Atlantic just behind SC.7, and there were three established operators, Ropner of West Hartlepool, Seager of Cardiff, and Nisbet of Glasgow with ships in each. The presence of the 1936-built tramp *Shekatika* (which had a design speed of 10¾ knots) in SC.7 was in fact the result of her being unable to keep up with a faster HX convoy. Whatever the case with the newer tramps, it is very difficult to understand why a three-year old motor tanker like the *Languedoc* with a design speed of 11 knots should have been consigned to a slow convoy. Britain had been relatively short of tankers at the beginning of the war, and although the addition of the large and modern Norwegian tanker fleet had partially re-set the balance, tankers were priority targets for U-boats and they thus represented an endangered strategic resource which should have been accorded the highest degree of protection.

Moving from the convoy's age to its nationality profile, 21 of the 36 ships involved flew the Red Ensign, of which four were owned by the Ministry of Shipping, one by the Board of Trade, and three by Canadian concerns, leaving 13 in the hands of domestic private sector operators. Of the 15 foreign ships, eight were operated by allied governments in exile: six being Norwegian and two Dutch. The other vessels – four Greek and three Swedish – were neutrals operating under charter from Britain. As far as ownership was concerned, this was a fair cross-section of the non-liner tonnage available in the North Atlantic in the last quarter of 1940. Of the European countries already overrun by Axis forces, only Belgium and Poland were not represented for, as we shall see, neither French nor Danish ships continued to fly their own colours. Non-European tonnage did not tend to operate in the North Atlantic theatre at this stage of the war. One other overall categorization is worth making. No fewer than 14 ships, more than a third of the convoy, were under 300 feet long, four flying the Red Ensign, and all six Norwegian, both Dutch and two of the three Swedish vessels. Of these, eight only measured 250 to 270 feet, the smallest vessels being the Norwegian *Havorn* at 1,527 gross tons and the Swedish *Gunborg* at 1,572 gross tons.

British Government-owned tonnage
It is only when we look beneath these age, nationality and size profiles, that the fascinating detail of SC.7's composition emerges. Starting with the 21 ships flying the Red Ensign, we begin with the four vessels operated for the Ministry of Shipping, each of which was representative of a different 1940 source of emergency tonnage. The oldest, the *Empire Brigade*, was the second convoy participant to have returned to the British flag. Built in 1912 as the *Hannington Court*, she had been sold to Italian owners in the 1930s and renamed *Elios*, but had been seized at Newcastle-on-Tyne when Italy entered the war. The other vessel to adopt Government nomenclature was the *Empire Miniver*, a product of the United States' Government's large First World War building programme. During 1940, the United Kingdom bought 92 old cargo vessels in the United States, 56 from private owners and 36 out of long-term lay-up from the United States

Maritime Commission. The *Empire Miniver*, built in 1918 as the *West Cobalt*, was one of the former, being purchased from Lykes Brothers.

The other two Ministry of Shipping vessels were the ex-Danish *Flynderborg* and the ex-French *Languedoc*. Poland, Norway, the Netherlands, and Belgium had all formed governments-in-exile and set up organizations to manage their tonnage under their own flag with their own crews on charter to Britain. Greece and Yugoslavia would follow suit in 1941 after Axis conquest. In the case of both Denmark and France, however, the home governments had surrendered and had no equivalent representation in the United Kingdom. To ensure control of ships caught in British ports or on the high seas, the United Kingdom Government had seized all Danish and French tonnage, operating it on the same basis as it did vessels either purchased by or built for the Ministry of Shipping, although usually retaining their original crews. Unlike other ships operated for the Ministry of Shipping, these vessels did not adopt *Empire* nomenclature, retaining their own names, but adding the suffix -II if there was already a ship of the same name on the British register. The *Flynderborg* had been caught in a Norwegian port when Germany attacked in April 1940. She had first been taken over for war service by the Norwegian Government, but sailed for the United Kingdom when she was threatened by the enemy's northward advance. She was finally taken over by the Ministry of Shipping at Newcastle-on-Tyne in August 1940. The tanker *Languedoc* was in the Caribbean when France left the war. She was intercepted by the Royal Navy off Curacao in July and taken into Trinidad where she was entered in the British registry on the last day of August. While a British master was appointed, she retained her original French crew, and the Chief Officer was the only other man aboard who could speak English.

A fifth ship was also under Government ownership, although she had been purchased before the war began. One of the provisions of The British Shipping (Assistance) Bill of 1939 – a piece of legislation largely concerned with subsidizing flagging new building by British ship owners – had been the provision of £2,000,000 to purchase British flag vessels and maintain them in reserve for emergency use. In the event, only four ships had been purchased by the Board of Trade before the scheme was overtaken by the outbreak of war. These were all at least 20 years old, and a typically uninspired Whitehall exercise in imagination produced the unfortunately named *Botavon* (built 1912), *Botwey* (1916), *Botlea* (1917) and *Botusk* (1919). The last of these, built as W.J. Tatem's *Molton*, and purchased as the *Transit,* sailed with SC.7, still under nominal Board of Trade ownership, but operated for the Ministry of Shipping under Reardon Smith management.

Under the Red Ensign – commercial operators
Of the other 16 British vessels, 12 were deep-sea tramps. Together, they represented a fair cross-section of the industry. The only pre-First World War ship was the London-registered *Creekirk* which we have already covered. Three more had been built in 1917 or 1918, and all were registered in north east England, Stag Line's *Clintonia* at North Shields, Hall Brothers' *Trident* at Newcastle-on-Tyne, and Ropner's *Sedgepool* at West Hartlepool. Five more had been built during the 1920s, the *Beatus* of 1925 and the *Fiscus* of 1928, both owned by W.H. Seager of Cardiff; Rowland and

Marwood's 1923-built *Scoresby* of Whitby; the *Corinthic* of 1924, originally built for Cockerline of Hull but now owned by Hartley Cooper and Co. of London; and George Nisbet's Glasgow-registered *Blairspey* of 1929. The final three were built in the 1930s, Ropner's second contribution to the convoy, the *Somersby* in 1930; and two post-Depression buildings in 1936, the *Shekatika* owned by Christian Salvesen of Leith, and the *Carsbreck* owned by William Honeyman of Glasgow.

The British liner sector contributed one rather eccentric vessel. Ellerman and Papayanni's *Assyrian* had been built in Germany in 1914 as the twin-screw motor ship *Fritz*. Handed over as a war reparation, she had been converted to steam propulsion several years after entering the Ellerman Group. Although she was aged, and at 2,960 tons a bit on the small side, she was chosen as the Commodore Ship for SC.7 because her relatively extensive passenger facilities could accommodate the Commodore and his staff.

The remaining three ships were Canadian rather than British. Although all had been built in the U.K., the *Winona* of 1906, the *Trevisa* of 1915, and the considerably more modern *Eaglescliffe Hall* of 1928 were all freshwater bulk cargo carriers, which normally operated on North America's Great Lakes and associated canal systems, coming no closer to the ocean than the St. Lawrence River. Their presence in the North Atlantic in late 1940 was the result of mass chartering by the U.K. for service in home coastal waters. Their original crews had been laid off at Montreal, where they were replaced by British crews from the Government-controlled Pool. While these Lakers were well suited to the British coastal trade, getting them across the ocean was much more of a challenge. It was entirely reflective of their limited seaworthiness that one of those assigned to SC.7 would turn back, while the other two straggled.

Clintonia at Bristol. [Bristol Series/J. and M. Clarkson]

The Allies – Norway and the Netherlands

The foreign component of the convoy was contributed by two Allies and two Neutrals. The largest was Norwegian, but while the size of the contingent was reflective of the overall size of the Norwegian merchant marine, its composition was not. Norway was one of the world leaders in the introduction of modern diesel-powered sea-going tonnage, but the six ships which sailed with SC.7 were all relatively small steamers which would normally have been more at home in the Baltic, North Sea or other short-sea/coastal trades. The presence of the convoy's three oldest ships, the *Thoroy* of 1893, the *Snefjeld* of 1901, and the *Havorn* of 1902 has already been noted. The remainder were all getting on in years, the *Karlander* having been built in 1914, the *Inger Elisabeth* in 1920, and the *Sneland I* in 1922. Every one of these ships were small, all being less than 300 feet long and four under 2,000 gross tons. While their size and age made them unlikely participants in trans-Atlantic voyages, they appear to have been well-found vessels. At least two, the *Karlander* and the *Sneland I*, had been trading in the Caribbean and on the United States east coast at the outbreak of hostilities, and the *Snefjeld* had already made one successful eastwards Atlantic passage with HX.61 in July-August 1940.

The other Allied power to contribute ships was the Netherlands, represented by the *Soesterberg* of 1927 and the *Boekelo* of 1930. While they were more modern than their Norwegian equivalents, they were no larger, both being significantly less than 300 feet long and designed for the north European short-sea trades. As was the case with Norway, the Dutch presence was not reflective of the overall composition of the country's merchant marine. In this case, however, the largest component of the fleet was made up of cargo liners, which, because of their size and speed, would not normally have been consigned to slow seven-knot convoys.

Somersby. [J. and M. Clarkson]

The neutrals – Greece and Sweden

There were seven neutral vessels in SC.7, four from Greece and three from Sweden. The Greek component came from what might be termed the lower end of the country's large deep-sea tramp fleet. All four vessels were owned by small operators, all were veterans of the previous world war, and three had been involved at some stage in a British corporate collapse. The newest vessel, the *Thalia* of 1917, was one of the 20 ships acquired by the Shipping Controller from Japanese builders, in this case as *War Lion*. The *Thalia* had served the Royal Mail Group subsidiary Elder Dempster as *Jebba*, before financial collapse triggered a mass sale of tonnage in 1932 and 1933, most of it to Greek buyers. The second youngest Greek vessel, the *Aenos* of 1910, was also the survivor of a British corporate failure, in this case coming from the insolvent Nautilus Steam Shipping Company as *Cedar Branch* in 1932. She was one of the most easily recognizable ships to sail in SC.7 because of the archaic bow-sprit which her builders Bartram of Sunderland had been fond of attaching to their ships in the years before the First World War. Of the two oldest vessels, the 1906-built *Dioni* had the more tortuous past. Built in Germany as the *Asgard*, she had been seized by Russia in 1914 and returned to her owners in 1918, only to be taken over by the Shipping Controller. She then went to the Greek Government before passing successively to two small private sector owners, changing names as she went. By contrast, the *Niritos* of 1907 had only flown two flags, but her career too had seen its share of drama. Originally the *Maylands* of a West Hartlepool owner, she had been one of the early purchases of Edgar Edwards' highly speculative Western Counties Shipping Company, following the latter's normal nomenclature to become *Maymead*. After Edwards' mortgagees foreclosed on him in 1922, she was re-sold to Walter Runciman at a fraction of her earlier cost, sailing as *Islemoor* for five years before joining the Greek flag.

The most notable of the three Swedish contributions was the 1917-built twin-screw *Valparaiso* of Stockholm's Johnson Line. One of the first generation of sea-going motor vessels, she featured the distinctive profile of her class, with a straight stem, counter stern, superstructure three-quarters aft, three raked masts and small exhaust pipes running along the aft mast in place of a funnel. She was part of a series of ten very successful near-sisters, two of which remained in service into the 1960s, and a third only going to the breakers in 1980 after 66 years in commission, the first 48 of them with her original Burmeister & Wain engines. In contrast, the other two Swedish ships, the *Convallaria* of 1921 and the *Gunborg* of 1930, were small short-sea traders, similar in size and design to those flying the Norwegian and Dutch flags.

Cargoes for war

If the composition of the convoy was reflective of the state of the Battle of the Atlantic in the last quarter of 1940, so too was the cargo it carried. Three bulk commodities formed the basis of the mixture of materials most frequently consigned to tramp tonnage. The first of these was wood products, particularly timber, pit props and pulpwood. No fewer than 17 vessels, including all the smaller Norwegian, Swedish, Dutch and Canadian ships were loaded with wood products. Another three ships carried part cargoes of wood products combined with smaller amounts of steel. Steel, scrap, pig iron and iron ore made up the full cargoes of another five

ships, while the third core commodity, grain, was carried by another three. Leaving aside the two tankers, the remainder of the convoy was carrying general cargo (three ships), sulphur (two) and flour (one).

In every case, the dependence on supplies from across the Atlantic had increased sharply in the first year of the war. Wood products had always been the major product from Canada's east coast ports, but the United Kingdom's wartime loss of traditional import supplies from Scandinavia and the Baltic had made it much more heavily dependent on these. The German conquest of Norway and Denmark had also shut down imports of Swedish iron ore either through Narvik or via the Kattegat and Skagerrak. Similarly, all steel imports from continental Europe had been lost; all this at a time when the rapid growth of warship, merchant ship, aircraft, tank and vehicle production had completely out-stripped the capacity of the domestic steel industry. In the last case, Britain's dependence on imported cereals had already been heavy, but the U-boat threat meant that grain ships from South America and further afield would join those from North America on the convoy routes.

The nature of the cargo carried could have a profound effect on the fate of a ship if it was torpedoed. At worst, a cargo of wood might slow down the rate at which a vessel sank after being torpedoed, a factor of great importance to smaller vessels with no realistic chance of surviving any such strike. At best, the cargo would keep a ship afloat and allow it to reach port either under tow or its own steam. At the other end, steel or iron ore could be a death warrant for crews. With little reserve buoyancy, torpedoed ships often sank in under two to three minutes, giving no time for those below to reach deck or those better placed to launch boats or rafts.

The naval protagonists

Before proceeding with the analysis of the convoy action itself, it is worth touching briefly on the naval escort and its German opponents. At this stage of the war, there were no permanently formed escort groups, vessels being assigned individually to convoys as they became available. There was normally only one Royal Navy ship assigned to cover each full eastward crossing, but it would be reinforced as it approached the danger area of the North-Western Approaches (normally between 15 and 20 west latitude) by ships which had escorted westbound convoys out to the point where they were dispersed. In the autumn months of 1940 there were very few destroyers assigned to the Atlantic escort forces, most of those not deployed on fleet duties being on anti-invasion watch in the south. Most of the escorts which were available were either pre-war sloops or the first of the new corvettes. Both types would play a full and distinguished role in the Battle of the Atlantic, but both were hampered by relatively low speed. Unless surprise was achieved, they could be out-run by a surfaced U-boat, and if pulled out of screening position either by a submarine hunt or the need to pick up survivors, they would struggle to get back. The ocean escort for SC.7 was the sloop HMS *Scarborough*. She was reinforced on 16th October by another sloop HMS *Fowey* and the corvette HMS *Bluebell*. A second pair, the sloop HMS *Leith* and the corvette HMS *Heartsease* would join on the night of 17/18th October.

At the beginning of October 1940, the German submarine force was smaller than it had been at the outbreak of war 13 months earlier. Losses had been relatively heavy, particularly to British fleet destroyers but, more importantly, new building had yet to be prioritised. Only 20 sea-going U-boats were in operational commission in mid-October, of which seven were in port or returning thereto, and another two had been deployed to distant waters off West Africa. From the eleven remaining boats, however, no fewer than eight would be deployed at some stage against SC.7, five of these together in a 'wolfpack' assault on the final night of the convoy battle. The achievement of such a concentration was partially a result of previous patrols having placed most U-boats on similar operational cycles. This said, the foundations of the new wolfpack approach were the re-deployment of the frontline boats from Germany to new bases at St. Nazaire and Lorient on the Bay of Biscay, and the deliberate concentration of resources for group attacks. The first of these factors added a week to ten days to the time a U-boat could spend on patrol and similarly reduced the time taken in transit to and from base. The second meant that only a few boats were assigned to outward patrol berths, the remainder being retained under central control to be used for a concentrated attack once a convoy had been detected.

The first losses

The 35 ships of SC.7 cleared Sydney on Saturday, 5th October. The convoy suffered its first casualty on the same night, when the aged Laker *Winona* was forced to turn back with a defective dynamo. The number of ships was restored to 35 on Monday, when the convoy was joined at sea by the *Shekatika*. This ship had sailed from Halifax with HX.68 a day before the Sydney convoy departed, but, despite being only four years old, had been unable to maintain the nine-knot speed of the faster convoy because of poor quality Canadian coal. While the weather was reasonable during the first few days at sea, it began to deteriorate on Thursday the 10th, and during that night four vessels lost touch with the convoy. Two of the stragglers were the remaining Lakers, the *Trevisa* and the *Eaglescliffe Hall*; the other two were both Greek, the 30-year old *Aenos* and the 33-year old *Niritos*. Only the last of these managed to re-join the convoy.

The straggling *Trevisa* became the first ship of SC.7 to fall prey to the enemy. She was found by *U 124* in the afternoon of 15th October, some way south of the track of the convoy. Having been missed in a first attack, she was sunk in the early hours of 16th October during a second. The torpedo wrecked the aft part of the ship, destroying the engine room and killing all three engineers (who ranged in age from 46 to 61), as well as the donkeyman, a fireman, the cook and the steward. The *Trevisa* was carrying lumber and sank slowly, allowing the remaining 14 men to take to two rafts, from which they were lucky enough to be found by a British destroyer after only a short time adrift. The *Aenos*, carrying wheat from Sorel, Quebec for Manchester, became the second straggler to fall victim to a U-boat

when she was intercepted by *U 38* on the morning of 17th October some distance to the north east of the previous engagement. A first torpedo also missed, but a second hit and the U-boat then surfaced and shelled the unarmed Greek steamer to destruction. Four crewmen died in the attack, but the rest were picked up by the *Eaglescliffe Hall* which completed her voyage unharmed.

Almost simultaneously, the main body of the convoy was experiencing its first attack. By this time, the escort had been bolstered by the arrival of the sloop HMS *Fowey* and the corvette HMS *Bluebell*. Despite these reinforcements, *U 48* had no difficulty in attacking from the port beam, torpedoing the *Languedoc* and the *Scoresby* in quick succession. The *Languedoc*, carrying fuel oil from the West Indies, was hit about 150 feet from the bow. She was soon awash from the bow to the bridge, and damage control efforts were frustrated when the French crew misunderstood orders to transfer steam to the pumps and moved it to the winches instead. The vessel was abandoned safely and the whole crew was picked up by HMS *Bluebell*. The *Languedoc* was briefly re-boarded to see if it was possible to pump oil aft, but the attempt was quickly abandoned and the ship was left in a sinking condition. The *Scoresby*, carrying pitprops from Corner Brook, Newfoundland, was hit in Number 4 hold just aft of the engine room. Her cargo slowed her demise, and by the time she sank vertically 30 minutes after being hit all the crew were away safely in the boats from where they were also rescued by HMS *Bluebell*. In the meantime, *U 48* had been attacked unsuccessfully aft of the convoy by a Sunderland flying boat. The attack was then taken up by HMS *Scarborough* which stayed behind to launch no fewer than five separate unsuccessful attacks, in the process leaving herself too far astern of SC.7 to catch up.

Around midnight on 17th October, the convoy experienced its second attack. The assailant on this occasion was *U 38* which had caught up with the main body after sinking the straggling *Aenos* the morning before. One of two torpedoes fired hit the *Carsbreck* on the port side in the way of Number 2 hatch. A third torpedo missed and the U-boat broke off the action. At the same time as this attack was taking place, further escort reinforcements in the shape of the sloop HMS *Leith* and the corvette HMS *Heartsease*

Scoresby of 1923. *[J. and M. Clarkson]*

had joined the convoy. The Captain of the former took over as Senior Officer and immediately detached the corvette to escort the *Carsbreck* to the Clyde. The latter was kept well afloat by her lumber cargo and was soon underway again. She would arrive safely on 22nd October, but HMS *Heartsease*, like HMS *Scarborough* the day before, represented a permanent subtraction from the strength of the escort.

The perfect storm

Up until now, the ships of SC.7 had been facing single U-boats, but all this changed as night fell on 18th October. Helped by early reports of the convoy and the coincidental arrival of several boats fresh from base, the German command had managed to concentrate no fewer than five boats across the path of the convoy: *U 46, U 99, U 100, U 101* and *U 123*. At this stage of the war, most U-boat captains were long-term professionals who had joined the submarine service before the war and had built up a year's combat experience either in command or as a watch officer. Even so, SC.7 was unlucky to fall foul of an exceptionally accomplished section of the U-boat arm. All eight men, the three who had already attacked and the five about to do so, would end their careers as holders of the Knight's Cross, and between them they would sink over 1,100,000 tons of Allied shipping.

It was *U 46* which initiated the major assault when she torpedoed the small Swedish pulpwood carrier *Convallaria* on the port side of SC.7 at about 8.30 pm, followed quickly by the *Beatus* with a mixed cargo of steel and lumber. There was no escort on this side of the convoy as HMS *Fowey* had been sent to carry out a dusk sweep astern and had not yet returned to position. HMS *Leith*, at the head of the convoy turned ninety degrees to port and steamed outwards at high speed for 10 miles. Sadly, this only left the convoy even more exposed and when attacks began to develop with increasing speed after 10 pm., the escorts were continually pulled out of position while rescuing survivors and standing by derelicts. Returning to the convoy, HMS *Leith* encountered four torpedoed ships, the *Beatus* and the *Gunborg* (also hit by *U 46*) and the *Empire Miniver* and the *Niritos* (hit by *U 99*), with HMS *Bluebell* already in attendance. She then sighted HMS *Fowey* with survivors from the *Boekelo* and *Shekatika* (both damaged by *U 100*) already aboard. There were no survivors from another victim of the first wave of attacks. The iron ore-laden *Creekirk* had taken her entire complement of 36 to the bottom with her after being hit by *U 101*, having sunk so quickly that her demise does not appear even to have been noticed at the time.

Two other ships were torpedoed before midnight, and their contrasting fates underline the extent to which cargo could be the difference between life and death for torpedoed crews. The lumber-carrying *Blairspey* had been one of the vessels hit in the spree of explosions after 10 pm. A torpedo from *U 101* hit her on the port side in the way of Number 1 hold, but although her engines were disabled by the shock,

she showed no sign of sinking. In the early hours of the 19th, she attracted the attention of *U 100*, which hit her with two more torpedoes, another forward and the second one in the engine room. Although abandoned after this attack, she still refused to sink and was eventually towed safely to the Clyde, having suffered no crew casualties. She would eventually be re-built with a completely new forepart and returned to service as the *Empire Spey*. Several columns to starboard, Seager's *Fiscus* suffered an altogether more terrible fate due to her full cargo of steel. She had fallen behind flying a flag indicating engine problems, but appeared to be returning to position when she was torpedoed by *U 99*. Hit on the starboard side of Number 2 hold, she appears to have dived straight under, her sole survivor being lucky enough to have grabbed the lashing of an unsecured piece of deck cargo as the ship went down. In another cruel juxtaposition of fate, *Fiscus* had lost 38 out of 39 men aboard, while her fleet-mate *Beatus* had not lost any of her 37.

A post-war view of *Blairspey* with a timber cargo. [J. and M. Clarkson]

After a short pause around midnight, the attacks and sinkings resumed in the early hours of 19th October. The Commodore's *Assyrian*, and the *Soesterberg* (by *U 101*), and the *Empire Brigade* (by *U 99*), were sunk in quick succession at the head of the convoy. Most of the *Assyrian's* large complement got away on lifeboats and rafts, but casualties were caused when pit props washed out of the sinking *Soesterberg* swept through the area, knocking men into the sea. A further four ships were lost before the night was out. The *U 99* rounded out a busy night by sinking the *Thalia* and the *Snefjeld*, and damaging the *Clintonia*, while the late-arriving *U 123* sank the *Sedgepool* and finished off the *Clintonia*, as well as despatching the derelict *Boekelo* and *Shekatika*. The crew of the steel-carrying *Thalia* was the third to be martyred by its cargo, only four out of 26 surviving when the ship was observed to go down in 45 seconds.

The crew of the tiny *Snefjeld* were the saviours of the *Thalia*'s survivors, and then embarked on what can justly be described as an odyssey of courage. The Norwegian master had stopped and launched all his boats when the *Thalia* went down. Having rescued the fortunate four, he had everyone back onboard and was just about to raise his boats when his own ship was hit in Number 2 hold. Both lifeboats were destroyed, but everyone got away safely in a small motor boat and a dinghy before their ship broke in two and sank. The motor boat's engine would not function, so both

The Commodore's ship *Assyrian*, seen in the Mersey. *[B. and A. Feilden/J. and M. Clarkson]*

craft began to row towards land. The next day they found an empty raft from the *Thalia* from which they recovered some supplies, and then an empty lifeboat from the *Empire Brigade* into which some of the men transferred. A short while later, a man was spotted standing on a piece of wreckage and rescued. He turned out to be the sole survivor from the *Fiscus*. With the smaller craft taking on water, all were eventually forced into the lifeboat, which they continued to row doggedly eastwards until they were finally picked up on 23rd October by the corvette HMS *Clematis*.

The reckoning
Overall, SC.7 had lost 20 of 35 ships, a total of 79,520 tons. The only real consolation was that, excepting the *Creekirk*, *Fiscus* and *Thalia*, crew casualties had been relatively light. Calm weather, good visibility and escorts devoting most of their time to life-saving meant that most of those who managed to abandon ship were picked up, many of them after only a short time adrift. The total number of men lost was 146, of which 96 had gone down with the three steel/iron ore-carrying ships, and another 17 with the *Assyrian*. No fewer than eight of the vessels sunk had suffered no crew losses at all, half of these being small ships carrying wood products.

As the surviving SC.7 ships sailed further east of Rockall and away from danger, one last act in the extended tragedy was being played out astern. Of the U-boats which had attacked SC.7, *U 99*, *U 101* and *U 123* had expended all their torpedoes and turned homewards, while *U 124* remained on patrol further out in the Atlantic. *U 47*, however, had arrived on station, and had sighted the next convoy in the cycle, the fast HX.79. She homed in the other boats still in the area, *U 38*, *U 46*, *U 48* and *U 100*. They attacked on the night of 19/20th October, just 24 hours after the climax of the SC.7 battle. The details of the action are beyond the scope of this study, but in brief, another 12 ships of 75,069

tons were sunk, again without any serious interference from the escort. Thus, just nine U-boats had sunk a total of 32 ships totalling just over 150,000 tons from two successive convoys in a matter of a few days. In terms of the number of ships lost, this was comfortably the worst extended convoy battle of the war. To put it in context, the bloodbath of the dispersed Arctic convoy PQ.17 cost 24 ships, but some of these were sunk by aircraft, and all but three of them after the disastrous decision to scatter was taken. In the Battle of the Atlantic, the next largest losses of ships were 16 from SC.42 in September 1941, 15 from SC.107 in October 1942, and 14 from ONS.154 in December 1942, but in each of these cases 16 to 19 U-boats were involved. Finally, the climacteric engagement of the Battle of the Atlantic involving SC.122 and HX.229 in March 1943 resulted in the loss of 22 ships at the hands of three wolfpacks made up of no fewer than 43 U-boats.

Later war casualties
The ships that survived SC.7 still had more than four years of war ahead of them, war that was particularly hard on older, smaller and slower vessels. Of the 16 vessels which reached the United Kingdom (including the *Winona* which crossed safely in SC.8), no fewer than 12 were lost. Two of these were sunk in the closing months of 1940. The 34-year old *Dioni* never left British waters, lasting only a matter of weeks before dragging her anchors, going ashore and being towed away for scrap. The Swedish motor ship *Valparaiso* was lost with all hands after straggling from HX.97 on her next eastbound Atlantic crossing and being torpedoed on New Year's Eve. Seven were lost in 1941, four (*Carsbreck*, *Corinthic*, *Flynderborg*, and *Somersby*) to U-boats, two (*Karlander* and *Trident*) to the Luftwaffe and one (*Botusk*) to a mine. Two more went down in 1942, the *Inger Elisabeth*, the victim of a U-boat in the St. Lawrence, and the *Havorn*, run down in the fog in the same river. Two of the U-boat losses, the *Valparaiso* to *U 38* in December 1940, and the *Corinthic* to *U 124* in April 1941, were at the

Corinthic, seen above on 23rd December 1932, survived SC.7 only to be lost on 13th April 1941 on passage Rosario to Freetown and the United Kingdom with a cargo of grain. *[J. and M. Clarkson]*

hands of submarines which has sunk ships from SC.7. It was, however, the last loss of the war, that of the *Sneland I* in May 1945, which was in many ways the most poignant.

The *Sneland I* had been trading in the Caribbean and along the United States east coast when Norway was invaded in April 1940. Her passage in SC.7 marked her arrival in U.K. waters, and thereafter she was very active in coastal and short-sea assignments, the latter including several voyages to Iceland and to Gibraltar and North Africa. Despite her small size, she also made six trans-Atlantic round trips, in each case surviving the eastwards passage in decidedly dangerous SC convoys. After compiling this extended war record, she failed to survive the conflict in Europe by a margin of less than two hours, thereby earning the melancholy distinction of becoming the last victim of the U-boat war. She was sailing in a five-ship convoy carrying coal from Blyth to Belfast. Just before 11 pm on 7th May 1945, the convoy was about two miles south of the Isle of May in the Firth of Forth when the vessel ahead of the *Sneland I*, the Canadian war-built Scandinavian type *Avondale Park*, was hit by a torpedo. *Sneland I* swung to port to avoid her consort, but within several minutes, she was hit by a torpedo on the starboard side in the way of Number 2 hold. The ship capsized before a boat could be launched, leaving her crew floundering in the water. Escorting trawlers managed to rescue 22, but seven died including the master and a 17-year old mess-boy from

Hull. The assailant had been *U 2336*, the only one of the new 'Electro' boats ever to launch an attack. The German surrender had already been signed, but was not due to come into effect until midnight on 7th May, just over an hour after *Sneland I* was sunk. German U-boats had been sent an order to stop all attacks and return to port on 4th May, but it is not clear whether *U 2336* did not receive the instruction or her novice captain turned a blind eye in order to take his one chance to register his first kills.

The survivors

Only four of the ships assigned to SC.7 were still afloat on VE Day 1945. The first of these to go was the ancient Norwegian tanker *Thoroy*, which would be just months short of her sixtieth birthday when she went to the breakers at Rosyth as the Panamanian *Anne De France* in 1953. Two of the other survivors were the Lakers *Eaglescliffe Hall* and *Winona*, both of which served as supply ships for the D-Day invasion of 1944. Both would remain well-travelled to the end. The *Winona* would be lost to marine hazard in the Far East under Chinese colours in 1956, while the *Eaglescliffe Hall* foundered off the British Columbian coast as the barge *Log Transporter* in 1961. The last survivor was the born-again *Empire Spey*, which returned to her former owners as *Blairspey* after the war, and went to the breakers in 1967 as the Greek-owned, Lebanese-flagged *Evandros*.

THE SHIPS OF SC.7

1. AENOS
3,554g 2,222n.
390.5 x 51.0 x 21.4 feet.
T.3-cyl. (28, 47, 78 x 51 inches) by John Dickinson and Sons Ltd., Sunderland; 484 NHP, 2,500 IHP, 12 knots.
21.6.1910: Launched by Bartram and Sons, Sunderland (Yard No. 217) for the Nautilus Steam Shipping Co. Ltd. (F. and W. Ritson, managers), Sunderland) as CEDAR BRANCH.
26.8.1910: Registered at Sunderland (8/1910).
29.10.1929: Mortgaged to the National Provincial Bank Ltd. to secure current account.
12.4.1932: British register closed on sale by the National Provincial Bank Ltd. as mortgagees to A. Lusi, Argostoli, Greece and renamed AENOS.
1938: Transferred to the 'Zephyros' Steamship Co. Ltd. (A. Lusi Ltd., managers), Argostoli, Greece.
17.10.1940: Torpedoed, shelled and sunk by the German submarine U 38 in approximate position 59 north, 13 west whilst on a voyage from Sorel, Quebec for Manchester with a cargo of 6,276 tons of wheat in convoy SC.7. Of her 29 crew, four were lost.

2. ASSYRIAN
O.N.143952 2,962g 1,759n.
331.4 x 44.7 x 22.9 feet.

The clipper-bowed *Aenos* off Montevideo in April 1938. *[J. and M. Clarkson]*

Two 2SCDA 3-cyl. (18.9 x 27.95 inches) oil engines by Blohm & Voss, Hamburg; 566 NHP, 9½ knots.
1924: Two T. 3-cyl. (16, 26½, 44 x 30 inches) by Cooper and Greig Ltd., Dundee; 219NHP, 1,400 IHP, 9½ knots.
24.2.1914: Launched by Blohm & Voss, Hamburg (Yard No. 207) for their own account (Woermann Linie, Hamburg, intended managers) as FRITZ.
1919: Taken over by The Shipping Controller, London.
13.12.1919: Registered at London (724/1919) in the name of The Shipping Controller (Glen Line Ltd., managers), London.
15.11.1920: Sold to Ellerman Lines

Ltd., London (Graham Smith, Liverpool, manager).
10.2.1921: Re-registered at London (75/1921).
14.2.1921: Re-registered at Liverpool (17/1921).
16.2.1921: Renamed ASSYRIAN.
1924: Re-engined.
1937: Management transferred to Ellerman and Papayanni Lines.
19.10.1940: Torpedoed and sunk by the German submarine U 101 in position 57.12 north, 10.43 west whilst on a voyage from New Orleans for Liverpool with general cargo including 3,700 tons of wheat in convoy SC.7. Of her 51 crew, 17 were lost.
24.10.1940: Register closed.

3. BEATUS

O.N.148281 4,885g 2,992n.
390.0 x 55.5 x 26.4 feet.
T.3-cyl. (26, 43, 71 x 48 inches) by
Blair and Co. Ltd., Stockton-on-Tees:
436 NHP, 2,000 IHP, 10 knots
23.1.1925: Launched by the Ropner
Shipbuilding and Repairing Co.
(Stockton) Ltd., Stockton-on-Tees (Yard
No. 548) for the Tempus Shipping
Co. Ltd. (Sir William Henry Seager,
manager), Cardiff as BEATUS.
2.3.1925: Registered at Cardiff (5/1925).
18.10.1940: Torpedoed and sunk by
the German submarine U 46 in position
57.31 north, 13.10 west whilst on a
voyage from Three Rivers, Quebec for
the Tyne with a cargo of 1,626 tons of
steel, 5,874 tons of lumber and a deck
cargo of crated aircraft in convoy SC.7.
37 crew; all saved.
29.10.1940: Register closed.

4. BLAIRSPEY

O.N.161892 4,155g 2,522n.
371.8 x 51.2 x 24.3 feet.
T.3-cyl. (22, 38, 63 x 42 inches) by J.G.
Kincaid and Co. Ltd., Greenock; 257 NHP.
5.2.1929: Launched by the Ardrossan
Dry Dock and Shipbuilding Co. Ltd.,
Ardrossan (Yard No. 344) for the
Northern Navigation Co. Ltd. (G.
Nisbet and Co., managers), Glasgow as
BLAIRSPEY.
18-19.10.1940: Torpedoed and damaged
by the German submarine U 101 and
subsequently torpedoed again by U
100 in position 57.55 north, 11.10 west
whilst on a voyage from Rimouski,
Quebec for Grangemouth with a cargo
of 1,798 standards of timber in convoy
SC.7. Remained afloat with timber
cargo and towed to the Clyde. Her
entire crew of 34 was saved. Re-built
with a new forepart.
21.3.1942: Returned to service for
the Ministry of War Transport (G.
Nisbet and Co., managers), Glasgow as
EMPIRE SPEY.
1946: Sold to the Northern Navigation
Co. Ltd. (G. Nisbet and Co., managers),
Glasgow and renamed BLAIRSPEY.
1961: Sold to Marfuente Compania
Naviera S.A. Beirut, Lebanon (J.P.
Hadoulis, Piraeus, Greece) and renamed
EVANDROS.
2.5.1967: Arrived at La Spezia to be
broken up.

5. BOEKELO

2,118g 1,253n.
281.2 x 42.7 x 19.0 feet.
T.3-cyl. (19½, 32, 52 x 36 inches) by N. V.

Ellerman's elderly Mediterranean cargo liner *Assyrian* was selected as the convoy Commodore's vessel because of her passenger accommodation. *[John McRoberts]*

Beatus was one of two ships owned in Cardiff by Seager's Tempus Shipping Co. Ltd. to be lost in SC.7. *[Warwick Foote]*

Although torpedoed and damaged in SC.7, *Blairspey* was towed home and became the convoy's last surviving ship. *[Fotoflite incorporating Skyfotos]*

Verschure and Co., Amsterdam; 208 NHP.
1930: Launched by A. Vuijk and
Zonen, Capelle a/d Yssel, Netherlands
(Yard No. 600) for N. V Stoomvaart
Maatschappij 'Noordzee', Amsterdam,
Netherlands as BOEKELO.
18.10.1940: Torpedoed and damaged
by the German submarines U 100 and
subsequently torpedoed and sunk by U
123 in position 57.14 north, 10.38 west
whilst on a voyage from Chatham, New
Brunswick for London with a cargo of
1,018 standards of timber in convoy
SC.7. The entire crew of 25 were saved.

6. BOTUSK

O.N.143449 3,091g 1,873n.
331.5 x 46.8 x 23.2 feet.
T.3-cyl. (25, 41, 68 x 45 inches) by
Blair and Co. Ltd., Stockton-on-Tees;
362 NHP, 1,900 IHP, 11 knots,
26.8.1919: Launched by the Ropner
Shipbuilding and Repairing Co. Ltd.,
Stockton-on-Tees (Yard No. 531) for
W.J. Tatem Ltd., London as MOLTON.
9.10.1919: Registered at London
(495/1919) in the name of The Right
Honourable Baron Glanely of St.
Fagans, Cardiff.
23.3.1920: Transferred to the Atlantic
Shipping and Trading Co. Ltd. (W.J.
Tatem Ltd., managers), London.
19.7.1921: Transferred to W. J. Tatem
Ltd., Cardiff.
11.5.1938: Sold to the Continental
Transit Co. Ltd. (David P. Barnett,
London, manager), London.
16.5.1938: Renamed TRANSIT.
11.8.1939: Sold to the Board of Trade,
London.
13.9.1939: Renamed BOTUSK.
1940: Transferred to the Ministry of
Shipping (Sir William Reardon Smith
and Sons Ltd., managers), London.
31.1.1941: Mined and sunk in a British
minefield about six miles north east of
North Rona Island whilst on a voyage
from St. John, New Brunswick for
Cardiff with a cargo of 4,221 tons of
grain. Of her 38 crew, four were lost.
18.2.1941: Register closed.

7. CARSBRECK

O.N.164092 3,670g 2,254n.
352.6 x 50.3 x 23.8 feet.
T.3-cyl. (22, 38, 63 x 42 inches) by
David Rowan and Co. Ltd., Glasgow;
346 NHP, 1,700 IHP, 10½ knots.
20.8.1936: Launched by the Ayrshire
Dockyard Co. Ltd., Irvine (Yard No.
518) for the Dornoch Shipping Co. Ltd.
(James S. Thomson, manager), Glasgow
as COULBEG.
10.9.1936: Registered at Glasgow
(34/1936).
30.11.1937: Sold to the Carslogie
Steamship Co. Ltd. (William C.
Honeyman, manager), Glasgow.
19.7.1938: Renamed CARSBRECK.
18.10.1940: Torpedoed and damaged by
the German submarine U 38 in position
58.46 north, 14.11 west. All 35 crew
were saved. Escorted safely to the
Clyde.
24.10.1941: Torpedoed and sunk by the
German submarine U 564 in position
36.20 north, 10.50 west whilst on a
voyage from Almeira for Barrow-in-

It took torpedoes from two U-boats to sink the Dutch steamship *Boekelo*, and thanks to her timber cargo her whole crew survived. *[M. Lindenboorn]*

Botusk survived SC.7 only to be sunk by a British mine some fthree months later. *[Roy Fenton collection]*

Carsbreck in the colours of William C. Honeyman's Carslogie Steamship Co. Ltd. *[World Ship Photo Library]*

Furness with a cargo of 6,000 tons of
iron ore in convoy HG.75. Of her 42
crew, 23 were lost.
27.2.1942: Register closed.

8. CLINTONIA

O.N.139879 3,106g 1,882n.
331.0 x 48.0 x 22.2 feet.
T.3-cyl. (27½, 36½, 62 x 42 inches) by
North Eastern Marine Engineering Co.
Ltd., Newcastle-on-Tyne; 275 NHP,
1,100 IHP, 9 knots.
8.2.1917: Launched by William Dobson
and Co., Walker-on-Tyne (Yard No.199)

for the Stag Line Ltd. (J. Robinson and Sons, managers), North Shields as CLINTONIA.

28.4.1917: Registered at North Shields (7/1907).

10.9.1918: Transferred to a new company of same name.

19.10.1940: Torpedoed and damaged by the German submarine U 99, and subsequently shelled and sunk by the German submarine U 123 in position 57.10 north, 12.30 west whilst on a voyage from St. Francis, Nova Scotia for Manchester with a cargo of 3,850 tons of pulpwood in convoy SC.7. Of the 36 crew, one was lost.

2.11.1940: Register closed.

9. CONVALLARIA

1,996g 1,145n.
280.4 x 40.2 x 19.1 feet.
T.3-cyl.(20, 31½, 53 x 36 inches) by Verschure & Co., Amsterdam, Netherlands; 194 NHP.

1921: Launched by Verschure & Co., Amsterdam (Yard No. 40) for Rederi A/B Activ (F. Borjesson, manager), Helsingborg, Sweden as CONVALLARIA.

1928: Management transferred to J. Gorthon.

18.10.1940: Torpedoed and sunk by the German submarine U 46 north west of Ireland in position 57.22 north, 11.11 west whilst on a voyage from St. John's, Newfoundland for Ridham Dock with a cargo 821 cubic fathoms of pulpwood in convoy SC.7. Her entire crew was saved.

10. CORINTHIC

O.N.147155 4,823g 3,023n.
390.1 x 55.6 x 26.2 feet.
T.3-cyl. (26, 43, 72 x 48 inches), by Richardsons Westgarth and Co. Ltd., Hartlepool; 335 NHP, 2,000 IHP, 10 knots.

20.5.1924: Launched by Irvine's Shipbuilding and Dry Dock Co. Ltd., West Hartlepool (Yard No. 617) for Sir Walter H. Cockerline, Hull.

20.6.1924: Registered at Hull (39/1924).

30.6.1925: Sold to Hartley Cooper and Co. Ltd., London.

13.4.1941: Torpedoed and sunk by the German submarine U 124 in position 08.10 north, 14.40 west whilst on a voyage from Rosario for Freetown and the United Kingdom with a cargo of 7,710 tons of grain. Of her 40 crew, one was lost.

10.7.1941: Register closed.

Although Stag Line's *Clintonia* was subject to torpedo and gun attacks by two U-boats, when she sank just one member of her crew was lost. *[Roy Fenton collection]*

Convallaria was a relatively small Swedish steamer sunk whilst carrying wood pulp from Newfoundland. *[World Ship Photo Library]*

Sir Walter H. Cockerline of Hull used a similar naming scheme to White Star and later Shaw, Savill, although his basic tramp ships could hardly be confused with ships of these prestigious companies. *Corinthic* was quickly sold, but without change of name. *[Roy Fenton collection]*

11. CREEKIRK

O.N.133032 3,793g 2,408n.
353.3 x 51.1 x 23.8 feet.
T.3-cyl. (25, 41, 67 x 45 inches) by
Rankin and Blackmore, Greenock; 334
NHP, 1,600 IHP, 10 knots.
21.2.1912: Launched by Robert Duncan
and Co. Ltd., Port Glasgow (Yard No.
319) for William S. Miller and Co.,
Glasgow as MARISTON.
19.4.1912: Registered at Glasgow
(37/1912) in the name of the Mariston
Steamship Co. Ltd. (W. S. Miller and
Co., managers), Glasgow.
17.4.1914: British register closed
on sale to Romania Prima Societate
Nationala de Nav. Maritima, Bucharest,
Romania and renamed MILCOVUL.
c.1916: Requisitioned by the Imperial
Russian Navy and placed in service as
Black Sea transport N.144.
2.5.1918: Captured by German forces at
Sevastapol.
11.1918: Recovered by owners.
1933: Sold to Ant. G. Yannoulatos
Sons, Cephalonia/Piraeus, Greece and
renamed HYPHAESTOS.
1938: Sold to the Cree Steamship Co.
Ltd. (Muir Young Ltd., managers),
London and renamed CREEKIRK.
9.2.1938: Restored to the British
register at London (37/1938).
18.10.1940: Torpedoed and sunk by the
German submarine U 101 in the North
Atlantic in position 57.30 north, 11.10
west whilst on a voyage from Wabana,
Newfoundland and Sydney, Nova Scotia
for Workington with a cargo of 5,900
tons of iron ore in convoy SC.7. Her
entire crew of 36 was lost.
26.4.1941: Register closed.

12. DIONI

4,227g 2,710n.
360.0 x 48.0 x 28.0 feet.
T.3-cyl. (25, 41, 69 x 48 inches) by
Richardsons, Westgarth and Co. Ltd.,
Sunderland; 372 NHP, 1,850 IHP.
24.7.1906: Launched by the
Northumberland Shipbuilding Co. Ltd.,
Howdon-on-Tyne (Yard No. 138) for
Midgard Deutsche Seevarkehrs A. G.,
Nordenham, Germany as ASGARD.
1.8.1914: Seized by the Russian
Government at Odessa.
10.1914: Placed in service with the
Imperial Russian Navy as AL'MA.
3.1915: Re-deployed as Black Sea
transport N.5.
17.3.1918: Recovered by German forces
at Nicolaiev.
7.1918: Returned to owners and
renamed ASGARD.

1919: Taken over by the Shipping
Controller, London (Evan Thomas
Radcliffe and Co., Cardiff, managers).
25.9.1919: Registered at London
(481/1919) in the name of The Shipping
Controller, London (Daniel Radcliffe,
Cardiff, manager).
23.10.1920: British register closed on
sale to the Greek Government Service
of Maritime Transport, Piraeus, Greece
and renamed VASILISSA SOFIA.
1923: Renamed LESVOS.
1927: Sold to G.F. Andreadis, Chios,
Greece and renamed DIONI.
8.11.1940: Broke moorings and drove
aground in Sandy Haven Bay whilst
on a voyage from Dublin for Barry in
ballast.
3.12.1940: Re-floated and towed to
Milford Haven where sold to T.W. Ward
Ltd. for breaking up.
1.1941: Breaking up began.

13. EAGLESCLIFFE HALL

O.N.160707 1,900g 1,204n.
253.0 x 44.1 x 18.5 feet.
T.3-cyl. (15, 25, 40 x 33 inches) by
Smith's Dock Co. Ltd., Middlesbrough;
81 RHP.
5.4.1928: Launched by Smith's Dock
Co. Ltd., Middlesbrough (Yard No. 846)
for the Hall Corporation of Canada,
Montreal, Quebec as EAGLESCLIFFE
HALL.
1955: Sold to Colonial Steamships
Ltd. (R. Scott Meisner, manager), Port
Colborne, Ontario and renamed DAVID
BARCLAY.
1959: Transferred to Scott Meisner
Steamships Ltd. (R. Scott Meisner,
manager), Port Colborne.
1959: Sold to the Powell River Co. Ltd.,
Vancouver, British Columbia.

Q1.1960: Converted to a barge and
renamed LOG TRANSPORTER.
25.10.1961: Foundered off Cape
Mudge, British Columbia whilst on a
voyage from Rivers Inlet for Teakerne
Arm, Redona Island.

14. EMPIRE BRIGADE

O.N.135157 5,166g 3,217n.
400.0 x 53.5 x 26.6 feet.
T.3-cyl. (27, 44½, 74 x 48 inches) by
Blair and Co. Ltd., Stockton-on-Tees;
440NHP.
10.10.1912: Launched by John
Priestman and Co., Sunderland (Yard
No. 239) for the Court Line Ltd.
(Haldinstein and Co. Ltd., managers),
London as HANNINGTON COURT.
9.11.1912: Registered at London
(191/1912).
1915: Managers re-styled Haldin and
Co.
13.5.1929: Transferred to the United
British Steam Ship Co. Ltd. (Haldin
and Philipps, managers), London.
2.12.1936: Register closed on sale
to Achille Lauro, Naples, Italy and
renamed ELIOS.
10.6.1940: Seized by the British
Government at Newcastle-on-Tyne.
20.7.1940: Entered service with the
Ministry of Shipping (Cairns, Noble
and Co., managers), Newcastle-on-
Tyne as EMPIRE BRIGADE.
20.7.1940: Restored to the British
register at Newcastle-on-Tyne
(12/1940).
19.10.1940: Torpedoed and sunk by
the German submarine U 99 about 100
miles east south east of Rockall in the
North Atlantic in position 57.12 north,
10.43 west whilst on a voyage from
Montreal and Sydney for Leith and

Laker *Eaglescliffe Hall* with a timber deck cargo.

the Tyne with general cargo, including 750 tons of copper, 129 tons of ferric alloys and 980 tons of steel in convoy SC.7. Of her 41 crew, six were lost.
4.11.1940: Register closed.

15. EMPIRE MINIVER
O.N.167629 6,055g 4,506n.
410.0 x 54.2 x 27.6 feet.
Double-reduction steam turbine by General Electric Co., Schenactady, New York; 2,500 IHP.
26.10.1918: Launched by the Columbia River Shipbuilding Corporation, Portland, Oregon (Yard No.11) for the United States Shipping Board, Portland, Oregon as WEST COBALT
12.1918: Requisitioned by the United States Navy, Naval Overseas Transportation Service as Transport #3836.
1933: Owners Lykes Brothers – Ripley Steamship Co. Inc., Galveston, Texas.
1938: Transferred to Lykes Brothers Steamship Co. Inc., Galveston, Texas.
1940: Sold to the Ministry of Shipping (A. Weir and Co., managers), London and renamed EMPIRE MINIVER.
16.8.1940: Registered at London (320/1940).
18.10.1940: Torpedoed and sunk by the German submarine U 99 310 degrees, 250 miles from Rathlin Head whilst on a voyage from Baltimore, Maryland for Newport, Monmouth with a cargo of 4,500 tons of pig iron and 6,200 tons of steel in convoy SC.7. Of her 38 crew, three were lost.
31.10.1940: Register closed.

16. FISCUS
O.N.148298 4,815g 2,948n.
399.0 x 54.5 x 25.2 feet.
T.3-cyl. (26, 42, 71 x 48 inches) by North Eastern Marine Engineering Co. Ltd., 432 NHP, 2,200 IHP, 10¾ knots.
6.3.1928: Launched by the Northumberland Shipbuilding Co. (1929) Ltd., Howdon-on-Tyne (Yard No. 401) for the Tempus Shipping Co. Ltd. (Sir William Henry Seager, manager), Cardiff as FISCUS.
16.4.1928: Registered at Cardiff (4/1928).
18.10.1940: Torpedoed and sunk by the German submarine U 99 in position 57.29 north, 11.10 west whilst on a voyage from Three Rivers, Quebec for the Clyde with a cargo of steel in convoy SC.7. Of her 39 crew, 38 were lost.
20.11.1940: Register closed.

17. FLYNDERBORG
O.N.165793 2,022g 1,203n.
280.1 x 40.1 x 19.2 feet.
T.3-cyl. (20, 31½, 53 x 36 inches) by William Gray and Co. Ltd., West Hartlepool; 194 NHP, 675 IHP, 8½ knots.
29.4.1930: Launched by William Gray and Co. Ltd., West Hartlepool (Yard No. 1044) for A/S Dampskibs Selskab 'Dannebrog' (C.K. Hansen, manager), Copenhagen, Denmark as FLYNDERBORG.
9.4.1940: At Nordfjord, Norway at time of the German invasion.
1.5.1940: Requisitioned by the Norwegian Government. Sailed to Kirkwall and taken over by the British Government.
1940: Placed in service for the Ministry

of Shipping, London (Hall Brothers, Newcastle-on-Tyne, managers).
28.8.1940: Registered at Newcastle-on-Tyne (21/1940).
3.11.1941: Torpedoed and sunk by the German submarine U 202 in the North Atlantic in position 51.21 north, 51.45 west whilst on a voyage from Parrsboro', Nova Scotia for London with a cargo of 2,125 tons of lumber in convoy SC.52. Of her 24 crew, three were lost.
26.11.1941: Register closed.

18. GUNBORG
1,572g 835n.
269.2 x 40.4 x 16.6 feet.
T.3-cyl. (17¾, 28¾, 47¼ x 30 inches) plis low pressure turbine with double-reduction gearing and hydraulic coupling by by Oskarshamns Mekaniske Verkstad A/B, Oskarshamn, Sweden; 122 NHP.
1930: Launched by Oskarshamns Mekaniske Verkstad A/B, Oskarshamn for Trelleborgs Angfartygs Nya A/B, Trelleborg, Sweden.
1940: Sold to Rederi A/B Sylvia (Alb. Billner, manager), Goteborg, Sweden.
18.10.1940: Torpedoed and sunk by the German submarine U 46 in position 57.14 north, 10.38 west whilst on a voyage from Halifax for Ridham Dock with a cargo of 850 cubic fathoms of pulpwood in convoy SC.7. All 23 of her crew were saved.

19. HAVORN
1,527g 913n.
257.6 x 36.3 x 17.0 feet.
T.3-cyl. (17½, 24, 48 x 33 inches) by

All but one of her crew of 38 were lost when the steel-carrying *Fiscus* was torpedoed in SC.7. *[Ships in Focus]*

Laxevaags Maskin and Jernskibsbyg, Bergen, Norway; 130 NHP.
1902: Launched by Laxevaags Maskin and Jernskibsbyg, Bergen (Yard No. 62) for P. Hamre, Bergen as ORN.
1908: Sold to S. L. Christie, Bergen, Norway.
1916: Sold to D/S A/S Sandvik (Ole Dahl, manager), Arendal, Norway.
1918: Taken over by The Shipping Controller (Wm. Brown, Atkinson and Co., managers), London.
16.3.1918: Registered at London (67/1918) in the name of The Shipping Controller (Arthur J. Atkinson, manager), London.
16.4.1919: British register closed on return of vessel to owners.
1919: Sold to: D/S A/S Orn II (Jespersen and Rabe, managers), Tonsberg, Norway.
1919: Sold to A/S Ulrikka (Chr. Mathiesen, manager), Haugesund, Norway and renamed ULRIKKA II.
1929: Sold to D/S A/S Havorn (Jacob Odland and Son A/S, managers), Haugesund, Norway and renamed HAVORN.
19.7.1942: Run down and sunk by the British steamship RADHURST (3,454/1910) in thick fog, while anchored off Ile aux Coudres in the St. Lawrence River in position 47.23.09 north, 70.27.07 west whilst on a voyage from Montreal for St. John's, Newfoundland.

20. INGER ELISABETH
2,166g 1,297n.
289.5 x 44.2 x 19.4 feet.
T.3-cyl. (22, 35, 61 x 36 inches) by Trondhjems Mekaniske Verksted, Trondhjeim, Norway; 223 NHP.
1920: Launched by Framnaes Mekaniske Verksted, Sandefjord, Norway (Yard No. 94) for A/S Cissy (Torp and Wiese, managers), Bergen, Norway as CISSY.
1927: Manager restyled Chr. B. Torp.
1928: Sold to A/S Sjofart (Sverre Sturlung, manager), Bergen, Norway.
1937: Management transferred to L. Pettersen.
1938: Management transferred to Jacob Kjode A/S.
1939: Transferred to A/S Inger (Jacob Kjode A/S, manager) and renamed INGER ELISABETH.
15.9.1942: Torpedoed and sunk by the German submarine U 517 in the Gulf of St. Lawrence in position 48.49 north, 64.06 west whilst on a voyage from Swansea and Sydney, Nova Scotia for

Port Alfred with a cargo of 3,400 tons of coal in convoy SQ.36. Of her 26 crew, three were lost.

21. KARLANDER
1,843g 1,092n.
265.2 x 42.1 x 18.9 feet.
T.3-cyl (20½, 33, 56 x 36 inches) by Nylands Verkstad, Christiania, Norway, 188 NHP.
1914: Launched by Nylands Verkstad, Christiania (Yard No. 242) for an unknown owner, and completed as VISNA for D/S Valkyrien A/S (L. Severin Skougaard, managers), Christiania as FROLAND.
1917: Sold to Friis and Lunds Rederi A/S (F. Friis and C.O. Lund, managers), Drammen, Norway.
1925: Sold to Rederi A/S Henneseid (Th. Holta, manager), Porsgrunn, Norway.
1930: Sold to Skibs A/S Karlander (H.T. Wilkens and Co. A/S, managers, Fredrikstad, Norway) and renamed KARLANDER.
14.5.1941: Bombed by German aircraft in position 55.38 north, 13.38 west whilst on a voyage from Hull for Curacao in ballast. The wreck was sunk by the British corvette HMS CAMPANULA. All 26 of her crew were saved.

22. LANGUEDOC
O.N.171459 9,512g 5,874n.
479.8 x 65.4 x 33.2 feet.
Two 2SCSA 7-cyl. ($19^{11}/_{16}$ x $35^{7}/_{16}$) oil engines by A/S Burmeister & Wain, Copenhagen, Denmark; 943 NHP, 5,600 IHP, 13 knots.
14.7.1937: Launched by A/S Burmeister & Wain, Copenhagen (Yard No. 627) for Neptune Shipping Ltda. S.A., Panama (Mosvold Shipping and

Agency, Farsund, Norway, managers) as ACTOR.
1938: Sold to Société Francaise de Transports Petroliers S.A., Le Havre, France and renamed LANGUEDOC.
8.7.1940: Intercepted by the Royal Navy off Curacao.
16.7.1940: Formally seized at Trinidad.
1940: Placed in service for the Ministry of Shipping (J.I. Jacobs and Co. Ltd., managers), London, registered in Port of Spain, Trinidad.
31.8.1940: Registered at Trinidad (1/1940).
17.10.1940: Torpedoed and sunk by the German submarine U 48 in position 59.14 north, 17.51 west whilst on a voyage from Trinidad for the Clyde with a cargo of 13,700 tons of fuel oil in convoy SC.7. All 39 of her crew were saved.
11.12.1940: Register closed.

23. NIRITOS
3,854g 2,452n.
345.0 x 50.1 x 25.0 feet.
T.3-cyl. (25½, 40½, 67 x 45 inches) by William Gray and Co. Ltd., West Hartlepool; 335 NHP, 1,500 IHP, 9 knots.
22.8.1907: Launched by William Gray and Co. Ltd., West Hartlepool (Yard No. 750) for the Wilson Shipping Co. Ltd. (Joseph F. Wilson and Co., managers), West Hartlepool as MAYLANDS.
18.9.1907: Registered at West Hartlepool (23/1907).
24.7.1919: Sold to Edgar Edwards and Trevor George Edwards, Cardiff.
31.7.1919: Transferred to Western Counties Shipping Co. Ltd., Cardiff.
22.1.1920: Fleet mortgaged for £1,000,000 with interest at 6½% by B.S.T. Ltd., London.
23.9.1920: Renamed MAYMEAD.
27.2.1922: Sold by B.S.T. Ltd. as

The Greek steamer *Niritos* under her original name, *Maylands*, owned in West Hartlepool by the Wilson Shipping Co. Ltd. *[Roy Fenton collection]*

mortgagees to the Moor Line Ltd., Newcastle-on-Tyne.

6.3.1922: Re-registered at London (79/1922) in the name of the Moor Line Ltd.

11.3.1922: Re-registered at Newcastle-on-Tyne (13/1922).

11.3.1922: Renamed ISLEMOOR.

9.4.1927: Register closed on sale to G.C. Dracoulis, Ithaca, Greece and renamed NIRITOS.

18.10.1940: Torpedoed and sunk by the German submarine U 99 in position 57.14 north, 10.38 west whilst on a voyage from Port Sulphur for Garston with a cargo of 5,426 tons of sulphur in convoy SC.7. Of her 28 crew, one was lost.

24. SCORESBY

O.N.137083 3,843g 2,310n.
360.1 x 50.0 x 22.9 feet.
T.3-cyl. (25, 42, 68 x 45 inches) by North Eastern Marine Engineering Co. Ltd., Sunderland; 340 NHP, 1,900 IHP, 10¼ knots.

18.12.1922: Launched by Robert Thompson and Sons Ltd., Sunderland (Yard No. 316) for Rowland and Marwood's Steamship Co. Ltd. (Headlam and Rowland, managers), Whitby as SCORESBY.

26.1.1923: Registered at Whitby (1/1923).

17.10.1940: Torpedoed and sunk by the German submarine U 48 in position 59.14 north, 17.51 west whilst on a voyage from Corner Brook, Newfoundland for the Clyde with a cargo of 1,685 cubic fathoms of pit props in convoy SC.7. All 39 of her crew were saved.

26.10.1940: Register closed.

25. SEDGEPOOL

O.N.139224 5,556g 3,408n
415.0 x 55.5 x 26.9 feet
T.3-cyl. (28, 46, 75 x 51 inches) by Blair and Co. Ltd., Stockton-on-Tees; 504 NHP, 2,500 IHP, 11 knots.

14.12.1917: Launched by Ropner and Sons Ltd., Stockton-on-Tees (Yard No. 520) for the Pool Shipping Co. Ltd. (Sir Robert Ropner and Co. Ltd., managers), West Hartlepool as SEDGEPOOL.

13.2.1918: Registered at West Hartlepool (3/1918).

19.10.1940: Torpedoed and sunk by the German submarine U 123 in position 57.20 north, 11.22 west whilst on a voyage from Montreal for Manchester with a cargo of 8,720 tons of wheat in convoy SC.7. Of her 39 crew, three were lost.

7.5.1943: Register closed.

26. SHEKATIKA

O.N.164365 5,458g 3,333n.
407.0 x 55.7 x 28.0 feet.
T.3-cyl. (21½, 36, 62 x 45 inches), by David Rowan and Co. Ltd., Glasgow; 341 NHP, 1,650 IHP, 10¾ knots.

1936: Launched by Caledon Shipbuilding and Engineering Co. Ltd., Dundee (Yard No.351) for the South Georgia Co. Ltd. (Christian Salvesen and Co., managers), Leith as SHEKATIKA.

7.3.1936: Registered at Leith (3/1936).

18.10.1940: Torpedoed and damaged by the German submarine U 100 and then torpedoed and sunk by U 123 in position 57.12 north, 11.08 west whilst on a voyage from Gaspe for Hartlepool with a cargo of 2,003 tons of steel and 6,000 tons of pitprops in convoy SC.7. 36 crew; all saved.

24.10.1940: Register closed.

27. SNEFJELD

1,643g 1,001n
270.0 x 37.6 x 18.4 feet
T.3-cyl. (20, 33, 54½ x 36 inches) by

Blair and Co. Ltd., Stockton-on-Tees; 182 NHP.

1901: Launched by N. V. Scheepswerf v/h Jan Smit, Czn., Alblasserdam, Netherlands (Yard No. 420) for N.V. Maatschappij Stoomschip Maastad (Driebeek & Zonen, managers), Rotterdam, Netherlands as MAASSTAD.

1909: Sold to N.V. Stoomvaart Maatschappij Nederlandsche Lloyd, Rotterdam, Holland and renamed OTTOLAND.

1915: Sold to A/S Snefjeld (Harald G. Martens, manager), Bergen, Norway and renamed SNEFJELD.

19.10.1940: Torpedoed and sunk by the German submarine U 99 in position 57.28 north, 11.10 west whilst on a voyage from Caraquet, New Brunswick for Preston with a cargo of 719 standards of timber in convoy SC.7. All 21 of her crew were saved.

28. SNELAND I

1,791g 1,054n
268.0 x 42.3 x 18.0 feet

A cargo of pit props helped ensure that the Whitby steamer *Scoresby* sank slowly enough for her entire crew to be rescued. *[R.M.Scott/Roy Fenton collection]*

Sedgepool was built by Ropner and Sons Ltd., Stockton-on-Tees for the fleet of Sir Robert Ropner and Co. Ltd., managers), West Hartlepool. *[Roy Fenton collection]*

T.3-cyl. (20½, 32¼, 55¼ x 35½ inches)
by Waggon und Maschinenbau A.G.,
Gorlitz, Germany; 155 NHP.
11.5.1922: Launched by Nuschke and
Co. A.G., Stettin, Germany for Reederei
Stange und Dreyer G.m.b.H., Stettin,
Germany as INGEBORG.
7.1922: Completed.
1925: Sold to D/S A/S Vestland
(Richard Amlie, manager), Haugesund,
Norway and renamed SNELAND I.
7.5.1945: Torpedoed and sunk by the
German submarine U 2336 in position
56.10 north, 02.31 west whilst on a voyage
from Blyth for Belfast with a cargo of
2,800 tons of coal. 29 crew; 7 lost.

29. SOESTERBERG
1,890g 1,119n.
278.5 x 40.2 x 18.4 feet.
T.3-cyl. (20, 33, 54 x 36 inches) by
North Eastern Marine Engineering Co.
Ltd., Sunderland; 214 NHP.
28.1.1927: Launched by Antwerp
Engineering Co., Hoboken (Yard No.
90) for N.V. Stoomvaart Maatschappij
'Hillegersberg' (Vincke & Co.,
managers), Amsterdam, Netherlands.
19.10.1940: Torpedoed and sunk by the
German submarine U 101 in position
57.12 north, 10.43 west whilst on a
voyage from Chatham, New Brunswick
for Hull with a cargo of 790 fathoms
of pitprops in convoy SC.7. Of her 25
crew, six were lost.

30. SOMERSBY
O.N.160769 5,170g 3,176n.
421.2 x 54.3 x 27.2 feet.
T.3-cyl. (26, 43½, 73 x 48 inches) by
Central Marine Engine Works, West
Hartlepool; 542 NHP, 2,500 IHP, 11 knots.
10.9.1930: Launched by William Gray
and Co. Ltd., West Hartlepool (Yard No.
1043) for the Ropner Shipping Co. Ltd.,
West Hartlepool.
16.10.1930: Registered at West
Hartlepool (5/1930).
13.5.1941: Torpedoed and sunk by the
German submarine U 111 in the North
Atlantic in position 60.39 north, 26.13
west whilst on a voyage from Halifax
for Loch Ewe and Hull with a cargo of
8,300 tons of grain in convoy SC.30.
All 43 of her crew were saved.
6.2.1942: Register closed.

31. THALIA
5,875g 4,278n.
385.3 x 51.2 x 25.5 feet.
T.3-cyl. (26, 43½, 72 x 48 inches) by
Kawasaki Dockyard Co. Ltd., Kobe,
Japan; 3,800 IHP.

Soesterberg was one of two Dutch-flag ships in SC.7 and its only ship built in Belgium. *[M.Lindenboorn]*

By the time *Somersby* was ordered by the Ropner Shipping Co. Ltd., the family's Stockton-on-Tees shipyard had closed and the order went to William Gray and Co. Ltd. of West Hartlepool. *[J. and M. Clarkson]*

The unusual crosstrees on *Thalia* identify her as one of the ships built in Japan to British account during the First World War and is seen at Montevideo on 12th October 1936 *[Raul Maya/J. and M. Clarkson]*

1917: Launched by Kawasaki Dockyard
Co. Ltd., Kobe, Japan (Yard No.
398) for The Shipping Controller,
London (Furness, Withy and Co. Ltd.,
managers), London as WAR LION.
30.1.1918: Registered at London
(26/1918).

28.10.1919: Sold to the African
Steamship Co. (Elder Dempster and Co.
Ltd., managers), London.
31.10.1919: Renamed JEBBA.
6.4.1933: Sold to the Tramp Shipping
Development Co. Ltd., London.
3.10.1933: Register closed on sale to

Xilas Brothers and A. Constaninidis, Syra, Greece and renamed THALIA. *19.10.1940:* Torpedoed and sunk by the German submarine U 99 in approximate position 57.00 north, 11.30 west whilst on a voyage from Montreal for Garston with a cargo of steel, lead and zinc in convoy SC.7. Of her 26 crew, 22 were lost.

32. THOROY

2,671g 1,518n.
294.0 x 39.6 x 26.8 feet.
T.3-cyl. (23, 37, 60 x 42 inches) by Wallsend Slipway and Engineering Co. Ltd., Wallsend-on-Tyne; 247 NHP, 1,400 IHP, 10 knots.
25.10.1893: Launched by Armstrong, Mitchell and Co. Ltd., Low Walker-on-Tyne (Yard No. 608) for the Bear Creek Oil and Shipping Co. Ltd. (C.T. Bowring and Co. Ltd., managers), Liverpool as SNOWFLAKE.
18.12.1893: Registered at Liverpool (78/1893).
27.12.1912: Sold to the S.A.J.C. Steamship Co. Ltd. (Lane and Macandrew, managers), London.
7.3.1913: British register closed on sale to Société Anonyme d'Armement, d'Industrie et de Commerce, Antwerp, Belgium and renamed KREMLIN.
1914: Requisitioned by The Admiralty for service as a Royal Fleet Auxiliary.
29.9.1914: Restored to the British register at London (135/1914) in the name of The Admiralty.
6.9.1919: British register closed on return of vessel to owners.
1922: Sold to Hvalfanger A/S Vestfold (J. Rasmussen and Co., managers), Sandefjord, Norway and renamed VELLOY.
1925: Sold to Bryde and Dahls Hvalfangerselskab (A/S Thor Dahl, manager), Sandefjord, Norway and renamed THOROY.
1947: Sold to Compania Panamena de Navegacion Santa Anna S.A., Panama (L. Reboul and G. Couteaux, Istanbul, Turkey managers) and renamed ANNE DE FRANCE.
12.1.1953: Arrived at Rosyth to be broken up by Metal Industries (Salvage) Ltd.

33. TREVISA

O.N.133573 1,813g 1,095n.
250.0 x 42.5 x 17.5 feet.
T.3-cyl. (16, 26½, 44 x 33 inches) by John G. Kincaid and Co., Greenock; 153 NHP, 835 IHP, 9 knots.
1.5.1915: Launched by the North of Ireland Shipbuilding Co. Ltd., Londonderry (Yard No. 61) for Swan,

Despite being the oldest ship in SC.7 the tanker *Thoroy* survived the convoy battle, and indeed the entire war, and was broken up at 60 years of age. *[J. and M. Clarkson]*

Trevisa photographed by Captain William J. Taylor, Master of a U.S. Lighthouse Service Tender, from his ship using a full plate camera. *Trevisa* was the only loss amongst the three Canadian vessels in SC.7. She had been built in Londonderry by a subsidiary of Swan, Hunter and Wigham Richardson Ltd., who made a specialty of building vessels for service on the Great Lakes. *[Captain J.N. Taylor/Jay Bascom collection]*

Hunter and Wigham Richardson Ltd., Newcastle-on-Tyne (Stewart and Esplen Ltd., Liverpool, managers) as TREVISA.
28.5.1915: Registered at Newcastle-on-Tyne (16/1915).
4.10.1915: Sold to the North of Ireland Shipbuilding Co. Ltd. (G.M. Stamp and A. Mann, managers), Newcastle-on-Tyne.
1919: Managers re-styled Stamp, Mann and Co.
23.5.1919: Sold to the Fairfield Steamship Co. Ltd. (Hugh Owen Jones and William Thomas Davies, managers), Cardiff.
6.11.1919: Sold to Harry Morgan Thomas, Cardiff.
7.5.1920: Transferred to the Tawe Steam Shipping Co. (H.M. Thomas, manager), Cardiff.
29.6.1921: Sold to John Waller, Montreal, Quebec.

20.7.1921: Re-registered at Montreal, Quebec (35/1921).
6.10.1921: Transferred to Export Steamships Ltd. (J. Waller, manager), Montreal, Quebec.
19.2.1923: Transferred to the Trevisa Steamship Co. Ltd. (J. Waller, manager), Montreal, Quebec
17.5.1928: Transferred to Canadian Lake Carriers Ltd. (J. Waller, manager), Montreal, Quebec [Keystone Transports Ltd.].
16.10.1940: Torpedoed and sunk by the German submarine U 124 in the North Atlantic in position 57.28 north, 20.30 west whilst on a voyage from Parrsboro', Nova Scotia to Aberdeen with a cargo of 460 standards of lumber in convoy SC.7. Of her 21 crew, seven were lost.
7.11.1940: Register closed.

34. TRIDENT

O.N.140697 4,317g 2,689n.
375.0 x 51.1 x 25.3 feet.
T.3-cyl. (25, 42, 69 x 48 inches) by
North Eastern Marine Engineering Co.
Ltd., Sunderland; 371 NHP, 2,000 IHP,
10½ knots.
8.8.1917: Launched by the Sunderland
Shipbuilding Co. Ltd., Sunderland
(Yard No. 293) for Hall Brothers
Steamship Co. Ltd. (Hall Brothers,
managers), Newcastle-on-Tyne as
TRIDENT.
20.9.1917: Registered at Newcastle-
on-Tyne (56/1917).
23.3.1937: Sold to the Quayside
Shipping Co. Ltd. (Connell and Grace
Ltd., managers), Newcastle-on-Tyne.
2.8.1941: Bombed and sunk by
German aircraft four miles off Buoy
20C, River Tyne whilst on a voyage
from Montreal and the Tyne for
London with a cargo of 6,000 tons of
grain and beans. All 43 of her crew
were saved.
14.8.1941: Register closed.

35. VALPARAISO

3,759g 2,259n.
364.5 x 51.4 x 22.1 feet.
Two 4SCSA 6-cyl. (23¼ x 35½ inches)
oil engines by A/S Burmeister and
Wain, Copenhagen, Denmark; 629
NHP.
21.12.1916: Launched by A/S
Burmeister and Wain, Copenhagen
(Yard No. 311) for Rederi A/B
Nordstjernan (A.A. Johnson, manager),
Stockholm, Sweden as VALPARAISO.
31.12.1940: Torpedoed and sunk by the
German submarine U 38 in the North
Atlantic in approximate position 60.00
north, 23.00 west whilst on a voyage
from Montreal for Glasgow with 6,181
tons of general cargo in convoy HX.97.
All 35 of her crew were lost.

36. WINONA

O.N.122851 2,085g 1,326n.
252.0 x 43.6 x 21.3 feet.
T.3-cyl. (20½, 33, 54 x 36 inches) by
MacColl and Pollock Ltd., Sunderland;
225 NHP, 1,200 IHP, 10 knots.
9.6.1906: Launched by Swan,
Hunter and Wigham Richardson
Ltd., Wallsend-on-Tyne (Yard No.
771) for the Winona Steamship Co.
Ltd. (Hamilton, Ontario) (R.O. and
A.B. Mackay, Newcastle-on-Tyne,
managers) as WINONA.
10.8.1906: Registered at Newcastle-
on-Tyne (17/1906) in the name of
Charles S. Swan, Wallsend-on-Tyne.

A plain funnel with a black top indicates that *Trident* was in the ownership of Hall Brothers of Newcastle-on-Tyne when photographed. *[J. and M. Clarkson]*

The classic Burmeister & Wain-built motor ship *Valparaiso* was one of three ships in SC.7 to carry general cargo. Although she survived the battle of SC.7 the Swedish ship was lost with all her crew within months. *[Roy Fenton collection]*

Winona laid up in the Toronto Turning Basin in 1939 with the Clyde-built *Kindersley* (1,999/1910) alongside. Neither would run again until they were requisitioned for wartime service. Despite her age *Winona*, one of three Canadian lakers in SC.7, came through unscathed and survived the war, although she was to be wrecked soon after her fiftieth birthday. *[A.C. King/Jay Bascom collection]*

28.8.1906: Sold to the Winona Steamship Co. Ltd. (Adam B. Mackay, manager), Hamilton, Ontario.
15.9.1909: Re-registered at Hamilton, Ontario (3/1909).
1913: Management transferred to the Inland Lines Ltd., Hamilton, Ontario.
25.5.1916: Sold to Canada Steamship Lines Ltd., Montreal, Quebec.

25.1.1946: Sold to the Ministry of War Transport (William France, Fenwick and Co. Ltd., managers), London.
18.3.1946: Re-registered at London (59/1946).
22.7.1946: Sold to Wheelock, Marden and Co. Ltd, London.
1947: Sold to the Eddy Steamship Co. Ltd., Shanghai and renamed EDDIE.

15.1.1947: Register closed.
1948: Sold to the Lien Yih Steamship Co. Ltd., Shanghai (W.H. Eddie Hsu, Taipei, Taiwan).
7.9.1956: Stranded in a gale on a sandbank off Aparri, Cagayan whilst on a voyage from Cagayan for Japan with a cargo of logs.

SOURCES AND ACKNOWLEDGEMENTS

We thank all who gave permission for their photographs to be used, and for help in finding images we are particularly grateful to Jim McFaul and David Whiteside of the World Ship Photo Library; to Ian Farquhar, F.W. Hawks, Peter Newall, Russell Priest, William Schell; and to David Hodge and Bob Todd of the National Maritime Museum, and to other museums and institutions listed.

Research sources include the Registers of William Schell and Tony Starke, 'Lloyd's Register', 'Lloyd's Confidential Index', 'Lloyd's Shipping Index', 'Lloyd's War Losses', 'Mercantile Navy Lists', 'Marine News', 'Sea Breezes' and 'Shipbuilding and Shipping Record'. Use of the facilities of the World Ship Society, the Guildhall Library, the National Archives and Lloyd's Register of Shipping are gratefully acknowledged. Particular thanks also to Heather Fenton for editorial and indexing work, and to Marion Clarkson for accountancy services.

South West Scenes: Falmouth part 3
Many thanks to Terry Nelder for photographs and information, and to John Bartlett quickly ran to earth an article on *Oriana* in 'Model Shipwright' No, 28 for June 1979 which mentioned her conversion to an experimental stern trawler.

John Cockerill's Tilbury Service
Interview and letters of Captain I.G. Camerlinck, former master of Cockerill vessels; documents of the late François Hermans, plus copies of 'The Belgian Shiplover', 'Wandelaer et Sur L'eau'; 'Transport Echo' and 'Sea Breezes'.

Aberdeen Motor Trawlers Ltd.
Newspaper cuttings from the 'Press and Journal' and 'Evening Express' held at the library of Aberdeen Journals Ltd.; the shipping registers for the port of Aberdeen held by Aberdeen City Archives; archive copies of 'Fishing News' held at Aberdeen Central Library.

John Priestman and Tower Deck ships
The few sources referring to Tower Deck ships include Thomas P.N., 'British Ocean Tramps' Waine Research Publications, Albrighton, 1992 which also has some details of Priestman's shipbuilding career. More on this is in Clarke, J.F., 'Building Ships on the North East Coast: A Labour of Love, Risk and Pain', Bewick Press, Whitley Bay, 1997. Oddly, Clarke's monumental two-volume work does not mention the Tower Decks. Smith JW and Holden TS 'Where Ships are Born: A History of Shipbuilding on the River Wear' Reed, Sunderland, 1946 also provides a brief history of Priestman, his yard and circumstances, and is widely quoted

on websites. None of the foregoing are completely accurate, and the ultimate source to launch dates and completions must be the World Ship Society yard list, and this was clearly used by Middlemiss, N.L. 'British Shipbuilding Yards Volume 1: North East Coast', Shield Publications, Newcastle-upon-Tyne1993, although he cites Kilmaho as an example of the Twer Deck ship, erroneously it is believed.

Union-Castle's Black Ships
Company documents: Union-Castle Mail Steamship Co. Ltd. documents used include Directors' Minute Books 1912-1975; Head Office Voyage Books 1926-1947 and 'Particulars of Fleet' issued 1912 and updated to 1926; *York Castle* building and engineering contract and related correspondence, 1901.

Books referred to include: 'Lloyds Register' (various years); 'Union-Castle Line A Fleet History' Newall, P., Carmania Press 2000; 'The Lost Ship *Waratah*' Smith P.J., The History Press 2009; 'The Nitrate Boats' Burrell, D., World Ship Society 1995; 'British Standard Ships of World War 1' Mitchell W.H. and Sawyer L.A., Journal of Commerce 1968; 'Fifty Thrilling Years at Sea' Whitfield, G.J., Hutchinson 1934; 'The Union-Castle and the War' Knight E.F., Union-Castle, 1920; 'Henry Blogg of Cromer - The Greatest of the Lifeboatmen' Jolly C., Harrap 1958.

Newspaper and journal articles include: 'British Cargo Ships and the 1940 Norwegian Campaign' Ships in Focus Record No 56, John de Winser; 'Daily Telegraph' Obituaries of Commodore Cuthbertson and John Coundley 'Magnificent Mail Motorships' Kohler P.C.

Ships of SC.7, October 1940
www.uboat.net proved the most comprehensive and up-to-date record of the German submarine campaign and of Allied merchant ship losses to U-boats.

Books consulted were 'Axis Submarine Successes 1939 1945' Rohwer, J., U.S.N.I., 1983 (the original reference book on U-boat sinkings, and still a valuable source for the digitally-challenged) and 'Night of the U-Boats' Lund, P. and Ludlam, H. Foulsham, London, 1973. The latter is the only narrative history devoted to SC.7. Perhaps a little dated, but it is based on extensive interviews with survivors, including no fewer than eight men who were masters of ships sailing in the convoy.

Whitwill, Cole
Some of the early history of Whitwill, Cole was sourced from research by the late Richard Parsons whose work was loaned by John D. Hill. Thanks to Nigel Jones for a review of the text and advice.

R.S. HAYES OF PEMROKE DOCK

Andrew Huckett

Following the cessation of hostilities in 1945, the ship repair and maintenance facilities which had flourished during the Second World War in part of the old naval dockyard at Pembroke Dock were no longer required. Although the RAF had taken over and developed much of the Royal Dockyard, part had remained available for ship repair work. It had also been used in the inter-war period by T.W. Ward for ship breaking.

During the war these facilities had been responsible for repairing and maintaining many warships and auxiliary vessels, including the boom defence vessels based at Carr Jetty which operated the booms across the entrance to the Haven. With the closure of the facility in 1947, the South Wales-based engineering firm of R.S. Hayes Ltd. was asked to open a ship repair yard to help improve the unemployment situation in Pembroke Dock caused by the closure of the wartime facility.

In response to the request a member of the Hayes family, Commander Richard Hayes, a former Royal Navy engineering officer, arrived in Pembroke Dock in 1947 to establish R.S. Hayes (Pembroke Dock) Ltd. It opened a yard utilizing what few facilities remained in the old Royal Dockyard, mainly centred round a graving dock. At its peak the company employed 500 people in a variety of trades, and in a diverse range of activities which included general engineering and the maintenance of RAF properties in West Wales.

It also undertook some ship breaking with six identified ex-naval vessels being broken up by the company in the years 1948/9. These were the 'Bangor' class minesweepers *Parrsboro, Peterhead* and *Poole,* a decoy ship *PC.74,* the ex-US Navy destroyer *Burnham* and the 'Flower' class corvette *Delphinium.* In 1923 the firm of R.S. Hayes Ltd. had broken up two ex-naval paddle minesweepers at Pembroke Dock, *Banbury* and *Hexham.*

However, the company's principal activity remained ship repair work. Over the years, until its closure in 1961, a great variety of ships came for repair or refit at Pembroke Dock. These included naval and RFA vessels, Trinity House tenders and lightships, Shell and Esso tankers, trawlers and general cargo ships.

In 1954 the yard began its biggest job to date. This was the conversion of a general cargo ship into a cable-layer. Taken over while on the stocks at Flensburg as war reparation, *Empire Foam* was completed in 1948 by her German shipbuilders for the Ministry of War Transport. In 1953 she was acquired by Submarine Cables Ltd., London, and arrived at the Hayes yard in Pembroke Dock on 21st February 1954. In the following year she emerged as the cable-layer *Ocean Layer.* Fitted with four cable tanks she was able to carry 1,100 nautical miles of coaxial cable or 1,875 nautical miles of deep-sea telegraph cable. The cable machinery was originally designed and manufactured by Johnson & Phillips for PLUTO (Pipe Line Under The Ocean), the system used to supply the Allied armies in France with fuel after D-Day.

Unfortunately, the *Ocean Layer* had a relatively short career in this role as, on 15th June 1959, while laying the second transatlantic cable between Newfoundland and France, she caught fire and was burnt out while working

Ocean Layer. [J. and M. Clarkson]

in the Western Approaches. The 86 crew and 12 US and French telephone and telegraph executives were rescued by Silvia Reederei's *Flavia* (3,355/1958). Initially leaving the scene the *Flavia* returned to the burning derelict, put on board her chief officer and six members of crew and secured a provisional towline. *Flavia* held *Ocean Layer* in position until the arrival of the German salvage tug *Wotan*, ex *Lenamill*-50, *Arngast*-47 (729/1939) to whom the tow was transferred. *Wotan* towed *Ocean Layer* into Falmouth where the fire was finally extinguished and she was handed back to her owners. The extensive damage meant the ship was sold for breaking up in the Netherlands.

The next major refit undertaken by the yard was for the Royal Navy. This was the refit of the 'Bay' class frigate HMS *Porlock Bay* between January and May 1956. Laid down as a 'Loch' class anti-submarine frigate she was originally to have been named *Loch Muick* but this was changed to *Loch Seaforth*. In 1944 she was altered to an anti-aircraft frigate while building and received the name *Porlock Bay*. She served as an active ship only between 1946 and 1949 when she was placed in reserve at Devonport. In March 1962 she was sold to the Finnish Navy and renamed *Matti Kurki*. She was withdrawn from service in 1975.

In 1956 it was announced that the newly established Federal German Navy was to acquire seven warships from the Royal Navy. One of these was the 'Hunt' class escort destroyer HMS *Eggesford*. Completed in 1943 by J.S White and Co., Cowes, Isle of Wight, she had seen service in the Mediterranean and the North Sea prior to serving in the Indian Ocean at the end of the war. After a year in a training flotilla at Rosyth she was reduced to reserve in November 1946. Her actual sale to the German Navy took place in November 1957. She then underwent a refit at Pembroke Dock before being commissioned, in May 1959, as a training ship for underwater weapons under the name of *Brommy*. She was broken up in 1979.

Over the years R.S. Hayes (Pembroke Dock) Ltd. also undertook some shipbuilding. The first build, in 1953, was a small twin-screw diesel tug name *Ramos*. Built for the Anglo-Saxon Petroleum Company she was designed to tow lighters on the rivers of Nigeria. She was the first new build to be launched at Pembroke Dock for 32 years. In 1955 and 1956 the company built four motor launches for H.M. Customs and Excise for their Gravesend station, *Pioneer*, *Despatch*, *Scout* and *Speedwell*.

The sixth build was a vessel which became a long-term resident of Milford Haven. The trawler *Norrard Star* was completed for Norrard Trawlers Ltd. of Milford Haven in December 1956. She was eventually broken up in 1995, not far from where she was built at Pembroke Dock. She was followed, in 1957, by the 959gt general cargo coaster *Kirtondyke*, built for the Klondyke Shipping Co. Ltd. of Hull. In 1975 she was sold to Greek owners as *Myrtidiotissa II*. After passing through several hands she was broken up in Yugoslavia in 1984 following a grounding the previous year.

The last vessel built by Hayes, described as a twin-hull firefloat, was *B.P. Firemaster*, completed in 1960 for B.P. Refinery (Llandarcy) Ltd. at Swansea. She was later converted into a diving tender.

In 1957 Commander Richard Hayes, while still General Manager of R.S. Hayes (Pembroke Dock) Ltd., obtained a RAF mooring contract with the Air Ministry under which he took over the running of the mooring and salvage vessels *Watchmoor*, *Salmoor* and *Rexmoor*.

In the following year he founded Milford Haven Marine Services Ltd. in anticipation of obtaining contracts with the oil companies to service the maritime needs of the oil terminals being built on the Haven. The base for the new company was established in what had been the western part of the Royal Dockyard. It was situated around the ex-RAF west basin alongside Hayes' ship repair yard.

After long negotiations the new company obtained joint contracts with Esso and B.P. for the mooring, storing and provision of all marine services for tankers at their respective terminals. As the number of oil installations increased so the company obtained contracts to service all the terminals on the Haven.

To provide its service the company needed to build up a small fleet of specialist vessels, as well as to train the required personnel to man the vessels and act as mooring gangs. Some of the first vessels acquired were ex-RAF marine craft, range safety launches and tenders, and all were given the *Pembroke* prefix and a bird name. All the company's vessels were similarly named. The role of the launches was to transport mooring gangs and personnel between the oil terminals. They were also advertised as providing cruises in the waters of Milford Haven, the lower reaches of the River Cleddau and around the Pembrokeshire coastline and islands. However, the launches proved too expensive in their projected oil role and the leisure aspect did not prove successful. One, *Pembroke Fulmar*, was sold in 1959 to the Milford Haven Conservancy Board as its first patrol launch, being renamed *Lady Dynevor*. The other launches were also sold. A harbour defence motor launch was also acquired, named *Pembroke Shearwater*, with the object of running as a waterbus between the oil terminals but as the necessary passenger certificate could not be obtain it was quickly sold.

Another requirement was of vessels to be used as rope-runners. Their task was to take the ship's ropes ashore as part of the mooring process. They had to be robust to withstand the sea conditions which can affect the Haven, as well as possible contact with a ship or the jetty piles on the oil terminals. The first acquired in 1957 was *Pembroke Grebe* which is thought to have been a Thornycroft-built

Kirtondyke sailing from Preston. *[J. and M. Clarkson]*

ship's boat from Canadian Pacific's *Empress of Canada*, ex *Duchess of Richmond*-47 (20,022/1929) which had caught fire and capsized in Gladstone Dock, Liverpool in 1953. In 1959 two ex-Trinity House boats were acquired and named *Pembroke Teal* and *Pembroke Pintail*. After long service with the company, on de-commissioning, *Teal* was burnt at Pembroke Dock and *Pintail* moved to Milford Docks for restoration in connection with a maritime heritage scheme. When the scheme failed it was broken up. The same fate befell *Pembroke Snipe*, one of four rope-runners acquired in 1964 and 1965. Another of the four, *Pembroke Heron* was burnt after being crushed by a tanker at the BP Terminal.

A third category of vessel was the store carrier. In 1958 an ex-RAF flying boat re-fueller was acquired as *Pembroke Guillemot* and converted into a stores carrier with the removal of its tank. She was sold in 1968.

In 1960 Milford Haven Marine Services acquired a number of motor and dumb barges at an auction in Liverpool following the liquidation of Liverpool-based Burton and Son Ltd. in the previous year. The purpose of the acquisition was to obtain vessels to carry stores and provisions to ships. Only three were actually used as such, the rest being laid up at Pembroke Dock. Those put into operation were the 1933-built dumb barge *Pembroke Mallard*, which was in service for just two years, and the motor cargo barges *Pembroke Cormorant* and *Pembroke Pelican*. They were broken up in 1968.

The following year a 1944-built motor fishing vessel was acquired, being renamed *Pembroke Provider*, to run stores to the ships. She was sold out of service in 1967. In 1965 the 1911-built steel lighter *Egbert* was acquired from Roy Eynon of Angle and renamed *Pembroke Skua* also to assist in the

transport of stores. Four years later, in 1969, the 1945-built water carrier *VIC 80* was acquired from the Admiralty. She was rebuilt and converted into a stores barge under the name *Pembroke Guillemot*. She was sold privately in 1989 after a period laid up.

For carrying lubricating oil the 1955-built motor barge *Helmsdale H* was acquired from John Harker Ltd. of Knottingley and renamed *Pembroke Helmsdale*.

The last acquisition for the company was a 30-foot, timber-built, rope-runner named *Pembroke Petrel* which was completed by Gayseng, Singapore, in 1975, although not commissioned until 1987.

In the late 1960s Milford Haven Marine Services Ltd. changed its name to Marine and Port Services Ltd. In 1977 the company was sold to the Milford Haven Conservancy Board, later the Milford Haven Port Authority, and the involvement of Richard Hayes ceased.

Helmsdale H at Liverpool. *[J. and M. Clarkson]*

Yard list

1. RAMOS Twin-screw motor tug
O.N. 196683 43g 3n.
56.5 x 14.6 x 5.7 feet.
Oil engine.
20.10.1953: Launched by R.S. Hayes (Pembroke Dock) Ltd., Pembroke Dock (Yard No. 500) for Anglo-Saxon Petroleum Co. Ltd., London as RAMOS.
1954: Transferred to Shell d'Arcy Petroleum Development Co. of Nigeria, Ltd., Lagos, Nigeria.
1966: Sold. Fate unknown.

2. PIONEER Motor launch
52 tons.
63 x 15 x 8 feet.
Oil engine by Ruston and Hornsby Ltd., Lincoln.
5.1955: Completed by R.S. Hayes (Pembroke Dock) Ltd., Pembroke Dock (Yard No. 501) for H.M. Customs and Excise as PIONEER and based at Gravesend.
1974: Sold.

3. DESPATCH Motor launch
52 tons.
63 x 15 x 8 feet.
Oil engine by Ruston & Hornsby Ltd.,

Lincoln.
6.1955: Launched by R.S. Hayes (Pembroke Dock) Ltd., Pembroke Dock (Yard No. 502) for H.M. Customs and Excise as DESPATCH and based on the Tyne.
1973: Sold.

4. SCOUT Motor launch
52 tons.
63 x 15 x 8 feet.
Oil engine by Ruston and Hornsby Ltd., Lincoln
1956: Completed by R.S. Hayes (Pembroke Dock) Ltd., Pembroke Dock (Yard No. 503) for H.M. Customs and Excise as SCOUT and based at Gravesend.
1.9.1963: S.I.S.

5. SPEEDWELL Motor launch
52 tons.
63 x 15 x 8 feet.
Oil engine by Ruston and Hornsby Ltd., Lincoln.
1956: Completed by R.S. Hayes (Pembroke Dock) Ltd., Pembroke Dock (Yard No. 504) for H.M. Customs and Excise as SPEEDWELL and based at Gravesend.
1974: Sold.
5.1996: Became work boat SCAPA COURIER at Stromness.

6. NORRARD STAR (M44) Motor side trawler
O.N. 300156 L.R. 5256472 167g, 56n.
101.0 feet x 23.2 feet.
2SCSA 4-cyl. oil engine by H. Widdop and Co. Ltd., Keighley.
1981: 4SA 12-cyl. vee-type oil engine by Poyaud-S.S.C.M.,Surgeres, France; 420 BHP.
10.7.1956: Launched by R.S. Hayes (Pembroke Dock) Ltd., Pembroke Dock (Yard No 505) for Norrard Trawlers Ltd., Milford Haven as NORRARD STAR.
12.1956: Completed.
1981: Re-engined.
9.1993: Sold to Cinca Ltd., Newry, County Down, Northern Ireland.
1995: Broken up at Pembroke Dock.

7. KIRTONDYKE Motor coaster
L.R. 5189174/O.N. 300379 959g 473n 1,275d.
214.6 x 35.5 x 13.3 feet.
2SCSA 6-cyl. oil engine by British Polar Engines Ltd., Glasgow; 900BHP, 12 knots.
11.6.1957: Launched by R.S. Hayes (Pembroke Dock) Ltd., Pembroke Dock (Yard No. 506) for Klondyke Shipping Co. Ltd., Hull as KIRTONDYKE.
10.1957: Completed.
1975: Sold to Emmanuel Xintarakos & Anastasios Papadopoulos, Piraeus, Greece and renamed MYRTIDIOTISSA II.

1976: Sold to Dragonara Shipping Co. Ltd. (Kytheraiki Marine Co. Ltd., agents), Piraeus, Greece.

2.12.1983: Whilst on passage from Rijeka to Preveze with a cargo of timber caught by gale force wind and deliberately run aground on Vrulje Islet to avoid capsizing when the cargo shifted.

3.12.1983: Refloated by the Yugoslavian tugs SIRIUS (208/1976) and ARIES (208/1977) but developed leaks while in tow to Mali Losinj and was beached on Kaludarac Islet.

11.1.1984: Refloated and laid up at Mali Losinj and later Rijeka.

1984: Sold to Starling Shipping Co. S.A., Panama (Kytheraika Marine Co. Ltd., Piraeus, Greece, managers).

6.2.1988: Arrived at Sveti Kajo in tow of Yugoslavian tug BORAC (430/1967) to be broken up and laid up in scrap yard.

3.1991: Demolition began by Brodospas. She was the last ship to be broken up there.

8. B.P. FIREMASTER Twin-screw twin-hull firefloat
 O.N. 168599 L.R. 5033014 88g 88n
 60.0 x 38.0 feet.

Kirtondyke. [World Ship Photo Library]

Two 4SCSA 6-cyl. oil engines by W.H. Dorman and Co. Ltd., Stafford; 290 BHP.
1959: Pontoons completed by J.S. Watson (Gainsborough) Ltd., Gainsborough (Yard No. 1764)
1.1960: Lengthened and completed by R.S. Hayes (Pembroke Dock) Ltd., Pembroke Dock (Yard No. 507) for B.P. Refinery (Llandarcy) Ltd., Swansea as B.P. FIREMASTER.
Converted into a diving tender.
Fate unknown.

EVERY PICTURE TELLS A STORY

This is an irresistible and possibly unique photograph of a ship in Blue Funnel colours, the *Dania* of 1904. It was taken whilst she was managed by Alfred Holt and Company for the Shipping Controller from May 1919 to October 1921. She is ignored by most histories of Holts.

The 3,898 gross tons *Dania* had been built by Reiherstieg Schiffswerft, Hamburg for Hamburg-Amerika Linie. With her sister *Bavaria* (3,898/1905), her enormous capacity for steerage passengers contrasting with her modest size and even more modest speed of 11½ knots indicates the intention to use for immigrants, and she is known to have worked between Hamburg and North and Central America. In 1915 the Kaiserlichen Marine requisitioned *Dania* and employed her as *Sperrbrecher 1*, literally a 'barrier breaker'. On 8th May 1919 she left Hamburg for the Firth of Forth to be claimed as war reparations, and was given to Holts to manage. But the Liverpool company were not keen on former German tonnage, disappointed by their one and only experience of buying one, the former Norddeutscher Lloyd *Brandenburg* which became *Hecuba* (7,540/1902). *Dania* made at least one voyage to New York where she is believed to have sunk in a collision during November 1920.

Presumably the Shipping Controller was pleased to get whatever her former owners were prepared to pay for *Dania*, and she returned to HAPAG on 1st October 1920. As *Tsad*, with a reduced passenger accommodation in first and third class, she was put on sailings to West Africa, from 1923 wearing Woernann Lines colours. Without its former colonies, Germany would have much reduced trade with Africa and in November 1924 *Tsad* was sold to Italy as *Assunzione*. Next she was with Marseille owners as *Caramanie* from 1925, but was laid up in 1928. Once more unloved, she was broken up in Italy during 1934. *[J. and M. Clarkson collection]*

Fleet in photos
STEVENSON OF LONDONDERRY

Reviewing the various types of ship featured in this issue, it was apparent that one of an editor's all-time favourites, the steam coaster, had been neglected. This gave an excuse to feature the five steamers of Londonderry owner Samuel B. Stevenson. Four out of five were photographed under their Stevenson names, and all are fully documented in registration records. Unfortunately, little is known of Samuel Stevenson himself, other than that he entered ship owning in 1919, having previously been in engineering, probably at Foyle Street, Londonderry where he first operated his ships, later moving to 25 Shipquay Street in the city.

Stevenson began business with a flurry, buying five steamers in less than a month during October and early November of 1919. He would have paid over the odds for this fleet, even though the steamers were up to 23 years old and had seen service for several owners, as the post-war boom in freight rates and with it ship prices had not yet given way to a deep recession. Indicative of a degree of pride in his ageing fleet, Stevenson bothered to rename them all. This was a process which required some administrative effort and was relatively unusual amongst steam coaster owners of the era, who often followed the practice of those running sailing vessels and never changed a name. Stevenson's names were mostly mellifluous although some were rather obscure, the exception being Islandmagee, from a peninsula between Larne and Carrickfergus on the Antrim coast.

Stevenson's steamers were all small, single-hold coasters, suited to working into small ports around Ireland. Naturally they served their owner's home port of Londonderry and the Lough Swilly ports of Buncrana, Letterkenny, Ramelton and Rathmullen, but also Bangor, Coleraine, Donaghadee, Drogheda, Dundalk, Larne and Portrush. In season they carried French potatoes to the Bristol Channel and occasionally traded on the East Coast out of Leith. But alas, the inflated prices Stevenson paid in 1919 were unsustainable once boom inevitably turned to deep slump in the early 1920s. Over the turn of the year in 1926 and 1927, Stevenson sold his three youngest – or perhaps it should be least old – ships, *Islandmagee* on the last day of December 1926, *Glencregagh* on 15th January and *Rossgarragh* on 28th February 1927. But the minimal prices he received did not rescue him financially, and his last two ships, *Thrushfield* and *Silversprings*, were repossessed by their mortgagees and sold on 18th June 1929. Built in 1896 and 1898 respectively, they were Stevenson's oldest, and some indication of their value can be had from the mere £300 *Silversprings* fetched when she went for scrap in the mid-1930s.

Samuel Stevenson was a brave man to buy five coasters in 1919, but it turned out to be a very inopportune time to make such an investment, and after ten years of struggling to make his expensively-acquired fleet pay, he had little to show for his efforts.

Possibly reflecting his training as an engineer, Stevenson favoured the well-built coasters from the Paisley yard of John Fullerton; the *May*, which became *Silversprings*, being the first of three acquired. This view, showing *Silversprings* with the characteristic list of a steam coaster whose coal in her port and starboard bunkers is not evenly distributed, shows her in Preston in 1937. By then owners were Percy Berrill of Bristol, and her funnel had been repainted. *[D.B. Cochrane/World Ship Photo Library]*

1. SILVERSPRINGS 1919-1929
O.N. 108625 236g 93n.
130.0 x 21.0 x 9.5 feet.
C. 2-cyl. by Campbell and Calderwood, Paisley; 50 NHP.

7.7.1898: Launched by John Fullerton and Co., Paisley (Yard No. 142).
15.8.1898: Registered in the ownership of Captain Thomas Burns, William Dunn and Thomas Matthews, Bangor, County Down

as MAY.
7.1.1915: Sold to Samuel Stewart, Belfast.
8.1.1915: Sold to Thomas M. Collier, Bray.
12.1.1915: Sold to Kynoch-Arklow Ltd., London.

Given her ownership in the port during the 1930s, this delightful photograph may well show the *Silversprings* in Bristol, although it would be good to have confirmation that in the late 1930s one J. Warriner did have a bonded warehouse in the town's docks. Note the queue of pedestrians waiting to cross the swing bridge, and the semaphore signal which may be controlling water or rail traffic. *[World Ship Photo Library]*

23.7.1919: Sold to John Kelly Ltd., Belfast.
6.10.1919: Acquired by Samuel B. Stevenson, Londonderry.
11.2.1920: Renamed SILVERSPRINGS.
18.6.1929: Sold to Wilson and Reid Ltd., Belfast.
6.1.1931: Sold to Percy Berrill, Bristol.
20.6.1935: Sold for £300 to T.W. Ward Ltd. for breaking up.
26.6.1935: Arrived at Briton Ferry.
27.8.1935: Register closed.

2. ISLANDMAGEE 1919-1926

O.N. 111275 227g 85n.
117.0 x 21.5 x 9.4 feet.
C. 2-cyl. by Muir and Houston Ltd., Glasgow; 35 NHP, 250 IHP, 9 knots.
28.6.1900: Launched by Scott and Sons, Bowling (Yard No.142).
6.7.1900: Registered in the ownership of Glasgow Steam Coasters Co. Ltd. (Paton and Hendry, managers), Glasgow as BONAHAVEN.

20.3.1919: Sold to Samuel Gray, Belfast.
4.4.1919: Sold to Alexander Montgomery Ltd., Londonderry.
25.10.1919: Acquired by Samuel B. Stevenson, Londonderry.
23.2.1920: Renamed ISLANDMAGEE.
31.12.1926: Sold to John G. Stewart, Glasgow.
20.6.1933: Sold by mortgagee to John A. Landsborough and Co., Glasgow.
3.10.1941: Sold to the Tay Sand Co. Ltd. (John Neilson, manager), Dundee.

Islandmagee sports a funnel which has a variant of the standard Stevenson colours, with the red which was normally just a band carried to the base. With her upright funnel and single mast, the 'Wee-Scotts' built coaster does not have the elegance of the Fullerton-built ships in the fleet. But handsome is as handsome does, and her total of 53 years of service made her by a narrow margin the longest lasting of the five coasters. Her last 12 years were spent in the River Tay sand trade, the double tragedy of her demise in October 1953 indicating that this was not the benign business it might sound. *[J. and M. Clarkson]*

26.10.1953: Left Dundee for Leith with a cargo of sand and disappeared with her crew of six. She is believed to have foundered off Fifeness early on 27.10.1953. Whilst returning to harbour after investigating flares which are believed to have been fired by the ISLANDMAGEE, the Arbroath lifeboat ROBERT LINDSAY capsized at Arbroath harbour entrance with the loss of six of her crew of seven.
23.6.1955: Register closed.

3. THRUSHFIELD 1919-1929
O.N.102463 249g 100n.
125.0 x 20.1 x 9.2 feet.
C. 2-cyl. by Ross and Duncan, Govan; 43 NHP, 400 IHP, 10 knots.
27.3.1896: Launched by John Fullerton and Co., Paisley (Yard No.129).
22.4.1896: Registered in the ownership of Robert Simpson, Whitehaven as ELLER.
6.10.1903: Sold to Thomas Coppack and Co., Connah's Quay.
23.2.1915: Sold to Kynoch-Arklow Ltd., London.
25.7.1919: Sold to John Kelly Ltd., Belfast.
30.10.1919: Acquired by Samuel B. Stevenson, Londonderry.
23.3.1920: Renamed THRUSHFIELD.
18.6.1929: Sold by mortgagees to Wilson and Reid Ltd. (Thomas S. Wilson, manager), Belfast.
4.2.1930: William Reid, Belfast appointed manager by mortgagees.
22.12.1930: Sold to William Reid Ltd., Belfast.
28.4.1936: Foundered six miles south east of Rathlin O'Birne, County Donegal whilst on a voyage from Birkenhead to Ballyshannon with a cargo of coal.
15.6.1936: Register closed.

4. GLENCREGAGH 1919-1927
O.N. 128493 322g 116n.
142.2 x 23.6 x 10.4 feet.
C. 2-cyl. by Ross and Duncan, Govan; 68 NHP, 450 IHP, 10 knots.
20.4.1909: Launched by John Fullerton and Co., Paisley (Yard No.210).
22.5.1909: Registered in the ownership of Edward England, Richard T. England and William Young, Cardiff as CARDIFF CITY.
9.6.1909: Sold to the Despatch Steamship Co. Ltd. (John Tyrrell, manager), Cardiff.
3.3.1914: Sold to the Wear Steam Shipping Co. Ltd. (Thomas Rose, manager), Sunderland.
31.3.1914: Renamed EDENSIDE.
6.3.1916: Sold to Kynoch-Arklow Ltd., London.
5.4.1916: Renamed RIVER AVOCA.
14.7.1919: Sold to John Kelly Ltd., Belfast.
30.10.1919: Acquired by Samuel B. Stevenson, Londonderry.
25.3.1920: Renamed GLENCREGAGH.
15.1.1927: Sold to William J. Ireland, Liverpool.
18.1.1927: Sold to Frederick E. Peters, Bristol trading as the Bristol Sand and Gravel Co. Ltd.
3.6.1929: Wrecked at Vazon Bay, Guernsey whilst on a voyage from Weymouth to Lizardrieux with a cargo of empty hampers.
1.7.1929: Register closed.

Four of Stevenson's five steamers had been in the fleet of the explosives company Kynoch-Arklow Ltd. which was disbanded in 1919, the ships passing to Stevenson through the hands of John Kelly Ltd. The oldest was the *Thrushfield*, another Fullerton product, seen above at Preston. It is indicative of the hazards which coasters and their crews faced over often long lives that, of the five ships featured here, three including *Thrushfield* were eventually lost. *[World Ship Photo Library]*

Glencregagh was the youngest ship in Stevenson's fleet, but the most frequently renamed. As *Cardiff City* she was built for Cardiff owners who wanted a steamer with a good turn of speed to compete in the seasonal, though profitable, trade in carrying vegetables grown in France to south coast and Bristol Channel ports. After she spent a few days in the hands of Liverpool coastal ship owner William J. Ireland, her final owner was a Bristol aggregate supplier, although she seems not to have been converted for dredging. Her last voyage was in the English Channel with what were presumably hampers destined for France to be loaded with vegetables.

5. ROSSGARRAH 1919-1927
O.N. 119143 281g 109n.
132.8 x 23.1 x 9.7 feet.
C. 2-cyl. by Bow, McLachlan and Co. Ltd., Paisley; 47 NHP, 370 IHP 9 knots.
16.6.1904: Launched by Bow, McLachlan and Co. Ltd., Paisley (Yard No. 175).
25.6.1904: Registered in the ownership of the Eglinton Limestone Co. Ltd. (Peter Rintoul, manager), Glasgow as GLENARM.
1.12.1910: Sold to John Faill and Peter Rintoul, Glasgow.
11.1.1911: Sold to Peter Rintoul, Glasgow becomes managing owner.
1.4.1915: Sold to Kynoch-Arklow Ltd., London.
22.7.1919: Sold to John Kelly Ltd. (Samuel

Kelly, manager), Belfast.
1.11.1919: Acquired by Samuel B.
Stevenson, Londonderry.
23.3.1920: Renamed ROSSGARRAGH.
28.2.1927: Sold to John Kennedy and D.
McA. Kennedy, Glasgow.

1.4.1927: Renamed ISLESMAN.
24.5.1937: Sold to Arthur C. Reynolds
(40/64), John C. Reynolds (12/64) and
Alfred N. Reynolds (12/64), Portreath.
22.6.1938: Sold to the Beynon Shipping Co.
Ltd. (Alfred M.C. Jenour, manager), Cardiff.

22.12.1954: Register closed on sale to
Oceana N.V., Holland.
3.1955: Sold to N.V. Maschinehandel
und Scheepsloperij 'De Koophandel' for
breaking up at Nieuwe Lekkerland.
6.1955: Work in progress.

Rossgarragh is seen in Preston, wearing Stevenson's regular funnel colours: black with a red band which bears a white letter S. The band was echoed on the owner's house flag, but whether this would have been flown regularly in the coastal trade is debatable. *[D.B. Cochrane/World Ship Photo Library]*

Another product of a Paisley shipyard, although Bow, Maclachlan's rather than Fullerton's, *Rossgarrah* is under her third name, *Islesman*. As such she lasted until the mass extinction of steam coasters in the mid-1950s, and is seen in the distinctive funnel colours of Beynon Shipping Co. Ltd. of Cardiff. In this post-war photograph taken near the Woolwich Ferry on the Thames (and in two other known photos) she has lost her mizzen mast but retains an open bridge. *[World Ship Photo Library]*

BURMAH OIL TANKERS

Andrew Bell

If India was the Koh-I-Noor ('Mountain of Light') diamond as the 'Jewel of the Crown' of the British Empire, Burma was a sapphire of great quality. Adjacent to India, its natural resources were almost limitless. The tropical hardwood forests measured in hundreds of square miles were rich in minerals ranging from tin to tungsten, a land so rich that its rice production could feed much of South East Asia and India. After a series of colonial wars from 1823 until 1886, the colony was annexed by the British and made a province of India. Exploited in the new era of colonial administration was crude oil, easily accessible from Yenangaung in the riverine lands through which the mighty Irrawaddy flows. Trade followed the flag and

An early Burmah Oil tanker was *Twingone* (1,771/1902). Sold to Anglo-Saxon as *Unio* after a fire at Tuticorin in 1913, she was sunk as *Cassala* in the disastrous German air raid on Bari in December 1943. *[J. and M. Clarkson]*

in the 1890s the James Finlay trading house of merchant venturers established the Burmah Oil Company which not only extracted the crude oil but, connected by a 275-mile pipeline, refined it at a plant at Rangoon. Not only was there a domestic market, but across the Bay of Bengal to the west was India with an insatiable demand for kerosene which much of the population who could afford it used in their cooking stoves.

Burmah's first tankers

In the ranking of the world's oil industry, Burmah Oil was never large. The peak of production was reached in 1937 with a total of seven million barrels: five million barrels refined at Rangoon and, by then, at Syriam south east and downstream of the capital. As early as 1899, when tankers were a new form of shipping, the company had Grangemouth build two vessels, the *Syriam* (1,426/1899-1924) and a sister ship the *Kokine* (1,426/1899). Lost by fire at Rangoon in 1900, the latter was replaced by the *Khodaung* (1,457/1901-1924). Thereafter small coastal tankers were delivered every few years and there were even two small suction dredgers in the local fleet. In 1937 Swan, Hunter and Wigham Richardson delivered the *Yenangyaung* (5,447g) which was Burmah Oil's first diesel-engined ship. The main engine was a Doxford opposed two cycle airless-injection type '...having its bedplate columns and entablature (an architectural term for structure above supporting pillars) of electric welded steel construction'. The main engine produced 3,500 BHP and gave a service speed of 12 knots.

The *Yenangyaung* established the 'Burmah Oil look' for, probably uniquely, she had two raked masts, a larger than usual block of accommodation amidships, a white funnel with black top on which there was an Admiralty cowl resembling a hat, a styling much favoured by Orient Line. Also unusually the officers accommodation was lavish to a level not equalled until the Onassis and the Niarchos newbuildings appeared in the 1950s. The navigating officers were housed

amidships, the engineer officers had the poop to themselves and, although with a duty mess aft, they were expected to use the midships dining saloon. All the 'native' ratings were accommodated in a large forecastle over which a complete awning was spread. The *Yenangyaung* was laid down on 19th September 1936; trials took place on 13th August 1937 and she sailed two days later for Rangoon. She reached 13.57 knots on trials and had a deadweight capacity of 7,000 tons on a fully-loaded draught of 26 feet six inches.

When, after years of exploration and political manoeuvring, British interests in Persia found oil in commercial quantities in 1901 it was to Burmah Oil, replete with experience, that the infant Anglo-Persian Oil Company (eventually to become B.P.) turned. This was done through the person of Charles (later Lord) Greenway (1857-1934) who as a prominent merchant in India had links with, and detailed knowledge of, Burmah Oil's production expertise. Part of the deal, which was later to cause much friction, was that Iranian refined products were not sold in India and also that Burmah Oil held a 26.5% shareholding. Even with the British Admiralty backing Anglo-Persian when it was running out of money to fund expansion in 1912, Burmah Oil had had enough and declined to subscribe more funds. This directly lead to the United Kingdom Government taking a majority shareholding just as the First World War broke out.

Troubled years

Throughout this challenging period and into the tumultuous 1920s the company was lucky to have Robert Watson (1878-1948) as its immensely talented corporate head. By 1926 Burmah Oil was supplying 65% of India's kerosene so it was no coincidence that the US oil majors schemed to break into this rich and expanding market. In the glamorous setting of St Moritz, Watson habitually spent each Christmas and New Year skiing and skating; so too did Shell's General Managing Director Sir Henri Deterding and it was in this setting that

Burmah-Shell Oil Storage and Distribution Co. of India, was conceived in 1927. To cement relations Burmah Oil spent £4.2 million buying 800,000 Shell (U.K.) shares. The new strategic venture did not buy peace because Standard Oil of New Jersey - Socony - had a deal to buy kerosene from Soviet Russia and needed an adjacent market into which to sell it: the result was a five-year turf war set in India. It was as well that Watson had a dour and pertinacious character, for concurrent with this period was the world trade depression of 1930 to 1933. Watson tirelessly lead measures to stabilise the international oil industry and without his efforts matters might have been much worse than they were. At the age of 73 Deterding died in early 1939 and one ungenerous obituary writer said of him 'He was everything that a good Dutchman should not be'.

By the Government of Burma Act of 1935 the colony became in 1939 a state free from India's suzerainty which triggered off unprecedented labour-relation problems for Burmah Oil. But all of these were as nothing to the tragedy of the Second World War when, in March 1942, the Japanese invaded Burma and as part of the British retreat towards Assam the company's two refineries and oil field were systematically destroyed. So thorough a job was done that the refineries burnt for eight weeks. As early as April 1945 Lieutenant General Bill (later Viscount) Slim, leading the Fourteenth Army drove the Japanese out of central Burma. The occupying forces had only been able to make minimal repairs to the oil fields and refineries. No written records of production were ever found but geologists calculated that the Japanese had raised only 2.7 million barrels in three years contrasting with Burmah Oil's seven million in 1941 alone. It took four years of ingenious improvisation to substitute the range of imported products by those of the indigenous industry. Worn out by three decades on the 'front line', ill health forced Robert Watson's retirement in 1947: he died a year later.

Meanwhile the Attlee Government's attitude towards the Burmah Oil Company was that it was 'quite comfortably off'. The company fought a court case for years with the British Government for compensation for the order to destroy its primary assets in 1942 and in 1964 won a famous House of Lords ruling, only to have the government enact retrospective legislation that avoided paying any claims brought under those grounds. With the future of India occupying Ernest Bevin's thoughts towards the sub-continent, the Attlee-Aungsan agreement with the long-established independence movement's leader in January 1947 took Burma out of the Empire one year later.

Burmah Oil's four ocean-going tankers must have operated under a whole constellation of lucky stars during the Second World War because they all survived. Under British government direction they voyaged all over the world. None were in their regular trades, Burma-India-Persian Gulf, when the Japanese conquest reached their home waters in 1942. The quartet comprised the *Badarpur* (8,079/1922-1958), *Masimpur* (5,556/1927-1952), *Singu* (4,928/1931-1953) and the *Yenangyaung* (5,448/1937-1960). So well did the last-named ship come out of the war years that in 1953 Swan, Hunter took three months to build a 30-foot section of additional cargo tanks which increased her deadweight by 1,000 tons. The accommodation was modernised with all the ratings being moved from the forecastle into a much enlarged poop structure.

In the same yard at the same time the second of a trio of new tankers was being built for the company. On the 1st April 1953 Mrs W. Harper, wife of Burmah Oil's managing director, named and launched the *Burmah Sapphire.* The sponsor was given a diamond brooch to commemorate the occasion presumably because Mrs Harper already had a collection of the local sapphires in her jewellery collection. In the speeches after the launch, J.W. Elliot, Swan Hunter's chairman, mentioned the then perennial subject at post-launch functions, that of the shortage of steel - of any quality - that made quoted delivery dates unpredictable. The 6,231g, *Burmah Sapphire* had a deadweight of 8,510 tons on a loaded draught of 25 feet 2 inches specifically intended for the trade westwards from Rangoon to ports in India. The four-cylinder Wallsend-Doxford main engine produced a service speed of 12 knots. All the officers were accommodated in the midships structure with the crew aft. Once again the two masts were raked, the forward one having a crow's nest for a lookout man, but the cowl funnel top was gone. Unusually there was a skylight over the wheelhouse and chart room and a permanent awning over the monkey island and much of the poop's accommodation. The two sister ships, *Burmah Emerald* (6,250/1952) and *Burmah Star* (6,250/l952) came from Cammell Laird's Birkenhead yard and had 3,500 BHP five-cylinder Sulzer engines.

Although in 1953 Burmah oil had manoeuvred its interests in the newly-independent state into a 50/50 joint venture with the government there was the inevitable 100% nationalisation in 1963 by which time commerce, industry and investment were in inexorable decline. It was in these circumstances that the famous United States economist John K. Galbraith (1908-2006) made the comment that the British with their Empire had founded three trading cities on the shores of the Bay of Bengal and he predicted that Singapore would become the modern version of Venice in the Middle Ages, Calcutta a living necropolis, and in one hundred years hence archaeologists would excavate the mound that had been Rangoon.

Masimpur was built in 1927 by Sir James Laing and Sons Ltd., Sunderland. Sold in 1952 she spent the next 12 years under the Panama flag as *Georgia*, being broken up by Brodospas at Split in 1964. *[Roy Fenton collection]*

Decline and fall

No sooner had the company withdrawn from Burma that it had to fight off a hostile takeover bid from Shell UK who had teamed up with B.P. to make it. The attackers motivation must have been that Burma was rich in assets, holding 25% of B.P.'s shares and 40% of Shell's quoted U.K. shares. This was a period of large scale diversification for the company which included the takeover in 1966 of Castrol, the specialist lubrication oil producing company, and which brought them into owning refineries in the UK. One of these at Ellesmere Port, on the Manchester Ship Canal, had them as neighbours of the Bowring group, long refiners of Peruvian oil from the Lobitos coastal oilfield, a location now better known for world famous surfing. A resultant rationalisation of the two companies' interests and a cross exchange of equities brought the Bowring tanker *El Lobo* (12,075g/15,000dwt/1959) into the fleet of Burmah Oil Trading Ltd. from 1966 until 1976.

In 1971 Burmah Oil Tankers Ltd. established headquarters in New York and London and the group began to speculate in a major way in trading a fleet of tankers to the extent that, by 1973, they controlled 42 ships of which 14 were owned, two leased and seven managed: the rest were chartered in, often changing their name to have a Burmah prefix. This expansion was done with borrowed money which, across the group, had doubled in 1973; the timing could hardly have been worse. The OPEC oil shock in the winter of 1973-1974 was such that with a massive cash deficit in early 1974 the Bank of England's resources were called in by the Wilson government to save the whole company, a move which was done by selling Burmah Oil's holding of 23% of B.P.'s shares at a very depressed price.

A new management regime under Government appointee Alistair Down (later Sir) (1914-2004) disposed of £865 million worth of assets in over forty subsidiaries in the period 1975-1983. By 1985 all but two of the tankers had been sold: they were hardly a talisman, brought so low

The name *Yenangyaung,* which needs to be spelt with care, was bestowed in 1937. This photograph is believed to have been taken in 1958, and therefore shows the tanker after she had been taken in hand *by her builders at Wallsend and modernised. This extended her life until June 1960 when the Hong Kong Chiap Hua Manufactory Co. (1947) Ltd. began breaking her up. *[E.E. Sigwart/J. and M. Clarkson]*

The Wallsend-built *Burmah Sapphire* of 1953 spent her entire life with Burmah, although this was probably cut short by a collision with the suction hopper dredger *Balari* (3,083/1913) in the River Hooghly on 10th September 1961, after which she went unrepaired to breakers in Hong Kong. *[Roy Fenton collection]*

A company photograph of one of the three post-war sisters, *Burmah Emerald, Burmah Star* and *Burmah Sapphire.* The second name has been partly retouched on the print, but it appears to shows the first of the three, *Burmah Emerald.* In 1963 she was bought by Indonesia and became *Permina 101,* a name held for 16 years until she was broken up at Kaohsiung in 1979. *[Roy Fenton collection]*

had been the company that had gambled in tanker trading. Here was Burmah Oil, who had given Burma an oil industry, had the foresight to open an offshore transhipment facility in the Bahamas to get crude oil imports into the USA, lead exploration into Prudhoe Bay on Alaska's North Slope and most notably been the first to find and produce oil from the North Sea. B.P. eventually took control of the company in 2000 and the name sank into history.

El Lobo of 1959 in the colours of Lobitos Oilfields Ltd. In 1967 ownership became Burmah Oil Trading Ltd., remaining under Bowring management. She was broken up at Faslane in 1976. *[J. and M. Clarkson]*

PUTTING THE RECORD STRAIGHT

Letters, additions, amendments and photographs relating to features in any issues of 'Record' are welcomed. Senders of e-mails are asked to provide their postal address. Letters may be lightly edited.

Grass to Granton

The caption on page 171 of 'Record' 63 states that *Trematon* was wrecked in 1912 on one of the Cape Verde islands while on a voyage with coal from Cardiff to Barcelona. No wonder she hit something – she was hundreds of miles off course! One wonders what really happened?

Thank you for illustrating my letter about esparto grass with the photograph of *Calfa* (page 149). I don't recall her bringing any cargoes to Granton under that name, but she did call more than once under her final name of *Ursula Peters* when she was in German ownership and part of the very small fleet owned by H. Peters. He was one of the owners included in my overall statement that, in addition to the five 'core' companies, Granton saw ships from a number of companies from time to time. He also had an older ship, the *Hinrich Peters* (1,234/1925), that brought cargoes a few times each year: my memory is that, like the *Calfa/Ursula Peters*, she was an inter-war ship that had been fitted with a new superstructure and a 'new' (probably second-hand) diesel engine in the early post-war years. His ships were usually in reasonably good external condition; the black funnel had a broad pale-blue band between narrow white bands with HP in white on the blue part. I was told at the time that he may have been a captain/owner.

I mentioned that there were five 'core' owners accounting for around 75% of the esparto grass trade to Granton. The other four, in addition to Hellenic Med, were:

Richard W. Jones of Newport (one of whose ships you illustrated in your superb book 'Tramp Ships') whose mostly war-built ships often took coal (or coke – also requiring some cargo to be carried on deck) out to the Mediterranean (primarily Italy), then ballasted over to Tunisia to load grass.

Constants of London, whose ships were early post-war and slightly larger than the Jones fleet, named after Kent villages (e.g. *Garlinge* (2,979/1951), *Hawkinge* (2,980/1952). I believe the Constants had been involved in South Wales coal mining, and the ships were the result of investing the proceeds from the nationalisation of the mines. Their cargo pattern was similar to the Jones ships.

Euxine Shipping of London, whose rather smart ships, built soon after the war, were like Hellenic Med in that they operated a non-conference regular cargo service out to the eastern Med (included frequent passages through the Suez Canal with military supplies to the RAF bases in Jordan and

113

the Sudan) and picked up what homeward cargo that they could before calling in Tunisia to top-off with grass. The company was part-owned (and largely operated) by Lambert Brothers; much of the capital came from the van der Zee family who were merchants (originally from the Netherlands) that had established a successful trading business – I think dating back to the 19th century – in Smyrna, then a Greek enclave on mainland Turkey (it was renamed Izmir after the disastrous Greek invasion soon after the First World War that was intended to widen the geographical scope of those enclaves but resulted in the Greeks being expelled altogether).

Marius Nielsen of Copenhagen, whose smart early 1950s ships carried Scandinavian timber out to the Mediterranean (or occasionally Moroccan Atlantic ports such as Casablanca) then went to Tunisia for a homeward cargo of esparto grass.

As I mentioned before, those five companies accounted for around 75% of the imports of esparto grass to the Forth ports. That involved around 12 cargoes a month to Granton, two a month to Methil and one a month to Grangemouth. Leith was occasionally used when Granton was congested (something that happened particularly when the outer end of the West Pier, where all the esparto cargoes were handled, became the terminal for cargoes of refined products shipped in for Regent Oil (later Texaco) which started using 15,000 deadweight tankers for deliveries: the size of those ships reduced the esparto berths from the usual three to two during the calls of the tankers). Other 'occasional but irregular' owners bringing grass cargoes included Borchard of Hamburg, John Nurminen of Helsinki, R. Nordström (another Finnish company), George Nisbet of Glasgow, and the ex-Hogarth steamer *Lorna* (3,330/1927), owned by a one-ship company of Estonian exiles but managed in Leith.

Finally, you mentioned the problem of fire in esparto grass. I think that as many as one or two ships a year that were heading

A typical trader with esparto grass, the *Uskside* (2,920/1946) of Richard W. Jones of Newport, photographed in August 1961 on the Bristol Channel. Sold to Greece in 1965 as *Gero Michalos*, she stranded at Akyab on 10th May 1968 and became a total loss. *[Fotoship/J. and M. Clarkson]*

A more modern version of the small, three-island tramp, Constant's *Hawkinge* (2,980/1952) on the pontoon at Penarth. After sale in 1965, she was in Greek and later Italian ownership until broken up at Vado Ligure in 1978. *[Fotoship/J. and M. Clarkson]*

Euxine Shipping's smart *Hendi* on the Thames in 1959. A ship that eventually carried seven names, as *Velba* she stranded at Alexandria on 3rd August 1973 and was subsequently broken up in Greece in 1974 under the name *Dirfis*. *[J and M. Clarkson]*

for the Forth caught fire at an earlier stage of their voyage: some were total losses, others were badly damaged and were often too old to be worth repairing. The fire hazard could, of course, come from sparks emitted from the ship's funnel but a much more common cause was spontaneous combustion. If the grass cargo became wet, and if the sea-water penetrated through to the heart of the cargo (several bales below the top surface), the chemicals naturally occurring in the sea-water reacted with the grass in those enclosed conditions to create a considerable rise in temperature which led in turn to the cargo setting itself ablaze. Even when the cargo did not actually catch fire, it was not uncommon to find during discharge that, despite the top cargo looking in perfectly good condition, the lower part of the hold could contain pockets of steaming, mushy grass.

COLIN MENZIES, 17 Bickenhall Mansions, London W1U 6BP

Colin's note on the loss of Artagan, *ex-*Trematon, *prompted a re-examination of our source, the World Ship Society's 'Hain of St. Ives', which gives the location of her loss as 'Carboeiros, Cape Verde Islands'. 'Lloyd's Register Wreck Returns' for 1912 states that she was 'wrecked off Carboeiro'. However, the Starke/Schell registers list the location as 'Cabo Carvoeiro' which is on the coast of Portugal and a much more likely site for the wreck. Ed.*

Right ship, wrong places

Two good photos of the *John Lyras* (page 152, 'Record' 63) but neither in the locations indicated! The top one is alongside the Collier Jetty in Cape Town (which despite its name was latterly a grain-loading berth). The give-away is the two motor fishing vessels in left foreground lying at what is known as the Cross Berth, adjoining the Collier Jetty. The name on the stern of the outer vessel is *Oubaas* (Afrikaans for 'Old Man' or 'Old Boss') – a vessel on which I frequently worked repairing her radio equipment whilst I was working for the Marconi Company in Cape Town.

Likewise, the upper middle shows the ship sailing from the Victoria Basin, Cape Town, fully loaded. In the background is the breakwater and the pilot tug in the foreground is either the *S.G. Stephens* or her sister the *R.A.*

Leigh (both 175/1952). Also note the South African courtesy flag flying from the signal mast. I suspect that the two photos were taken within a day or two of one another.

As you say, the *John Lyras* was sold to Durban owners in 1970 and probably did one or two trips for them before being renamed *Boundary*.

Thanks, as always, for your most interesting journals.
DAVID WITTRIDGE, 25 Fairlawn Close, Rownhams, Southampton, SO16 8DT.

Firstly may I say how much I enjoy 'Record'. I have gradually worked my way through each copy and consider that it sets the standard for this type of work with much of interest that would not see the light of day elsewhere.

I know that you strive hard for accuracy and therefore feel that I should comment regarding the photograph of *Fort Constantine* that appears at the bottom of page 124 of 'Record' 62. The caption indicates that the photograph was taken 'probably in Vancouver', however this is not the case and she is at Woolloomooloo in Sydney (Australia). The photograph has been taken from the Domain Gardens and is looking across the finger wharf towards Kings Cross and Potts Point on this hill. The finger wharf still exists and has now been converted into luxury apartments. The wharf sheds above the bow of *Fort Constantine* have long since gone and this now forms part of the Royal Australian Navy's Fleet Base East precinct.

For a long time the finger wharf at Woolloomooloo was the Orient Line wharf. However, in the more recent past it was used as a general wharf and as an overflow passenger wharf. Incidentally when I arrived in Australia aboard Chandris Lines *Australis* as an 11-year old migrant in 1975 with the rest of my family, we were berthed at No.7 Woolloomooloo which is the far side of the finger wharf from where *Fort Constantine* is seen. At the extreme right of the photograph the number '8' can be seen on the wharf shed.
DAVID ROBINSON, 14 Lomond Crescent, Winston Hills, NSW 2153, Australia
The editor who wrote all these captions has promised to get out more.

Lorna, built as *Baron Tweedmouth*, was the last surviving Hogarth pre-war steamer when broken up at Split in 1974. Registered owners from 1954 to 1968 were the Liberian Steamship Corporation Ravala, but her beneficial owners were exiles from the Baltic. She was managed at Leith by Neil and Hannah Ltd. *[J. and M. Clarkson collection]*

Coast Lines at Falmouth

Falmouth was a regular call on Coast Lines' routes from the Mersey and Ireland to London, and one of the best-known cargo-passenger steamers on the service was *Southern Coast* (1,972/1911), seen here on 17th July 1932. She was built by the Greenock and Grangemouth Dockyard Company, Grangemouth as *Dorothy Hough* for Coast Line's precursor Samuel Hough Ltd., Liverpool.

In October 1936 she was sold to the Falkland Islands Co. Ltd., London and renamed *Lafonia*. On 26th March 1943 she was sunk in collision with the steamer *Como* (1,205/1910) in dense fog in the North Sea whilst on ballast passage from London northabout to Greenock. *[Ships in Focus]*

Falmouth provided calm waters for transhipment of cargo bound to and from smaller ports in the South West, and here the motor vessel *Atlantic Coast* (890/1934) services three small craft alongside. These include what is probably the motor ship *Cornish Coast* (219/1937) to port and, outside to starboard, the tiny steamer *Pennar* (130/1907). *Harfat* (128/1911) carried out similar work, and is almost certainly the vessel inside *Pennar*. *[J. and M. Clarkson collection]*

Right: A single-hatch Coast Lines steamer at Freeman's Wharf, Penryn, probably loading granite blocks. She is the second *Irish Coast* (249/1900) in service from 1922 to 1938. She had been built at Larne for Belfast owners as *Mayflower*. As *Arcliff* under later owners she soldiered on until 1951. *[Ships in Focus]*

Local wreck and rescue

Top: *Renwick* (664/1890) after going aground on Gyllyngvase Beach near Falmouth on 27th-28th February 1903. She had left Devonport in ballast for Burryport, but after seeking shelter in Falmouth Bay she dragged her anchor and went aground. Fortunately she was so close in that the coastguards' rocket apparatus was able to rescue all 13 on board.

    Renwick was part of the fleet operated by Fisher, Renwick and Company of Newcastle-upon-Tyne who ran a regular steamer service between Manchester and London. *Renwick* was refloated and returned to service, but her luck ran out on 27th December 1911 when she sank following a collision with the French steamer *St. Pierre et Miquelon* off Green Island east of Halifax. Renwick was on a voyage from Port Hastings to Bridgewater, Nova Scotia with a cargo of coal. *[Gibson/J. and M. Clarkson collection]*

Middle: Everard's coastal tanker *Allegrity* (797/1945) was blown on to rocks near Portscatho in a south westerly gale on 13th December 1961. She floated off, but went ashore again near Greeb Point, rolling heavily. The Falmouth lifeboat managed to get alongside and took off all but two of the crew. The complete rescue required two further runs alongside the tanker, one to persuade her master to leave, and the second involving lifeboatmen going aboard to assist the last crew member who was in shock. Although salvage attempts were made, *Allegrity* eventually rolled over and was abandoned. She had been on a voyage from Le Havre to Stanlow with lubricating oil. *[Everard archives, courtesy Captain K. Garrett]*

Bottom: The Atlantic Transport Line's *Minnehaha* (13,403/1900) was notoriously accident-prone. This depicts the aftermath of one of her more serious incidents when she struck rocks on Bryher, Scilly Isles on 18th April 1910. Her forward three holds were open to the sea, and it was only thanks to the skill of her salvors, plus a fortunate spell of calm weather, that she was got off on 12th May. Falmouth connections included the local tugs which are in attendance, plus a brief call whilst *Minnehaha* was being taken to Southampton for repair by her builders, Harland and Wolff. She resumed her London to New York service on 27th October 1910.

    Minnehaha met her end on 7th September 1917 during a voyage from London to New York when torpedoed by U 48 off Fastnet. *[E.A.Bragg/J. and M. Clarkson collection]*

Dry docks

Top: In the left-hand dry dock is the Furness, Withy steamer *Alleghany* (4,262/1901). Built at the group's own yard at West Hartlepool, she was initially registered in the ownership of the British Maritime Trust Ltd., but in 1903 was transferred to the Chesapeake and Ohio Steamship Co. Ltd. She was employed carrying live cattle on the North Atlantic, and her three island profile is distorted by the 500 stalls in her wells and along her bunker hatch. In November 1909 *Alleghany* was transferred to the parent company, Furness, Withy and Company, and this dry docking may coincide with this change, as the 'C&O' logo on her funnel has been painted out.

In 1912 she was sold to Japan and sailed as *Saigon Maru* until wrecked on Hokkaido on 23rd May 1929.

Middle: *Strathlyon* (4,400/1907) on fire at Falmouth on 21st January 1908. The Burrell steamer was 300 miles off Land's End outward bound from Antwerp to New York when she began to take in water, and put back to Falmouth for repair. Whilst in dry dock number 2 a careless carpenter set her ablaze.

Strathlyon was trapped at Luleå, Sweden in August 1914 and was sold to local owners as *Mertainen*. She continued in Swedish service until sunk by the Luftwaffe on 20th April 1940.

Bottom: Excavation of the Queen Elizabeth Dry Dock at Falmouth, which began in 1956. *[All: Terry Nelder collection]*

Dismasted

Top: Falmouth Roads would be the first port of refuge for sailing ships dismasted in the Atlantic. Here is the wooden Danish barque *Sörine* (398/1891) which has staggered in under a stump of a foremast and a jury rig. She had been built and was owned in the port of Nordby. *Sörine* drops out of 'Lloyd's Register' between 1910 and 1912. *[Opie/J. and M. Clarkson collection]*

Middle: Of similar rig and vintage is the wooden Norwegian *Sirrah* (467/1891), but the Grimstad barque looks to have suffered even more with both her mainmast and foremast reduced to stumps. In this condition she has, presumably, been towed into Falmouth Roads. *Sirrah* drops out of 'Lloyd's Register' between 1912 and 1915. *[Opie/J. and M. Clarkson collection]*

Bottom: The steel barque *Zeus* (391/1896) was built at Kristiansand in Norway for Gunder Olsen of Arendal. Here she has been struck by lightning and, although her mainmast rigging has been partly brought down, she looks to have been able to sail into Falmouth. A local craft is alongside, inspecting damage.

Zeus was certainly able to sail again, and in 1912 went to Fécamp owners as *Étoile Polaire*. She remained in French hands until 1928 when sold to a Genoese who had her name translated into Italian as *Stella Polare*. Her fate is unknown as she was simply deleted from 'Lloyd's Register' in 1931. *[Terry Nelder collection]*

Partially saved

Whilst on a voyage from London to Buenos Aires with a cargo of bagged cement, *Highland Fling* (3,822/1890) put into Falmouth on 2nd January 1907 to have a leak beneath her boiler examined. She was patched up and allowed to proceed to Cardiff for permanent repairs but on 7th January off The Lizard she ran into dense fog and went aground in Kennock Bay near Cadgwith. Although several tugs got ropes aboard, she could not be pulled off. Falmouth tugs involved in these unsuccessful attempts included the *Eagle* (103/1883), *Victor* (153/1898) and the *Triton* (173/1900) of the Falmouth Towage Company.

Discharge of her cargo began, and she was handed over to a salvage contractor, whose steamer is probably the one working alongside in the upper photograph.

Difficulty refloating her necessitated use of explosives to cut away her forepart. The stern section complete with engines, seen in the middle photograph, was then towed into Falmouth on 20th January.

Despite all this effort, it was decided not to build a new forepart, and the *Highland Fling* was unceremoniously scrapped, probably in the dry dock which she is seen occupying in the lower photograph.

Highland Fling had been built at Hebburn for Turnbull, Martin and Co. of Glasgow as *Morayshire*. In 1898 she was sold to James Westray, London and was soon renamed *Duke of Portland*. She passed to Nelson Line (Liverpool) Ltd. in May 1905 to become *Highland Fling*. [E.A. Bragg/J. and M. Clarkson collection; J. and M. Clarkson collection]

Top: Also only partially saved was Anders Jahre's Panama-flagged tanker *Janko* (9,720/1928) which broke in two during a storm 50 miles west of Corunna in the Bay of Biscay. The forepart later drifted ashore near the entrance to the Rio Mino, whilst the afterpart was towed into Vigo.
Middle: In March 1951 the surviving part of *Janko* is assisted into Falmouth by local tugs, having been brought from Vigo by *Bustler* (1,100/1942).
Bottom: *Janko* was dry-docked in Falmouth, but was broken up at Newport arriving on 19th September 1951.

This was the second time the twin-screw motor tanker had fallen apart. As *Jaguar*, a name given when acquired by Anders Jahre from Swedish owners in 1938, she first broke in two on 17th January 1939 in the North Atlantic whilst on a voyage from Mexico to Germany. She was towed in, and a new fore part built at Amsterdam and fitted in December 1939. As *Janko* she was subsequently put back into service for Jahre under the Panama flag. From 1941 to 1947 she ran as *Norsktank*, then reverted to *Janko* and the Panama flag until lost in 1951. *[Terry Nelder collection (2); J. and M. Clarkson collection]*

121

Falmouth for orders

Top: Sailing ships heading for Europe would often not know their final destination, and would put into Falmouth to learn where they were bound. *Muskoka* (2,357/1911) was a latecomer to the ranks of steel four-masted barques, completed by Richardson. Duck and Company of Stockton-on-Tees for owners in Windsor, Nova Scotia. The photograoh may have been taken in April 1902, at the end of a 96-day voyage from Australia with wheat. After transfer of ownership to London in 1902, *Muskoka* was sold in 1909 to Bordes et fils of Dunkerque who renamed her *Caroline*. Bordes were major owners of the French 'bounty ships' described by John Naylon in 'Records' 54 and 55. Her end came on 19th July 1920 when she was beached at Antofagasta with her coal cargo on fire. *[Opie Ltd./J. and M. Clarkson collection]*

Stationary training ships

Middle: The 84-gun HMS *Ganges* was built at Bombay between 1819 and 1823 and gave the Royal Navy long service, mostly in the Pacific. She arrived at Falmouth in 1865 for training recruits, remaining in St.Just Pool, off Mylor, until 1899 when she moved to Shotley, near Harwich. Moving to Devonport in 1906 she was renamed several times before being broken up at Plymouth in 1930. The captain's cabin is believed to survive as part of the Burgh Island Hotel in Devon *[Terry Nelder collection]*

Bottom: Photographed at Falmouth in July 1931, HMS *Implacable* was a ship with a remarkable history. Launched in 1800, she fought at Trafalgar, but on the French side as the *Duguay-Trouin* and was one of only four French ships which escaped. She was, however, captured within a month at the Battle of Cape Ortegal, and commissioned into the Royal Navy as HMS *Implacable*. She saw considerable action, in the Napoleonic Wars and beyond, and was not taken out of commision until 1842. By 1865 she was a training ship for boys.

Given her historic significance, second only to that of HMS *Victory*, there were repeated attempts to preserve her from 1908 onwards. In 1949 these were abandoned, as not even the French were prepared to fund her. With the White Ensign and the Tricolour flying side by side, she was towed out to near the Isle of Wight and scuttled. The outcry was loud, but did have the effect of ensuring that the preservation of the *Cutty Sark* was funded. *[J. and M. Clarkson collection]*

Sail training ships

This selection of present-day sail training ships was photographed in Falmouth in the early 1960s when ships gathered for the start of one of the first 'Tall Ships' Races. All three of those pictured here were built as training ships and all were fitted with auxiliary oil engines.

Right: The ship *Georg Stage* is Danish, built at Frederikshavn in 1935. The smallest of the three shown at just 123 feet, she looks well with a 'traditional' black hull. She replaced an1882-built iron training ship of the same name, which was renamed *Joseph Conrad* and, after being sailed round the world by Alan Villiers, became a yacht in the USA and is currently afloat at Mystic Seaport, Connecticut.

Middle right: the ship-rigged *Christian Radich* was built at Sandefjord in 1937 as a training ship for the Norwegian merchant marine, and is based in Oslo.

Bottom right: The Norwegian barque *Statsraad Lehmkuhl* is the oldest of the three and the largest at 258 feet. She was built in 1914 at Geestemunde as the training ship *Grossherzog Friedrich August* for the German merchant marine. Since1924 she has been based in Bergen.

Below: *Christian Radich* with *Statsraad Lehmkuhl* astern.
[All: J. and M. Clarkson]

US cruisers, German captives

Above: USS *Tennessee* and *North Carolina* amongst captured German ships in Carrick Roads in August or September 1914 having brought funds for U.S. citizens stranded in Europe. *Tennessee* also sailed to the Hook of Holland with further funds and evacuated U.S. citizens from France. Right middle: Hapag's *Prinz Adalbert* (6,030/1903) was seized in Falmouth on 4th August 1914, and was initially commissioned by the Admiralty as the repair ship HMS *Princetown*. After a spell of mercantile use she was sold in 1917 to Compagnie de Navigation Sud-Atlantique of Bordeaux to become *Alesia*. Germany soon had its revenge, and bound from Cardiff to her home port on 6th September 1917, *Alesia* was torpedoed twice, once by UC 69 and again by UC 50. *[Opie/J. and M. Clarkson collection]*

Salvage tug

Right bottom: Until at least the 1970s, large tugs were stationed at Falmouth in the hope that there might be profitable salvage work to be had in the Western Approaches. Here waits the Overseas Towage and Salvage tug *Neptunia* (798/1938), one of the world's most powerful tugs at the time of her completion by Cochrane and Sons Ltd. at Selby in August 1938. She certainly looked the part but her career was to be tragically short. She was taken over by the Admiralty on 9th September 1939 and almost immediate sent out from Falmouth on a rescue mission. But just four days later the German submarine U 29 sank her with gun and torpedo. *[J. and M. Clarkson collection]*

Failed to make Falmouth

Top: Despite her name beginning with a letter T, HMS *Torrid* was an 'R' class destroyer completed by Swan, Hunter in May 1917, and serving with the Harwich destroyer force. Placed in reserve in Februay 1919, she was sold in 1937, one ot the last of her class to go, but on 16th March 1937 she went aground on her way into Falmouth and had to be broken up on Trefusis Point. *[J. and M. Clarkson collection]*

Middle: One of the most famous ships not to have made Falmouth was the *Flying Enterprise* (6,711/1944). The C1-B type *Cape Kumukaki* was sold to Isbrandtsen in 1947 and renamed. During a voyage from Hamburg to the U.S.A. she hit storms on Christmas Day 1951, and after sustaining structural damage took a 46-degree list. Help was summoned, and the British salvage tug *Turmoil* (1,136/1945) took her in tow 300 nautical miles from Falmouth. With the list increased to 60 degrees, the tow line broke on 10th January when she was just 41 miles from Falmouth and she sank shortly after Captain Kurt Carlsen and Kenneth Dancy, *Turmoil's* mate, were taken off. If she had been heading for the nearest port, Cork, rather than Falmouth, she might have been saved. *[J. and M. Clarkson collection]*

A significant oddity

At Exchequer Quay, Penryn, north of Falmouth, lies a vessel as odd looking as the warehouse against which it is moored is picturesque, but one of exceptional significance to the British fishing industry. It was universal practice in this industry for the nets to be hauled in over the side of the vessel, and one which persisted long after steam trawling had been introduced. Elsewhere, especially in the Mediterranean and in North America, it was common practice to haul nets over the stern, and some in the British industry considered that this might offer significant advantages.

Hence, at the end of the Second World War the ageing steam yacht *Oriana* (128/1896) was bought by Fairfield Shipbuilding and Engineering Co. Ltd. and extensively modified as an experimental stern trawler. The Cornish photograph clearly shows the rollers fitted on the stern, and the Oropesa floats which may have been used as well as traditional otter boards. Winches for hauling the nets were fitted on to her comparatively clear deck abaft the funnel.

As a prototype, the *Oriana* seems to have proved the concept, as thereafter stern trawlers were increasingly built for British owners. The advantages over the traditional 'sidewinders' included the ability to handle larger catches, as the nets were hauled by machinery, also reducing the heavy and dangerous work of hauling manually. Not needing to have nets hauled over the side meant that the stern trawler could have greater freeboard at this vulnerable point.

Oriana was hired by the Admiralty as an auxiliary patrol yacht during the First World War, but was seemingly too old to be of use to their lordships in the Second World War. Her fate is not known to the editors: she was soon sold by Fairfield to owners in southern England. The 'Falmouth Packet' of 7th July 1950 reported that *Oriana* had been converted

from a trawler back into a yacht after laying derelict at Penryn for many months. The work was carried out by Advance Industries at Ponsharden Shipyard, Penryn, She then sailed for Shoreham. The rebuild gave her a new lease of life and she seems to have lingered on in the 'Mercantile Navy List' for some years. Information on her fate would be welcome. *[Keith Hancock]*

BOSUN'S LOCKER

Two intriguing photographs are included in this issue, both probably showing the aftermath of an accident.

Petrolea (below) poses two mysteries: which of five known tankers of the name is depicted here, and was it responsible for the large gap in the jetty behind (there are some marks on her bow)? Between 1908 and 1924, British Petroleum had a German-built steam tank barge of this name (202/1905), but she is unlikely to have had a clipper bow and so much rigging. More likely is an auxiliary schooner built at Delfzijl as *Aleks Pelander* (149/1913) and from 1920 owned as *Petrolea* by a Finnish branch of Nobel. But the jetty looks British – possibly on the Thames – and would a small Finnish vessel venture so far? Suggestions as to identity and place welcome.

The rather substandard photograph of the Greek steamer *Maria Kyriakides* (1,556/1921) (right) was taken at Ilfracombe in 1930. Her careworn appearance, and the interest of the onlookers, is explained by her having been stranded on Lundy on 24th March 1929, and not refloated until 13th August 1930. She had been on a voyage from Cardiff to St. Malo with coal. She had probably been abandoned to her underwriters, as in 1931 she was sold to William Tulley and Co. Ltd. of Hull who ran her as *Newlands*.

Her fate was both unfortunate and unusual, as on 26th March 1945 *Newlands* was torpedoed and sunk by a German midget submarine with the loss of three lives whilst carrying oilcake from

Liverpool to London. Her position 51.28 north, 01.25 east would put her east of Deal.

It is surprising that her builder, Bow, McLachlan of Paisley, completed her for a Greek owner, N.G. Kyriakides of Andros. It is likely that whoever ordered her defaulted on payment and she was sold cheaply. The next yard number to hers, 390, is blank in the yard list, suggesting that a sister ship was also ordered but cancelled.